EARLY CHILDHOOD EDUCATION SERIES

Leslie R. Williams, Editor
Millie Almy, Senior Advisor

THE
FULL–DAY
KINDERGARTEN

DORIS PRONIN FROMBERG

TEACHERS
COLLEGE
PRESS

Teachers College, Columbia University
New York and London

Published by Teachers College Press, 1234 Amsterdam Avenue, New York, N.Y. 10027

Library of Congress Cataloging in Publication Data

Fromberg, Doris Pronin, 1937–
  The full-day kindergarten.

  (Early childhood education series)
  Includes bibliographies and index.
  1. Kindergarten — Methods and manuals. 2. School day —
United States. 3. Kindergartens — United States —
Curricula. I. Title. II. Series.
LB1169.F76 1986   372'.218   86-14506

ISBN 0-8077-2833-0
ISBN 0-8077-2821-7 (pbk.)

Manufactured in the United States of America

92 91 90 89 88 87   1 2 3 4 5 6

This book is dedicated to
MELVIN S. FROMBERG

Contents

10. Establishing a Full-Day Kindergarten 229
     Ongoing Arguments About Full-Day Kindergarten 229
     Administrative Conditions 231
     Highlights of the Full-Day Kindergarten Curriculum 233
     Proposed Ways to Plan: Daily, Weekly, and Beyond 234
     Purposeful Teaching 236
     Reflections 237

     References 241
     References to Children's Literature 251
     "Great Books" for Beginning Readers 253
     About the Author 257
     Index 259

Preface

The half-day kindergarten was first introduced into American education in the latter part of the nineteenth century, but for many years its incorporation into the public school curriculum varied widely from locality to locality. Acceptance of public kindergarten gradually increased, and during the last decade in particular, such programs have been added in many regions where none had previously existed. More recently, there has also been an increase in public full-day kindergartens and extended-day variations.

The full-day kindergarten has continued to expand in the United States despite the fact that it has been a subject of controversy. It is a controversial subject because both protagonists and antagonists raise questions about where kindergarten children should spend their time, with whom, doing what, and how they should be doing what they do.

The issue for our discussion is not whether there should be a half-day or a full-day or an extended-day kindergarten. It is a bit late for that consideration. The public school extended day is a reality already chosen in many communities across the United States, without even considering what is offered in private education or in the schools of other nations.

This book deals with the reality of what already exists: Given that there is an extended kindergarten day, then what can teachers do with the additional time and how can they work in order to make a worthwhile, humane learning experience take place? The process of answering this question will take place as we consider how teachers interact with children who come to school with a diverse range of backgrounds, abilities, and needs. A major purpose of this book is to demonstrate how different children doing different things at different times can have equivalent experiences.

A basic question in need of answering is how to retain the right of kindergarten children to have a distinctly human and satisfying learning experience in school while keeping open the possibility for great expectations in their lives. This question is central to our thinking about the full-day kindergarten because there are political pressures on kindergarten teachers to use the additional time for creating a workbook-oriented program devoted mainly to teaching the three R's as separate subjects in a linear way.

Since all questions predispose a range of possible answers, the particular position of this book may be evident in the questions that follow. Teachers will come away from reading this book with specific ways to answer the following questions:

- How can I set up, organize, and maintain a full-day kindergarten?
- How can I help to strengthen children's self-concepts?
- How can I break down tasks and skills in ways that can help children of differing abilities to learn successfully?
- How can I develop alternative techniques that can influence children's learning?
- How can I build on children's strengths and capacity for joy in learning?
- How can I help children become focused, organized, independent, and responsible learners?
- How can I stimulate, keep open, and extend young children's imaginative and creative ways of thinking?
- How can I help children to learn skills that are applicable to their own concrete construction of conceptual knowledge in a playful environment?
- How can I develop curriculum and adapt commercial and generic materials?
- How can I interpret the kindergarten program to parents?

A POINT OF VIEW ABOUT HUMAN EXPERIENCE

As implied by the preceding questions, this book presents a particular point of view about human experience in the full-day kindergarten. Neither the three R's alone nor socialization in a random environment constitutes an adequate human experience. Offering only the three R's devalues and undermines the children's capacity and limits the amount of time for connection-making and problem-solving activity. The unstructured socialization position dispossesses children from the joys inherent in challenge. Both the three R's and the random socialization positions put a ceiling on children's academic and intellectual achievements.

Children need both skills and content. Indeed, skills should support content. The three R's and other skills exist to serve content, ideas, connection making, and cooperative socialization, rather than being ends in themselves.

Thus, the full-day kindergarten curriculum design in this book consists of four interconnected features:

Child Development. Children's developmental capacities direct the ways in which teachers can help children learn best.

Disciplines. Content includes consideration for the knowledge bases and ways of working in organized disciplines.

Interdisciplinary Experience. Content evolves over time as teachers and children interact and activities become connected across disciplines, through the experiencing of perceptual models.

Skills. Skills are applied in content-based concerns about meaningful ideas, feelings, and attitudes.

The basic business of the full-day kindergarten should be to provide concrete experiences that raise questions that help children and teachers make connections and leave children and teachers feeling both satisfied and thirsting for more.

A POINT OF VIEW ABOUT TEACHING YOUNG CHILDREN

The teacher and the children both have active roles in this interaction; therefore, you cannot learn to teach only by reading a book. A book can share some ways of looking at the work, some ways of approaching the interaction with children, and some ideas about materials and activities that can be shared with children. A book also can provide notions about how children develop, learn, and feel; how they might be likely to behave in certain situations; and alternate ways in which teachers can plan their work. This book will provide some such direct information.

However, to convey some sense of the interactive nature of the process and the cooperative feeling of learning, there will be some sections that not only describe but ask that you, as a teacher, imagine yourself in different classroom settings and moments. Dialogue, examples, simulated visits, and occasional stream-of-consciousness techniques will be used to approach these experiences.

Beyond reading this book and others, you will need to try out these ideas, working with children in a setting where you can have feedback about what you are doing. The feedback, through coaching by an experienced colleague or supervisor, using audiotapes or videotapes and verbatim written records, is essential. Even if you have taught older children, learning to "read" the behavior of kindergarten children is a new behavioral language or dialect for you.

In order to develop your own teaching style in relationship with young children you will need to develop the ability to select and focus teaching strategies and alternatives and to use them when you want and in ways that you intend. This book is only one step in this interactive process. In a sense, you will finish writing it in your work with children.

I thank the staff of Teachers College Press for their support and enthusiasm. In particular, Director Carole Saltz has been a dynamic and helpful force. Lois Patton, formerly Executive Editor, persevered in stimulating the start of this project. Professor Leslie Williams of Teachers College made valuable and generous suggestions.

THE FULL–DAY KINDERGARTEN

PART I

The Interactive Context of the Full–Day Kindergarten

1

A Full Kindergarten
Day Is . . .

The main purpose of this chapter is to share a feeling of both the child's and the teacher's experience of kindergarten. We will begin with two looks at the five-year-old, first from the child's own perspective and then from the teacher's. We will then consider what learning in a full-day kindergarten looks and feels like, particularly as teacher and child interact in *relation* to each other. These relative views will be elaborated throughout the book, for they provide the best means of imparting a true understanding of what a full-day experience in kindergarten can be.

THE FIVE-YEAR-OLD

The Child's View

Imagine yourself to be a five-year-old, beginning kindergarten. You were born sixty-three months ago and spend your time at home with your mother, father, older sister, babysitters, grandparents. . . . You find toys and pictures in the supermarket and notice the giant inflated banana hanging over the produce counters.

New flowers in spring thrill you, and you feel that you will never forgive the gardener in the park who must have destroyed the crocuses. You try to capture birds with your jacket and bring a bowl of milk to the stray cat near your house. When thunder wakens you at night, you feel your heart beat faster as you race to your parents' bed. That's one good thing about thunder.

You walk to your neighbor's house to see if he can play ball with you, but he tells you he cannot come over because he cannot bear to part with his best friend, who is visiting. You ask your mother to play with you because you feel so lonely and there's nothing to do. It feels good when your mother tells you what a great checkers player you have become.

You feel puzzled to see your older sister's face contort with disgust when she takes the spoon you have handled. More often, she wants to take what you have long before you want to give it to her. You will hate Harold all your life for pushing you on the steps and reopening your scraped knee. You will miss your friend Stanley if his family moves away. He taught you to count to one hundred and shared your horror when the doll baby's paint came off in the water. You play card games together, and he taught you how to stack the deck in his favor. You talk about favorite television shows together and race to your mother's side because the commercial tells you to tell your mother to go right out and buy it. You can sing every commercial you hear and ride your two-wheeler.

You feel guilty when you eat more candy than your mother said you could have. You don't understand why your mother's not wanting to send the dentist on vacation is a reason not to eat candy. You watch the older children sneaking cigarettes in the park while their heavy school books sit on the ground.

You have been delighted by Curious George, the peddler and the monkeys, and other storybook characters; you can look repeatedly at the pictures in the monster book, *Cars*, and *Ask Mr. Bear*.* Everybody wonders why you keep collecting yogurt tops. You have piles of red, green, blue, brown, and orange ones in a shoe box. The blueberry and vanilla covers are both blue, but the blueberry has more letters on it. Everybody says that you will learn to read when you go to the big school. Then you will be able to tell the difference between the cherry, the plain, and the strawberry tops, all of which are red.

It is clear that you have had many experiences — social, aesthetic, psychomotor, emotional, and intellectual. You have devoted your entire attention to solving a problem. You have readily repeated skills again and again, and feel satisfied and supported in this activity.

The Teacher's View

As a teacher, you have considered that each child has had many experiences, some different from others, and that each child needs a different amount of time to satisfy his or her need for repetition to gain mastery —

---

*The books referred to here — Rey's *Curious George*, Slobodkina's *Caps for Sale*, Sendak's *Where the Wild Things Are*, Rockwell's *Cars*, and Flack's *Ask Mr. Bear* — and all other children's titles mentioned in the text are included in the References to Children's Literature section that follows the main bibliography at the end of this book.

whether the task was tying shoe laces, riding a bicycle, pouring liquids, writing a name, or fixing a puzzle. As you have walked with young children, you have seen, heard, and appreciated what might otherwise have been a lost world of novelties. You have caught a glimpse of the connections they made that sometimes felt poetic.

Your work has made you aware that young children learn most effectively when they can have physical contact with concrete materials. The kindergarten children's direct involvement is the basis for their motivation. When you have been able to provide such direct involvement, you have been able to help them build on the strengths of their experiences. The children's ways of working have been an effective vehicle for carrying out the school's purposes.

In short, young children's ways of learning and the kindergarten teacher's ways of teaching are largely social, affective, aesthetic, and physical. Yet schools are the single institution charged with the major task of intellectual development. For full-day kindergarten education, the issue is not *either* intellect *or* socialization. The issue is helping young children achieve academic and personal success by using experiential means, through concrete experiences that are largely physical, aesthetic, affective, and social. The bulk of this book is devoted to elaborating and representing this issue through concrete ways of working with children during an extended school day.

The most caring teacher can hurt children unless she or he is skilled in translating the human fund of knowledge (Dewey, 1933) into activities in which children can feel competent. Wedding what is taught with how it is taught is more important than either content or method alone. The value of kindergarten education derives much more from its ability to help the child develop internal structure than from isolated instances of information processing, skills building, memory cramming, or verbalization. After all is said and done, little remains of the bits of information. What remains forever are the residual feelings and attitudes that ultimately dictate how individual human beings will behave and receive experience in life. This view concurs with Whitehead's (1929) belief that wisdom lies in the use of knowledge. Use implies action: If you think back to the most satisfying residues of your own early education, you are likely to find active participation — sometimes painful, pleasurable, or actively stimulating — serving as a window back in time. The full-day kindergarten within this framework is a time that is valuable in itself, rather than only as a preparation for next year.

As teachers, we know that children enter school with many rich experiences, even if they are disturbing rather than harmonious ones. We need to harness these experiences and build upon them, because they are sources of strength for the children and the basis for building a sense of academic competence.

SIMULATED VISIT TO A FULL-DAY KINDERGARTEN CLASSROOM

As we move together through an imaginary visit, we can see how a particular organization works. The following section attempts to share an image of what learning in a full-day kindergarten looks and feels like.

Arrangement of Space and Materials

MATHEMATICS AREA.   One area, enclosed on three sides by shelves, contains mathematics-related materials. There is a balance scale with labeled boxes of beads, pine cones, sand, buttons, cotton balls, beans, discs, and other items. There are Cuisenaire rods and Dienes multibase arithmetic blocks. There are also rulers, card games, and board games, some of which appear to be teacher-made. Transparent measuring cups of varying sizes and shapes sit in a tub.

SCIENCE AREA.   Three children sit at a table, sorting materials into two piles on the basis of whether they do or do not absorb water. Nearby, two others are changing the newspaper in a guinea pig's cage. On another table, tadpoles at various stages of development swim in an aquarium, while a salamander adds color to the terrarium.

SOCIODRAMATIC AREA.   The sociodramatic area contains a hospital section, a store-front/puppet stage made of large hollow blocks, and wooden floor blocks on shelves. Boxes, shelves, and pegboard enclose an area containing a woodworking bench, carpentry tools, and pine lumber in a basket.

READING AREA.   At the opposite side of the room from the sink, arts area, and science area, there is a corner created by bookshelves and a storage cabinet. Book jackets hang on a bulletin board. A box of spaghetti and the book jacket for the book *Strega Nona* (de Paola) are hung from two lengths of blue yarn attached to the ceiling. Two children are seated on carpet squares, three are seated at a small round table, and two are sitting together in a soft, slightly battered armchair. All are reading different books. There are two mats on the floor upon which two children lie with books. One of the reclining children holds a stuffed toy. There is also a large boothlike box in which the top of a curly-haired head can be seen.

WRITING AND INDIVIDUAL MANIPULATION AREA.   Six children are seated at several tables that face a wall and two room dividers. Four children are writing in personal books that they have illustrated, copying sentences from preprinted words set on a stand. Three-sided folders stand in front of each of the children, forming individual-study carrels. These materials are part of the *Breakthrough to Literacy* (Mackay, Thompson, & Schaub, 1978) language-experience program (detailed in chapter 9). One child is working on a puzzle, another on a card-matching game.

ARTS AREA.   Near the sink and easel, two children are weaving jersey loops at a table, while still another child writes her name with a pencil at the top of a crayon drawing. She uses a teacher-made namecard attached to her own photograph as a model. (The teacher explains later that almost all of the children can write their names independently but that this child is developmentally delayed. The photograph helps the child find her own name or that of others in the class independently when she wants to write.)

TEACHER'S INSTRUCTIONAL AREA.   A child who had made his own picturebook with felt-tipped colored pens dictates narrative as the teacher records his comments beside each picture. They are seated at a curved table in the corner where the teacher's chair is in a position so that she can observe the entire classroom.

The Teacher's Activities

When the picturebook maker returns to the writing area, the teacher helps another child begin a two-sided sewing card in the arts area. She also obtains additional gummed paper for a collage maker, adjusts wire for a hanging mobile construction, and hangs a child's finished twelve-by-eighteen-inch painting on a bulletin board that contains an unoccupied white oaktag frame.

When she sees that everybody seems reasonably occupied and can be expected to continue for a while, she sits in the mathematics area with four children, the balance scale, some standard weights, and a blindfold. The weights, while all the same size, are marked differently according to their densities. The teacher explains that she is isolating the weight from its appearance and tries to help the children develop seriation skills, ordering first two, then three, then five weights.

She further explains to the visitor that she plans parallel activities with other materials. These children have had prior experiences with sorting, by touch, the lengths of wooden Cuisenaire rods placed in bags. They also have used Lavatelli's (1970) seriation pictures. These pictures are on ten identical cards, with picture size as the only variable. Two series of ten pictures, one of a child wearing rain clothing and one of an umbrella, are then matched, using one-to-one correspondence after the pictures are seriated.

However, the teacher continues to note that the published materials are teaching conveniences. The children have many seriation experiences in their everyday lives, such as comparing sizes of berries, toys, sticks, houses, body parts, and people. This teacher also has constructed a series of cylinders using discarded paper rolls, plastic containers, lids, and buttons. She reflects that the longer day makes it possible for her to provide, in varied forms, several experiences with a concept and to plan alternatives for those children who need them. This variety solidifies and reinforces learning.

Figure 1.1 summarizes the way in which one teacher alternated direct teaching and circulating around the room. While she circulated, she engaged in a variety of organizational and teaching functions, which are listed within each time period.

While each teacher plans ahead and prepares materials, some of the most valuable learning takes place in a teacher's spontaneous awareness of a "teachable" moment. Replanning on-the-spot, doing "fleeting" teaching, and matching the child's need with an appropriate activity are some of the skills that a kindergarten teacher uses. In this respect, the teacher in the full-day program has more opportunity for learning a great deal by being a sensitive observer, listener, recorder, and assessor of children's readiness for a range of experiences.

Observing the Child's Day

So far, our visit has looked at the teacher's flow of activity. Now we need to replay the day by following a few children through their experience of it. Each of us needs to pay more attention to the way children have perceived their day. In this way we as teachers have a better chance of learning what activities children are asking for with their behavior as well as their overt requests.

TERRY, A HESITANT CHILD

Terry entered the classroom with a stonelike expression, put a small bag in the shopping bag hung from a name-bearing hook, and brushed past several children until he sat down near the chart paper. When the teacher made eye contact and smiled, Terry nodded grimly in return.

During the group planning, Terry stared at the chart paper, picked at a fingernail, and moved slightly away from another child. When it was time for four children to select a place at the sociodramatic area, the teacher invited Terry, who shrugged and nodded.

When everyone had dispersed, one group at a time, to their respective areas, Terry remained close to the teacher until she walked with him to the sociodramatic area on her way to the science area. As he began to remove blocks, the teacher smiled encouragingly and moved on. When another

Figure 1.1: Kindergarten Teacher's Flow Map

ACTIVITY	CIRCULATION
8:50 Children arrive together Greeting (store personal effects, sit on floor facing chart paper)	**8:52** Store materials Assist with materials Appreciate Question Answer questions
9:00 Whole-group planning Meeting area (record activities for day and who begins where)	**9:15** Assist with materials Encourage Observe Answer questions
9:27 Science area (water activity)	**9:40** Redirect social behavior Assist with materials Appreciate Question Fleeting teaching
9:45 Teacher's instructional area (writing group)	**10:05** Record keeping Assessment Fleeting teaching Display child's work Plan ahead Encourage Assist at snack table
10:14 Mathematics area (balance scale: seriation)	**10:30** Plan ahead Mediate Redirect social behavior Encourage Appreciate
10:32 Expand activity	**10:35** Close-down, 5 minutes' notice, beginning with socio- dramatic and arts areas Appreciate Answer questions
	10:40 Redirect children to meet- ing area; cleanup details
10:50 Whole-group sharing	
11:05 Leave for gym class	

(continued)

9

Figure 1.1 (continued)

ACTIVITY	CIRCULATION
11:40 Whole-group story; meeting area (teacher reads story)	
12:00 Lunch in school lunchroom, then to playground	**12:50** Assist with books for silent independent reading
12:52 Teacher's instructional area (reading group skill instruction)	(N.B.: Science and art areas are closed) **1:10** Redirect reading group Close-down notice for form-ing of puppetry group members
1:12 Sociodramatic area (puppetry group and tape recorder; play development and values discussion)	**1:24** Assess Encourage Appreciate
1:28 Teacher's instructional area (reading group skill instruction)	**1:42** Redirect reading group Observe Fleeting teaching Extend sociodramatic area, questioning, and encouraging
1:52 Teacher's instructional area (individual reading with three children in turn, alternating circulation)	**1:56** Observe Replan Answer questions Do record keeping
1:58 Individual	**2:05** Appreciate Do record keeping
2:10 Individual	**2:15** Close-down, 5 minutes' notice Appreciate
2:20 Whole-group activity; meet-ing area (teacher reads poem) Discuss trip to seashore List on chart Sing sea songs (teacher plays guitar)	
2:50 End of day	

child's building grew closer, they merged their construction. The other child chatted amiably and Terry offered brief suggestions. Half an hour later, they were cheerfully pouring and drinking juice at the snack table near the sink.

Terry's building partner went to paint at the only open easel, and Terry went to the reading corner the long way around, past the games and media area, the teacher's instructional area, and the science and mathematics areas. As he circulated, he would stop to watch what was happening, listen to a conversation, and pick up and examine various objects along the way.

Figure 1.2 shows Terry's movements. As you analyze what he did, several patterns are present:

> Terry alternately engaged in an activity and then circulated, observed others, and touched materials.
>
> When not engaged in a clearly social activity, he appeared to seek time alone, for example, on a mat or a designated private space, distancing himself from close contact with others.
>
> Terry made eye contact with the teacher, noting and sometimes returning her smiles.
>
> He seemed to alternate active and sedentary activities independently.

It is important to notice that the flexible structure of this setting made it possible for Terry to choose many activities independently. In turn, the teacher could see when Terry needed the social potential of the sociodramatic area and adapted her plans by suggesting and encouraging his activity. It was comfortable for him to receive the teacher's suggestion because there were many other times when he could make independent choices.

When a teacher schedules and plans most of a child's time, there is less opportunity for that child to feel capable, independent, and responsible. When a teacher changes activities frequently in other, more rigid settings, children learn not to invest their energies in school activities because the activities change too soon. There is a sense that just as they begin to get involved in something, they are interrupted.

By contrast, in this setting Terry could invest attention and commitment because his teacher had allowed for long blocks of time. Clearly, when some people say that young children have short attention spans, we need to ask ourselves, "To what?" Kindergarten children can spend as long as an hour doing those things to which they feel committed. The full-day scheduling provides an opportunity for this kind of active scholarship.

PAT, AN IMPULSIVE, SOCIABLE CHILD

The crash of a paint can, the clatter of a long-handled brush, and calls for help from Pat punctuated the arts area. At that very moment, the teacher was helping a group of seven children in the nearby science area to organize

Figure 1.2: Terry's Flow Map

ACTIVITY	TEACHER CONTACT
8:50 Terry arrives--stores personal effects; sits on floor facing chart paper for planning session	Eye contact Smile
9:00 Terry listens	Eye contact Suggests activity Walks alongside Terry
9:20 Sociodramatic area--blocks	Observes Encouraging smile
9:25 Parallel play with other child	
9:30 Building together	Teacher stops at blocks, appreciates, questions
9:55 Snack table--brings snack from closet; shares raisins with other child; conversation with other child	
10:05 Tours the room--observes others; examines and handles materials	Teacher passes, smiles, and says, "Think about what you might do next."
10:08 Reading area--lies on mat with a book	
10:20 To toilet then returns to mat	
10:30 Finishes second book and brings a puzzle to the mat	Teacher stops to look at Terry's book; discusses briefly
10:50 Whole-group sharing Chatting alongside block-building companion as group gathers	Asks Terry and other block builder to talk about their structure; teacher writes out large label for various parts; Terry places labels on parts

12

Figure 1.2 (continued)

ACTIVITY	TEACHER CONTACT
11:05	
Gym class--passes ball over head; Terry blushes as he takes lead position	Gym teacher says,"OK, Terry!"
Laughing as participates in vigorously shaking parachute with entire group	
Jogs around outside of gym	Eye contact with gym teacher
11:40	
Drinks water at fountain	
Listens to story	Eye contact
Silent during discussion	
12:00	
Lunchroom--keeps distance from others at food line; eats quickly and then slowly, looking at children across the table	
12:25	
Playground--jogs; asks aide for a ball; bounces and plays catch with another child; after balls are collected, the children roll along incline and giggle	Aide provides ball
12:52	
Teacher's instructional area, with five other children	Teacher models word game, plays with children, gives feedback as they play together
1:10	
Children play word card game together twice	Leaves group, with writing followup
1:20	
Terry copies words from cards into personal notebook, which remains in teacher's area	Appreciates
1:28	
To toilet	
Easel--paints two pictures; hangs them on rack to dry	Teacher observes quietly
2:00	
Washes paint from hands with lots of suds	Unties smock in passing(2:05)

(continued)

13

Figure 1.2 (continued)

ACTIVITY	TEACHER CONTACT
2:05 Games area--observes other children; when they finish a game and one leaves, the other invites Terry to play a board game with a die; they play, with comments	Teacher stops, observes, appreciates(2:15)
2:20 Whole-group meeting Terry offers addition to list; sings along with group, taking deep breaths	Teacher leads discussion Teacher appreciates and asks Terry to tell more about undertow
2:50 Keeps distance as group gathers to leave room	Teacher smiles and nods

materials for experimenting with water absorption. She made sympathetic eye contact with Pat, whose pained expression was noticed by other children in the area. One child who was coming from the water fountain brought a large sponge and handed it to Pat, who recoiled for a moment after accepting it.

By the time the teacher had disengaged herself from the science-area activities, Pat had artfully smeared paint over several square feet of the linoleum floor beyond the newspapers that were spread under the easel. The teacher helped her rinse the sponge and brought more newspapers to cover the wet area. Her sympathetic, matter-of-fact, helpful attitude helped Pat to relax about the mishap. Pat eventually carried fresh paints to the easel, and the teacher returned to the science area.

This child painted one picture and hung the painting to dry. Pat gave her hands a fast splash of water and a casual wipe on her jeans on the way to the snack table. She stopped off to pick up an apple from the shopping bag labeled with her name and immediately entered into a brisk discussion of a television character's pratfalls with the other children at the snack table. Figure 1.3 traces Pat's movements in this classroom.

This flexible schedule gave Pat the opportunity to bounce along, expressing her enthusiastic, chatty exuberance in many ways. Even though Pat sought out contacts with others, this option was often available. Her needs to be social, to be noticed by the teacher, and to have ready access to

Figure 1.3: Pat's Flow Map

ACTIVITY	TEACHER CONTACT
8:50 Pat arrives--playfully tackles another child, approaches the teacher with some news about home, and stores personal effects; sits next to another child and converses; turns toward chart paper for planning session after teacher begins the meeting	Conversation, smile Eye contact
9:00 Pat listens, comments to adjacent children occasion- ally, and raises hand for art area	Eye contact Responds to Pat's comments
9:30 Art area--drops paint mate- rials, cleans up, and paints	Eye contact Assists with materials
9:50 Snack area	Assists with materials
10:14 Mathematics area (balance scale: seriation)	Direct instruction
10:32 Laying out materials with partner and outlining on chart in sequence	Direct instruction
10:50 Ambles to whole-group shar- ing with math partner and chart, partially completed	Asks Pat and partner to show group their chart and explain their next steps
11:05 To toilet then joins the last of the children on their way to gym Gym class--jogs around gym and joins the end of the ball-passing group, chat- ting to child in front Races to take a place next to math partner for the parachute; laughs hard, occasionally dropping an edge	 Gym teacher redirects Pat

(continued)

15

Figure 1.3 (continued)

ACTIVITY	TEACHER CONTACT
11:40 Slides into space in front of teacher and tells her about the parachute Listens intently to story; comments during discussion	Teacher smiles, listens, questions, and comments appreciatively
12:00 Lunchroom--chatting and jostling with other children; talks through the meal, sucking noisily at the straw in the milk container	
12:18 Playground--climbs on apparatus with several others, playing at space travel	Aide cautions holding on with both hands
12:50 Reading area--shares armchair with math partner as they look together at books, commenting quietly and pointing	Teacher nods encouragement
1:10 To toilet then puts on earphones at media center	
1:25 Looks up as teacher places hand on shoulder; listens awhile longer and joins reading group	Teacher gives notice for instructional group
1:28 Teacher's instructional area, with four other children	Teacher shows children a sorting activity of pictures and captions and gives the children feedback on their sorting and sequence
1:35 Children take turns, sharing and explaining their sequences to one another; they discuss the action	Redirects reading group

Figure 1.3 (continued)

ACTIVITY	TEACHER CONTACT
1:50 Pat takes the materials to the writing area and records the sentence sequences in a notebook	
2:10 Returns notebook to the teacher's instructional area Takes a drink of water and heads directly to another child, who is playing with Tangrams (ESS); comments and makes suggestions	Teacher nods and smiles
2:20 Joins whole-group activity, shoving in closer to the teacher; contributes to the discussion and sings along, swaying with the children on either side	Comments, appreciates, and asks questions
2:50 End of day	Teacher smiles and holds eye contact

personal routines were met in this setting. Even sociable Pat took some time alone with the earphones. The teacher, recognizing and accepting Pat's social activity, provided a balance in the reading group, where individual work, physical manipulation of materials, and sharing were involved.

Less reflective, more confident looking than Terry, Pat went directly to activities such as the easel and "Tangrams" (Elementary Science Study, 1976b). For both children, the full-day kindergarten offered academic challenges as well as exploratory, joyful activities.

TEACHER-CHILD CONTACT

Children tend to initiate contact with the teacher for five basic reasons, and each of these requires its own response from the teacher, as listed below; the child's motivation for contact is given in regular type, and the appropriate teacher response follows in italic type (the teacher responses are also behaviors that teachers sometimes initiate).

1. Approval of work: *Appreciation, approval*
2. Attention: *Attention, encouragement, commentary, discussion, eye contact*
3. Information, verification: *Provision of information, suggestions for improvement*
4. Mediation of disputes: *Redirection of behavior; mediation*
5. Exchanging of plans, discussion of what to do next: *Commentary, discussion, preplanning*

Traffic jams and demands upon teacher time are sometimes tangential and avoidable. For example, children who repeatedly ask for materials or help in getting them, or those who seek attention and approval in disruptive ways or by interrupting instruction can be a constant source of distraction to the teacher who has not anticipated these problems. The following three guidelines will greatly help in minimizing such disruptions:

1. Anticipate what materials will be needed and prepare them before the children arrive; store materials near the areas in which they are used; make these locations known to all the children beforehand.
2. Arrange to circulate regularly and schedule times for sharing and appreciating children's accomplishments.
3. Discuss the problems with the children and ask them to suggest alternative ways of coping.

REFLECTIONS

As you reflect on the experiential, full-day kindergarten, imagine hearing what is happening. There is conversing: children with other children, and the teacher with individuals and small groups of children. There is a rather steady buzz of meaningful sound. Occasionally, you hear a dramatic exclamation or the clatter of fallen materials. As a visitor, you feel welcome but not necessarily noticed. Children seem to be involved in their activities and with each other as the teacher listens responsively to children's comments. The teacher seems to be enjoying the children and the active pace.

Sometimes you will see individual children or the teacher observing, perhaps while walking around. Sometimes you will see a child lie on a mat, savoring a few moments of solitude. There may be room-divider shelves or tables facing the wall, forming individual carrels where children will write, draw, read, or manipulate objects.

Teacher and children learn from each other. They live *in relation to one another*, the behavior of each one influencing the actions of the other. This is a shift in emphasis from the traditional setting in which children are loyally polite to the teacher as an "authority," or where children are "honest" and become "problems." Maria Montessori's (1965) pioneering conception can serve us well: The child should not learn for love of the teacher or for fear of the teacher, but for the love of the learning. When children have the opportunity to learn for love of the learning, they experience a sense of power, competence, and well-being. Later on in this book, in chapter 4, I will describe how teachers organize classrooms so that children can feel joyful in school and learn for the sake of the learning, in fulfillment of their natural sense of curiosity and their need to make connections. First we will take up in the next chapter some significant ways in which teachers work in order to create and support this kind of worthwhile learning experience for kindergarten children who are in school during the full day.

2

Professional Roles for the Teacher

When children spend the full school day in kindergarten, it is inevitable that the longer day will influence more aspects of their lives than would a shorter day. The greater responsibility for children's development suggests that teachers should be that much more aware of the impact they have on children; therefore, it makes sense to consider ways in which teachers function as they interact more extensively with children. This chapter looks at some professional roles that teachers can play in the full-day kindergarten in order to create and maintain a worthwhile learning experience. The functions of these roles include the following:

Mediating social behavior
Appreciating positive behavior
Questioning
Inquiring into learning conditions
Integrating learning experiences
Disseminating accomplishments to adults (parents, teachers, administrators)
Scheduling

MEDIATING SOCIAL BEHAVIOR

On a hot August morning before beginning kindergarten, Lee asked his father for ice cream money. Lee's father rummaged through his pockets and extricated five dimes, which he held out to his son. "No, Daddy, I need two quarters. Mr. Mack always gives me ice cream when I give him two quarters." "But Lee," his father said, "five dimes is the same as two quarters.

He'll give you the ice cream. You'll see." Lee protested, "No, he won't. It's not the same." After some repetition, Lee started crying pitifully as his father, who clearly had not read Piaget on the development of the conservation of quantity, fumed and shouted at him to stop crying about such nonsense or he would get no ice cream at all. Overflowing with tears and integrity, Lee missed an ice cream treat for his "stubbornness." Some time later, however, pained doubt about his contention nagged near the surface of his awareness.

Perhaps each of us has been Lee or met Lee and can retrieve the emotional power by which we acquired concepts. Whether or not we can recall, Lee's experience is a reminder that when children have trouble understanding, they may become anxious, aggressive, impulsive, or depressed. While early childhood educators have often cared deeply about children's feelings, we need to be sure to recognize and appreciate the interaction between feelings and thought. It is interesting to note that an entire remediation program for preadolescents is based on the recognition of this relationship and focuses attention on the *processes* of cognitive functioning rather than the end of *production* alone (Feuerstein, 1980). In a similar way, successful kindergarten teachers work at the processes of learning and interacting as they develop activities that stimulate in their children a sense of successful achievement.

Lee was learning about his self-concept when his father called him "stubborn." This child was being honest about how he understood quantity, which was on the basis of concrete appearances rather than by any abstract concept of an invariant amount. His father's response makes us wonder if Lee will risk honesty as readily in future.

Children need help with other concepts in school that may have an impact on social interaction and feelings. As mediators, teachers will need to help children toward building independence and inner controls by accepting their feelings and helping them to take responsibility for their behavior and, to a degree, control it. These purposes require that teachers create and support varied cooperative learning activities. Some issues and examples of the mediating functions follow.

Sharing and Cooperating

Some kindergarten children need help in classifying "mine," "not mine," and "ours." Children share more easily when they have a sense of possession. Generosity is also a cognitive attainment even though it looks like a purely social accomplishment.

A personal storage space and a personal writing booklet are easily provided basics that will give children an understanding of "mine" and "not mine." Along with this grows the sense of "ours," which successful teachers model by sharing with a helpful and cooperative attitude. Beyond "our" toys we have "our" jobs. "When we have materials to put away, you can finish with what you used and then help a friend." If everyone has a sense of everybody being responsible for replacing materials, children can look forward together to engaging more quickly in a forthcoming special activity. It is also helpful when you choose language carefully. For example, saying "I want you to . . . " places children in the role of satisfying the teacher's purpose. It is useful instead to say, "Now is the time for . . . " or "How would you suggest doing that?" Instead of saying what you *do not* want them to do or to stop what they are doing, ask them *to do* what it is time to do. (See Figure 2.1 for some other examples of positive language choices.)

Children can be asked to suggest how they can help one another when the teacher is occupied. Some kindergarten teachers and children have an understanding that all children in a group of two or four have to agree that they cannot help each other before they can seek help outside their group, whether from other children or from their teacher. This is a variation of the "quality circles" concept (Johnson, Johnson, Holubec, & Roy, 1984).

There are times when you can provide substitute materials to children who are struggling over possession. At other times, you can help children negotiate waiting and taking turns. "Now" and "later" are concepts that children need to classify through repeated experiences in which their expectations are fulfilled.

Activities that require mutual effort are useful, such as murals planned and executed together. Since children can be expected to have an egocentric notion of which side is up, a tablecloth worked from all four sides with felt-tipped pens is an ideal mural project. It could be offered for use at a parents' meeting. Dramatic play activities are also social activities that can take many forms. Children have created puppetry productions together, showing some of their productions and self-made puppets to other groups. This is a way they can receive additional recognition for focused work.

In order to avoid frustration and negativity when cooperation is sought, the teacher should try to anticipate difficulties. For example, if a teacher is planning a group discussion for the class, a child who speaks little English will do better with an activity in which there are concrete referents. This might mean planning a separate activity for that child, such as a puzzle, a painting, or earphones and a tape recorder with a story told in his native language. One teacher had had the foresight to arrange for a bilingual colleague and parent to tape record a translation of several classroom books.

An activity needs to make sense to a child before she can be expected to do it. If she refuses to participate or withdraws, there may be a variety of reasons. The activity may seem too difficult or too easy, and she may have trouble putting this into words. She may simply test the limits of her power by saying no. This negativity may be in part the child's way of corroborating her understanding of the situation or of asking for more information. There are other times when a child is already engrossed in an activity and nothing else seems as relevant. The teacher might say, then, "You seem to prefer to do this now" (respecting her feelings). "It is important for you to have a planning meeting with me sometime today. Do you prefer to meet before lunch or right after lunch?" (giving her responsibility and a degree of control).

The way in which the teacher makes a request or offers a choice will influence a child's perception and response. Children who are having their first school experience may need the teacher to explain that even newcomers are included when the teacher asks "all" or "everybody" to do something.

Competition is inevitable, but it does not have to be encouraged. While we may not value or seek out competitive pastimes, there are times when some people come out ahead of others. The winners have been rewarded by winning; therefore, the best that teachers can do is acknowledge accomplishment in a low-key way rather than magnify it. Instead, we may consider magnifying the efforts of everybody who played fairly, showed commitment to the larger group effort, and enjoyed the camaraderie and the effort itself. When children are worried about their standing in relation to others, competitive feelings grow. It is contradictory when a teacher urges helpfulness but operates a public chart with stars or points.

A positive force for cooperative work takes place when a group shares a problem together and builds group procedures. The teacher acts as an important model by accepting children's feelings and expecting responsible behavior where it is possible.

Aggression

There is hardly a situation where human beings gather in which aggression does not occur from time to time. Besides dealing with aggression that occurs at school, teachers must be prepared to help children who come to school already brutalized. Much aggressive behavior at school can be traced to these roots and will manifest itself in varied forms ranging from hurting others, destructiveness, verbal aggression, and other attention-begging behavior to apathy.

HURTING OTHERS. When children hurt other children, they need to be restrained. After the hurt child has been comforted, the aggressor must be spoken to and alternatives to violence must be explored. Teachers have used some of the following statements successfully in dealing with aggression:

"Come with me. We need to talk alone."

"We'll come back to the others when you are ready."

"When you learn to build with this, then you may have it."

"That hurt him. Tell him with words if you don't like what he did."

"If you want her attention, tell her with words."

"You need some time out." (A place and brief procedure should be discussed with all of the children ahead of time.)

"Let's talk when you've calmed down."

While a kindergarten child who is out of control can be removed physically from a situation, this is only a temporary measure. Teachers who find themselves physically dragging away children who do not respond to words must take stock of other more appropriate techniques and means of prevention, since the goal is to make children take responsibility for and bear the consequences of their own behavior. Certainly any teacher who hits a child is a negative model for the other children and has abandoned a professional role. Helping children to build inner controls is an important educational purpose.

Teachers can prevent a lot of aggression by setting up as few restrictions as possible. When children are constantly being prohibited from activities, they may ignore an essential prohibition because it is not noticeable among all the other restrictions. The following questions can be used as guidelines for an actively positive approach (see also Figure 2.1).

- How can you give children legitimate, varied choices?
- Are you giving children enough time to pace themselves?
- Are you giving enough notice before ending an activity?
- Are you frequently circulating, appreciating, and planning ahead?
- Are you sharing your appreciation of children's efforts when they are working in a positive way?
- Are you planning activities that create success experiences?
- Can you set up more situations in which children can make friends through working on a common task?
- Are there times when you welcome fun and giggles?

All children, and especially those who come to school feeling powerless, need to experience success in activities that they have chosen. They need to feel accepted and appreciated for their efforts. Daily activities should include legitimate, supervised projects that help children feel powerful. Especially relevant are activities for which there are varied interpretations, including the use of malleable materials such as clay, other art media, water play, woodwork, and sociodramatic play. Other large-muscle activities could include using balance scales or a pendulum or playing in a contained area in which marbles or beads can be rolled and aimed. Besides being legitimate ways to socialize, many of these activities possess aesthetic potential.

DESTRUCTIVENESS.　　When a child destroys equipment or another child's work, it may be accidental, a result of curiosity, or impulsive handling. Teachers should look at the child's intent and act accordingly. Assume positive motives for children. There also are physical considerations. Children need sturdy materials, and furniture and materials should be arranged properly. Perhaps classroom traffic needs to be rerouted by changing the placement of a table or a shelf. Some equipment might be moved outdoors. Still other equipment might be scheduled for use at a different time.

VERBAL AGGRESSION.　　When a child calls another a name or an insult or uses toilet words or sex-related words, it is usually in an angry tone. Rather than force the issue of apology by putting empty words in the child's mouth, a teacher would do better to see what the behavior means to the user. She might be copying older children, trying out new words whose meanings are unclear. She may also be testing the teacher's limits or trying to get attention. If she used to hit others and now uses words, then this can be seen as progress, an interpretation that should be shared with her. It also may mean that she needs more stimulating activity. Whatever the motives, it is reasonable to let children know that "When you call a person by that name you hurt his feelings." "It upsets some people to hear those words, and we do not like to hear those words used here."

Many teachers treat toilet talk as a phase or an attention-getting mechanism. They have been most effective in reducing and eliminating its presence by ignoring it in group settings, a model that the other children have followed.

ATTENTION-BEGGING BEHAVIORS.　　When a child takes things from others or takes home school toys as a way of feeling potent, an appropriate response is to pay special attention to him when he is working well, in terms of who he is. Notice and appreciate his positive efforts. When a teacher enjoys a child's activities or just enjoys his enjoyment, a message of acceptance and success is sent to the child. It may help to show sympathy toward his desire for an object that is not his and to accept his feelings, at the same time making it clear that his behavior is not acceptable.

May (1972) suggests that human beings show at least three types of responses when they feel threatened: "fight," "flight," and a "delayed response" (pp. 183–84). Fighting is dangerous. The flight reaction may or may not directly hurt anybody, but adults do become anxious when a child runs away or disappears. Unlike these impulsive actions, the "delayed response" is a more civilized attempt to consider alternatives. Children who fight or flee are sending a clear message that they need more positive attention and stimulating activities from parents and teachers, in the form of frequent appreciation of their work and their very childhood itself. To this end, it is useful to plan a regularly scheduled individual time to meet each child. The longer kindergarten day permits a more frequent, regular schedule. Even in a decentralized classroom, it is possible to miss regular contact with the quieter children.

APATHY VERSUS POSITIVE ASSERTIVENESS.   When legitimate forms of assertiveness are unavailable, human beings tend to turn aggression against themselves. One historian has documented the tendency among a suppressed group to teach their children to deny or control anger (Genovese, 1974). This denial has sometimes resulted in difficulties with real self-assertion, which can lead to apathy. Sometimes obstinacy, performing a task very slowly as if bored, or "forgetting" to do something are symptoms of such feelings. Apathy harbors the threat of leading to explosive violence.

Aggression has a positive side that we need to acknowledge. When you assert yourself, you risk action. For a child, assertiveness may involve testing limits. Aggression as well as apathy may be the only ways that a child can express her growing independence and communicate that legitimate self-assertion has been blocked.

Teachers have a chance to help children toward positive assertiveness by accepting their feelings and helping them to express their anger in forms that group life can support. When it comes to aggression, it is fruitless to fight fire with fire. In order to put out the fire, the fueling source must be removed and water added. In searching out the source of fuel for hostility, teachers will find that dependence and overly controlled situations make their contribution.

Children need to develop independence through legitimate responsibilities. When children feel secure enough to take risks, to try new activities, teachers have succeeded in helping them to feel competent and challenged. When children are legitimately active, they do not have the time or need to be mischievous. At most, they may use humor as a way of showing their power, as when a child knowingly matches objects incorrectly in jest. Children thus show that they know what they are doing and feel competent enough to play with their acquisition. Teachers can appreciate their humor and see it as a clue that they need additional challenges.

It is worthwhile to plan ways of working that reinforce cultural values. Shigaki (1983) found that Japanese kindergarten teachers expressed cultural

values that were present in school practices and observed in children's behaviors. Whereas "thinking" appeared among the Japanese teachers' values,
it followed after empathy, cooperation, perseverance, and creativity. With
the pressure in many school districts for academic achievements in the full-
day kindergarten to be narrowly defined by testing for the three R's, it is
important for teachers to increase public awareness of other values and
alternative means of achieving them.

APPRECIATING POSITIVE BEHAVIOR

When appreciation is given for children's processes as well as their
products, teachers can influence some of the cultural priorities that they
value. There have been concerns recently that teachers have become "flat"
(Goodlad, 1984) and "bland" (Sadker & Sadker, 1985) in classroom interactions. It is clear that children need to see models of enthusiasm, caring,
cooperation, and curiosity, if they are to develop into human beings who
display these traits. Figure 2.1 includes some examples of language that
teachers can use in modeling and encouraging positive values.

Plan activities in which children can learn to appreciate each other.
For example, one youngster at a time can be chosen to sit on the teacher's
lap as the other members of the group take turns saying something nice about
the target child (Donna Barnes, personal communication, 1978). During and
just after cleanup time are good opportunities to highlight children's efforts
and achievements. Plan activities where children can see their own progress
and the cooperative products of others. Examples include

Cumulative individual writing and mathematics booklets
Cooperative class books on topics such as beauty, friendship, and other
    values
List of books read by the class members
Collaborative class science fair, social studies display, or children's arts
    and crafts exhibit
Schoolwide multicultural fair with dancing and other arts

These ways of working have been used successfully with kindergarten
children who have varied learning needs. Their sense of challenge, which
should include a perceivable chance for success, will motivate their attention
to activities. When children feel that they have useful responsibilities, can
be active in their learning, and are pursuing important questions, they are
likely to spend more time involved in their schooling.

Figure 2.1:   Examples of Positive, Appreciative Instructions

Say it with words.	Please ask.
Use your indoor voice.	Share your idea with us.
Please speak one at a time.	What do you have to tell us?
Do you need help?	Take your time.
Can you hear her?	Please sit down.
Catch him when he's done.	Now is the time to...
You should be at the table.	We need to wait until lunch.
Take a little at a time.	It's safer to slide off.
You did it very well.	Please walk.
Let's do that together.	Look how nicely Tom's working.
Thank you for helping.	It's your turn.
Please hang up the...	Finish in the next ten minutes

It's his turn to speak now and then you can tell us your idea
Use this now; you can have a turn with that in a few minutes.
"Pretend that you are a [person] who knows how to share."*
I notice that you work better when you're quiet.
Let's listen to what Mel has to say.
It was hard to do but you did it.
You really seem to understand that.
It's great when you try out new ideas.
How can you solve that in a friendly way?
What other suggestions does anybody have?
That's one idea. Tell us how you got that.

*Paley, 1984, p. 87.

QUESTIONING

When one new kindergarten teacher asked how many children had had hot cereal for breakfast, three-quarters raised their hands. When she asked how many had had dry cereal for breakfast, three-quarters raised their hands. It was her dawning realization that often children will answer a question because they want to be right or agreeable, regardless of what might be the correct answer.

She began to notice how the ways in which she phrased questions influenced the quality of children's thinking and responses. She noticed that children came up with different responses when she asked questions *conditionally* (e.g., "What might, could, or would you or somebody else do . . . ?") than when she phrased her questions more *emphatically* (e.g., "What is," "Who can," or "Why do . . . ?").

Next she tape recorded group discussions and individual conferences and noticed how many yes-or-no questions she asked unintentionally. With practice, she built up a stock of alternative ways of phrasing questions. Instead of asking, "Did you ever get picked for something?" or "Did you ever feel sad because someone wouldn't play with you?" she began using descriptive questions, such as "What happened when you got picked . . . ?" "When were you . . . ?" "Tell us about a time when . . . " and "What might you want to do next time?"

When the content of activities and discussions called upon children's attitudes, opinions, feelings, and evaluations, they had plenty to say. Instead of a cycle of teacher-child interaction, there was much more interaction among the children, who listened to each other and elaborated upon one other's statements. Other types of questions that elicited expanded comments from children included some of the following:

- What does it mean when . . . ? Why might . . . ? How did you do that? (Explanations)
- What might happen if . . . ? How would things be different when . . . ? Suppose that . . . . Pretend . . . . (Guesses)
- Why would you pick . . . ? What do you prefer . . . ? (Choices)

These examples illustrate that the act of questioning alone will not serve best the aims of good education, but that careful attention must be paid to the content of questions. (See Aschner, 1963; Hyman, 1979; and Taba, Durkin, Fraenkel, and McNaughton, 1971, for extended treatment of this subject.)

Discussion Techniques

With less rushing in the full-day kindergarten, there is time for more significant, focused discussions. Experienced kindergarten teachers automatically use various group discussion techniques. For example, the teacher sometimes needs to refocus the group's attention on individual contributions as often as every second or third time he speaks:

Let's listen to Mary.
Van, can you hear Jamie?
I wonder what Phil is going to tell us.
Let's see if Dan agrees with you.
Imagine how far that game piece could move.
Let's all listen/look to see what will happen when . . .
What do you think about what Ali said?
It's great to see how interested you are. Now try to remember what you want to say, and you'll have a turn to say it after Jerry finishes.
Let's listen to Jerry finish his idea first.

Sometimes the group will refocus when a teacher lowers her voice abruptly or even whispers, providing a contrast while retaining eye contact. Abruptly pausing or changing the pace of speech may get attention. Overly enthusiastic children may be seated next to the teacher, where they may be reminded with a gentle hand motion to wait their turn. Occasionally the teacher might summarize what the group has agreed upon, in order to bring together different viewpoints. This is different from repeating each statement that a child makes, which might encourage children to listen only to the teacher's repetition rather than to the other children.

The subject matter of a discussion needs to allow all children to feel successful. When the purpose of an activity permits only a single correct response, some individuals may feel inadequate. It does little to help a child's self-concept if other children "help" the target child in a public situation. Consider the feelings of the "helped" child. In these situations the same child usually ends up getting help and could become a target for scapegoating. To avoid such experiences, it is preferable to plan group discussions in which varied interpretations are solicited.

The best questions to ask are those for which there may be more than one response. A teacher's feeling relief at getting a "right" answer from one child may come at the expense of another child's right to feel successful. It often helps to say that different people may have different ways of thinking about these things. Kindergarten children can be encouraged to reflect upon their responses: "First think about this question before you let us know what you think"; "Fold your idea into your hand/close your eyes/sit on your answer before we share." This is a way of building some early self-awareness (meta-cognition), as well. "Thinking first" also permits individual children to formulate their own responses before they are closed off by hearing somebody else's views.

Techniques for Aiding Comprehension

It can be exciting to share ideas during a discussion that follows hearing a story, seeing a film, taking a trip, or engaging in any stimulating activity. These kinds of discussions can be self-contained or lead to prewriting activities, experience charts, role playing, future planning, values discussions, or problem-solving sessions. Teachers help children to become more active and responsible for learning when engaged in discussions that encourage them to question and expand their contributions through predicting, experiencing directly, and comparing.

PREPARATION.   Before a story, film, trip, or other activity, it makes sense to prepare by predicting what might happen and by developing imagery. Questions could include

- What do you suppose you/we might find? Why do you think so? Where might the people be coming from/going? Why would they need to . . . ?
- Why do you think the other children are laughing at her?
- What are some other things that we might find?

Another set of questions, suggested by the "Wolf and Hounds" game by Dennis Sullivan (Downie, Slesnick, & Stenmark, 1981, p. 58), focuses on math and science skills. These questions encourage developing imagery as a strategy for problem solving:

- Who has the best chance of winning? Why?
- What would happen if . . . ?
- What are the best (and worst) places on the gameboard for . . . ?
- What moves should the hounds avoid?

Finally, instead of the usual practice of a teacher asking children splendid questions, consider McNeil's (1984, p. 30) suggestion that you ask children, "What questions do you have about this picture?"

FOLLOW-UP.   When children have shared an experience, you can help to sharpen their comprehension and critical skills by highlighting their reactions:

- What part of the story/film/trip did you like the best? Why? Other views? Why?
- What part did you like the least? Why? Other views?
- Which part did you find the most exciting/interesting/funniest? Why? Other views?
- Which character did you like the best/least? Why? Other views? Why do you dislike/like the character?
- Why do you agree/disagree with (name of classmate)?
- Think about this: What else could this character have done?
- What might have happened if he had not . . . ?
- How did this character feel? When was a time when you felt the way he did? What might have made him feel this way?
- If you had been this character, what might you have done when . . . ? How might you have changed what happened?
- If you could ask the characters questions, what would you want to know?

Role playing after children have had experiences helps them to express their understanding and to connect their comprehension with other feelings and experiences that they have had. This activity begins with some questions that help children to place themselves inside a character:

- Let's imagine that you could become that person. What would you want to do? Say? Ask? Know? Have happen? Why?
- What might be happening in this picture? Other views? Why do you think so?
- How do you feel about what Robin said? What else might be happening? Why?

The teacher then asks the class to agree on one problem and try to act it out. Children can then take turns trying out other problems and solutions. (See McCaslin, 1980; Paley, 1984; Shaftel & Shaftel, 1967; and chapter 5 of this book for other role-playing ideas.)

Values questions often arise. Questions such as the following tend to encourage children to consider alternative viewpoints:

- Why do you suppose that was important/worthwhile to them? When might they have begun to see it that way?
- What would happen if you were there?
- How might you help them to find a peaceful/friendly/honest/solution?
- Why is that important to you?
- What are some things she bought that you wouldn't buy? Why? What would be more important for you to buy?
- What if you/they felt differently?
- How might they do it differently the next time?
- If that happened to you, how might you feel?
- Why do you think that some people tell lies? What are some ways to get people to believe you?
- What might make him more friendly toward you?
- Why would you choose that way?

In the expanded interaction that is likely to result from such questions, teachers may find that, after planning half a dozen questions, only one or two are used in a particular session because children have raised other relevant issues that are discussed together.

NETWORKING IDEAS.   The networking or mapping of ideas and feelings after a discussion is one way of reinforcing content and comprehension. Usually networking takes the form of a structured experience chart, a constellation of pictures, or pictures with labels. It is possible to explore and represent an issue by making a kind of inventory. For example, using a "feely box" of textured items, teachers have asked children to feel an unseen object, always an attention-getting and suspenseful activity. Then they have created three lists and shared (1) how they would feel if they were to "become" that texture (or fragrance or appearance or shape), (2) what they might be, and (3) what they might do.

After reading a story, one teacher asked children to select a feeling from the story to use in a "semantic map" (McNeil, 1984; Pehrsson & Robinson, 1985). The children selected anger. Then they used arrows, pointing toward and away from anger, outlining areas that served to answer the questions, "What other feelings does anger remind you of?" "What other things that happened does anger remind you of?" and "What things could you do to feel better?"

Problem Solving

Solving problems involves recognizing patterns and making connections, and hence seeing things in new ways. Analogies are among the devices that help us to see things in new ways, and "synectics," a metaphorical way of learning and knowing, is a systematic approach to using analogies (Gordon & Poze, 1973, 1980). In looking at the other side of Dewey's (1933) notion that teaching is "making the strange familiar," Gordon and Poze (1980) make the point that creativity and problem solving "make the familiar strange." The conscious use of analogy and connection making are tools that help learning, creating, and problem solving because they help us find some familiar elements upon which to build solutions.

In synectics, the discussion leader's role in problem solving is "to form questions, keep the group within the process, and record the group's responses" (Synectics Education Systems, n.d.). The following are some synectics procedures that are useful in group or individual problem solving.

1. *State the problem.* State the problem briefly in up to ten words.
2. *Make a direct analogy.* What are some "living" analogies to the problem? For example, what animal acts like that?
3. *Define the differences.* How is that animal *not* like that? The sentence pair, How is _____ like _____? and How is _____ *not* like _____? is helpful in building stretch or distance between the referent and the analogue in direct analogies. In direct analogies, we try to compare a living thing with a nonliving one, in order to build greater stretch. We will find greater stretch as children have more experience and can deal with the transformation of functions between their referent and their analogue.

4. *Make a personal analogy.* Imagine that you are that animal, "become" the animal. What might you, as the animal, do? Say? Feel? How do you, the animal, feel when your friend brings you a treat? Takes away the toy? Wins the race? Breaks your sand castle?

The personal analogy phase is a sort of role-playing situation in which children can show how they feel or what they can do in their analogous role. It is useful to explore how the analogy is like and not like its referent, in order to suggest new possibilities.

In order to solve a problem, to make connections, there needs to be a knowledge base (Frederiksen, 1984). When compared with an adult, a young child who tries to solve a problem may focus on different variables. This happens because young children perceive things in unique ways. For example, faced with an overflowing bathtub because of a broken faucet, the young child may focus on the surface image of bailing it out. An adult might pull the plug and call a plumber (Elizabeth Meng, personal communication, 1982).

Young children may focus on surface variables in understanding or trying to solve a social problem. When children build rules together, and with their teachers, they tend to become more independent as they come to see other points of view. Piaget's (1950) concept of decentration reflects this interaction of affect and cognition and supports the notion that "logical thought is necessarily social" (p. 164). Through social interaction, thinking becomes more flexible. The teacher's role as a questioner who welcomes children's questions and curiosity is pivotal. Kamii (1984) suggests that, if children have had opportunities to develop a questioning attitude in general, then they are likely to develop a questioning attitude toward moral questions.

INQUIRING INTO LEARNING CONDITIONS

Let us think back for a moment to the questioning teacher mentioned earlier, who tape-recorded group discussions and individual conferences. She noticed her pattern of asking yes-or-no questions, decided that she did not prefer to use these, and then expanded her questioning techniques. By wondering about the impact of her questions, finding a way to collect information, and then trying out alternative, preferred types of questions, she became an inquirer, a researcher into her own teaching. There are a variety of ways in which successful teachers study their own teaching, some of which they take for granted without labeling them as inquiry or research. Observation is one of these ways, record keeping is another, and looking at children's work is still another.

OBSERVATION.   Observation begins as the teacher greets each child in the morning and intuitively experiences his mood, energy level, or state of health. Observation continues as the teacher circulates and teaches throughout the day, assessing what children have accomplished, where they need help, and what they need to be taught next. More systematic observation may take place after identifying one child's need for frequent attention whenever he is nearly finished with an activity and needs help in planning a transition to the next activity.

RECORD KEEPING.   When a teacher finds, for example, a child who has problems with other children or with work, and the teacher is not sure what to do, it may be helpful to keep brief anecdotal records about problem moments for a week or two, to gather information. If the teacher needs to know more about what a child is doing, she may want to jot down what he is doing at regular intervals for a day or two. When she reviews these notes after some time has elapsed, a pattern of behavior and a possible alternate way of working often emerge. Such records also have been shared with other teachers, who may provide fresh ideas for handling a problem.

PRODUCT SAMPLES.   When looking at children's behavior and the products that they create, a teacher can find additional insight into how to work with them. For example, several months into the school year, a teacher found that one child had never painted. Others have found that the drawings as well as the play of children who have been sexually abused may reveal their victimization (Koblinsky & Behana, 1984). The writing attempts of kindergarten children and their art work also show you their coordination, perseverance, and readiness for new experiences.

REFLECTIVE INQUIRY.   In various ways, we are in a position to find out more about children's behavior, our own actions, procedures that we can use, and content that we might present. The more reflective we are as professional teachers, the more able we will be to restructure our ongoing work. The process of such reflective inquiry involves the following steps:

Defining a problem, whether it is child behavior, the teacher's procedures, or the context
Collecting information about what is happening
Trying alternative procedures or materials
Collecting information over time and comparing old findings with new ones

There are limits to each teacher's personal informal observations or even more systematic "action research." Some teachers have found that collaborating on such inquiry and involving others such as school support or local college personnel provide for stimulating work conditions and an intellectual challenge (Elliott, 1979; Stenhouse, 1980). Ultimately, as institutions redefine the roles of teachers and college personnel and provide support for expanding the teacher's inquiry role with such things as time and personnel, we can create a stronger professional teaching practice and improved working conditions for all (Fox, Anglin, Fromberg, & Grady, 1986).

INTEGRATING LEARNING EXPERIENCES

It is not enough only to mediate effectively, appreciate appropriately, question relevantly, and inquire meaningfully. All of these various functions must be integrated in a balanced way. Examples of these functions are present throughout this book. Since activities are important to integrating curriculum, this section discusses technology and trips as two kinds of integrative activities that may take place during the longer kindergarten day. Although they can easily become isolated events in children's lives, they also can be integral to the task of providing rich experiences for kindergarten children.

Computers and Other Technical Resources

Computers and audiocassettes are resources in many full-day kindergartens. When they are well integrated, they conform to a number of consistent criteria, represented by the questions in Figure 2.2. Working with computers in an interactive way, there are times when you might stimulate children's critical thinking skills and perhaps tickle a sense of self-awareness, for example, by using the question pair: How did you do that? What might you want to do next time?

There are several recent articles on the use of microcomputers with young children including those by Barnes and Hill (1983), Burg (1984), Cuffaro (1985), Gilliland (1984), Hill (1985), Kreinberg, Alper, and Joseph (1985), and Swett (1984). There are also relevant materials that deal with the use and impact of television and film culture on young children (Honig, 1983; Paley, 1984; and Winn, 1977). Since it is apparent that computers and television are realities in the lives of children, teachers must be prepared to use them in appropriate ways.

We will need to consider the ongoing direct changes in children's play themes as we face the growing challenge of sorting out children from themes. Despite the strides that have been made by minority groups, women, and people with disabilities in recent years, the cultural impact of the mass media

Figure 2.2: Guidelines for the Use of Computers and Other Technology in an Integrated Kindergarten Curriculum

---

-Can children use the technology independently?
  Consider that an initial introduction to the resource may
  require that you show children how to use it and that you
  monitor periodically. Does excessive adult monitoring
  time take away from other priorities?
-Does the material add to the children's concrete knowledge
  base?
-Does it minimize the time available for the more
  worthwhile, concrete, manipulative activity for which it
  is a less effective substitute?
-Does it reinforce, introduce, demonstrate, or teach
  something worthwhile?
-What provisions have been made so that children can feel
  comfortable with the medium?
-Is equal access provided for girls as well as boys, so
  both may gain a sense of comfort in using the computer?
  With kindergarten children, perhaps comfort with the
  medium, rather than computer literacy itself, is a
  reasonable purpose.
-Can children set their own problems and explore
  alternative ways of solving them?
-When children find problems to solve, are there
  opportunities for alternative ways of solving them?
-Are there opportunities for cooperative work among
  children? While an individual audiocassette usually is
  used by one child alone, it also may be an opportunity
  to create materials that other children may use. A
  computer may invite use by dyads or small groups who are
  working together on a problem or game, quite as much as
  it may be used by individuals. Kindergarten children
  often use the computer together and the audiocassette
  alone.
-Is there some content-based learning that can be
  reinforced by these resources? For example, the
  perceptual model of indirect progress, where a player
  might sacrifice a turn in order to gain some other
  advantage, might be experienced in a computer game just
  as it might in a game of checkers. However, the
  graphics in a LOGO format might more flexibly represent
  indirect progress than would numerous variations on
  paper.
-Is the expenditure justifiable in relation to other budget
  needs and priorities? Parental and community pressure is
  sometimes a persuasive consideration regardless of how
  this question is answered.

---

continues to be a demonstration of stereotypical imagery and expectations. Therefore, we will need to integrate inclusionary curriculum consciously, planning for underrepresented groups to have opportunities and taking proactive steps to develop a relativist, egalitarian curriculum.

There is also persuasive evidence that parents need help in integrating computers and television into children's lives. Perhaps it is most important to influence parents to help children become selective, critical users of these resources while they maintain time for children to be alone quietly, to be with other children of different ages, and to be with the family at meals and other extended opportunities for conversation.

Trips

Somehow trips seem to abound in the springtime in northern climates; however, learning is supposed to take place throughout the year. Are trips less valuable at other times? There are certainly plentiful ideas for brief educational trips within and directly around the school, if only for environmental studies and even if the school has a hard-surface playground (Russell, 1973). Teachers should consider looking further at what places are worth visiting in their region, so they can extend and tie together school experiences with such visits. Some criteria for taking trips are represented by the questions in Figure 2.3.

Teachers find that the longer kindergarten day provides for more meaningful trips. All on the same day, they can accomplish what otherwise would be separated into several days, possibly diluting the educational impact. There is time for the following steps to take place:

Planning together with the children
Considering what they might find and predicting the possibilities
Taking the trip
Discussing and comparing their experiences
Creating a variety of graphic and symbolic representations of their
    experiences

Children can retain more connections this way than by waiting until the following day or after a weekend has passed.

A basic consideration in integrating any resource would be that it is consistent with the teacher's expressed values about worthwhile education for human beings. A real pressure upon the teacher will be the needs of the community as they are expressed directly and as they are interpreted by school administrators.

**Figure 2.3: Guidelines for Use of Trips in an Integrated
Kindergarten Curriculum**

-Can children see things on the trip that are otherwise not
available directly?
-Has time been taken to plan and prepare together with
the children? Have children planned questions?
-What are the reasons for believing that a particular
trip is relevant and that the children are likely to be
receptive to this particular exposure? Is this trip an
activity on which all of the children can focus, even
with different degrees of commitment and understanding?
-Can teacher mediation during a trip help the children to
see familiar things in new ways? For example, while all
of the children might have been to a supermarket with a
parent, they may or may not have focused systematically
on the setting of buying priorities, on the monetary
transactions, or the various roles of employees. The
teacher might arrange for a visit when the class could
observe deliveries as part of a study of the food cycle.
A study of the economic cycle might take the class on a
visit to farms and processing factories.
-Can a trip serve as material for reinforcing skills and
making comparisons and connections?
-Will there be sufficient time to allow for some follow-up,
preferably on the same day? With a full-day schedule,
teachers find that they can do a same-day follow-up,
retaining some of the strength and enthusiasm of the
experience before intervening events dissipate its impact
(S. Terens, personal communication, 1984).

DISSEMINATING ACCOMPLISHMENTS TO ADULTS

It is reasonable to state that parents want their children to achieve well in school without much suffering. While this may seem to be a fairly negative statement, it contains a degree of accuracy on the face of it. That is, parents generally perceive that it is worthwhile for children to "work hard" at school, but they complain when they perceive that a teacher is harsh or does not appreciate their child. This interface between teachers and other adults has another aspect to it as well. Kindergarten children who are active and learning should be using concrete materials and engaging in cooperative work with other children. To some parents, active children look as if they are enjoying themselves too much. Unless teachers take time to explain this look of learning in kindergarten, some administrators and many parents may dismiss what they see as "just playing around with toys."

There are several points at which we might communicate with other adults about how significant learning is taking place in the full-day kindergarten. Important areas in the classroom can be labeled, such as "Mathematics Area," "Science Area," and so forth. We can prepare educational bulletin boards and displays in the classroom and corridors that explain children's work and learning. Just before children leave at the end of the day, we can discuss briefly what they did that day and remind them of one or two highlights. In this way, they may acquire the necessary language with which to retain something to share, other than a puzzled expression or shrug, with parents who meet them after school.

Teachers can report on individual and group learning activities by arranging for parent conferences and parents' group meetings, and sending one-line notes home to a few parents each day. There could be a periodic — perhaps quarterly — one-page kindergarten newsletter. It is particularly important to let parents know which skills the children are learning as they engage in concrete, playful-appearing activities. It is also important to communicate similarly with administrators and first-grade teachers.

We should be sure to tell what we are doing to help children learn the skills that other adults understand and care about, while we can de-emphasize those methods that we do not value. For example, chapter 9 suggests a four-part approach to reading and language arts instruction. There are materials that children use and products that they create which are concrete and visible. Chapter 7 suggests a seven-part approach to acquainting other adults with mathematics education in the kindergarten. Chapter 5 presents concrete activities that reflect how children move toward more mature understanding of their social lives and the social sciences. These approaches focus on active, cooperative experiences that are meaningful and reflect how young children learn.

SCHEDULING

How activities are scheduled each day reflects the teacher's priorities. There are important ways in which scheduling can contribute to a positive learning atmosphere in the full-day kindergarten. Research findings have shown that full-day kindergarten programs have helped children to achieve more academic skills and have helped to reduce the necessity of repeating grades in later school years, and that parents and children have shared a positive view of the kindergarten experience (Adcock, 1980; Humphreys, 1983; Nieman & Gastright, 1975; Winter & Klein, 1970). Unfortunately, the researchers are less clear about what curriculum models were used in their studies.

Many half-day kindergarten teachers say that they need more time with the children. How they would use additional time reflects a broad range of philosophies for kindergarten curriculum development.

This book supports an experiential full-day curriculum that has clearly defined intellectual and social purposes in a caring, egalitarian context. Curriculum develops through ongoing interaction rather than as a body of plans fixed on the calendar. This book proposes that skills need to be learned not as ends in themselves but by being applied to substantive activities. The real work of education is to extend children's knowledge base and their capacities to think critically and make new connections. This experiential position exists in full-day kindergartens and in their flexible, varied schedules.

Teachers should keep in mind that what they schedule and how they make their decisions about curriculum reflects how they really feel about children. If children are seen as curious, active builders of knowledge, teachers will be likely to follow children's pacing needs, encourage options, and organize longer time blocks. When the deepening of conceptual knowledge and connection making is seen as a major purpose of the extended day, then the focus will be on substantive, content-based activity to which skills are applied and through which skills are learned. If we see the full-day kindergarten as an interactive relationship involving the teacher, the children, and the nature of meaningful knowledge, then it will make sense to us that different children doing different things at different times can have equivalent experiences.

The possibilities for scheduling daily and longer-term curricula are determined by the following three broad categories of kindergarten structure:

The full-day kindergarten with a single teacher responsible for the class

The full-day kindergarten with different morning and afternoon teachers

The half-day kindergarten with a single teacher, providing alternate full days for part of the class

The most enlightened school districts subscribe to the first of these alternatives. They expect the full-day kindergarten teacher to provide an integrated learning experience and use the additional time to deepen and extend the usual kindergarten pursuits. In this format, it is expected that the teacher will integrate and teach

More appropriate systematic readiness and skills

A deeper knowledge base that grows out of varied ways of knowing and interdisciplinary development

Activities in the arts and humanities

An experiential, intellectual curriculum based heavily on concrete, direct activities is possible in this format. Figure 2.4 represents some alternatives.

Figure 2.4:   Experiential Full-Day Schedule

8:50 Arrival
     Whole-group planning
9:20 Activity period. Teacher circulates and works in turn
     with three small instructional groups and individuals
     in reading, writing, mathematics, or science.
     Variety of self-paced activities in all subject
     areas, including reading, mathematics, sociodrama,
     science, media, arts and crafts, and games. How
     snacks are handled depends on teacher philosophy,
     which suggests either an integrated or a separate
     snack time. Integrated snack means that children
     can have a snack at their own pace, alone or with
     another child or children, or with the teacher alone
     or in a small group. A separate time denotes a
     setting where everybody takes their snack at the same
     time. Ideally, in either arrangement, the teacher
     would join the children in snack time and extend
     conversation and collegiality.
10:50 Whole-group sharing
11:05 Gym. Music, dance, group games, or calisthenics;
      indoors or out
11:40 Whole-group story time and discussion
12:00 Lunch/playground; activity period or planning
12:50 Quiet time, reading, or listening with headphones.
      The time directly after lunch/playground is often
      designated a rest time, a quiet time, or a diminished
      activity time. Sometimes music is played.
 1:10 Moderate activity period. Teacher circulates and
      works in turn with three small instructional groups
      in either reading, writing, mathematics, science, or
      social science. Variety of self-paced activities,
      excluding woodworking. In general, a less active
      time; fewer large-muscle activities are available.
 2:20 Whole-group sharing.
      Social studies discussion/planning; experience chart;
      creative dramatics; or special event. A special
      event denotes such occasions as a birthday time each
      month, other celebrations, the visit of a resource
      person, planning a trip, recounting and recording a
      trip, taking a short trip in or around the school,
      learning to use new equipment, cooking, or viewing a
      film.
      Day ends with singing, clapping, riddles, poetry. . .
 2:50 End of day

Some districts have tried to economize by using two teachers for each
half of the children's full day. Usually one half-day teacher is paid at the
contracted scale and the other teacher is paid at a lower, hourly rate. The
scale-paid teacher is expected to provide more academic work and the hourly
teacher more exploratory and recreational activity. The meaning of "aca-

Figure 2.5: Schedule for Half-Day Kindergarten with
Alternate Afternoon Programs

8:50 Arrival
     Group planning, discussion and sharing
9:25 Activity period. Teacher circulates, alternately
     working with small instructional groups. Children
     self-pace activities in reading, mathematics,
     science, sociodrama, media, arts and crafts, and
     games. May or may not include snack.
10:45 Whole-group sharing
10:55 Gym. Music, dance, group games, calisthenics;
      indoors or out
11:30 Creative dramatics, science subgroups, special event
12:10 Whole-group story time and discussion
12:30 End of day* for some children. Lunch for small group
      remaining. Size of small group can be six to twelve,
      depending on whether children return one or two
      afternoons each week.
1:00 Quiet time, reading, or listening with headphones.
     Individual instruction in concepts, reading, or
     writing.
1:20 Language arts, mathematics, or science lesson, using
     concrete materials. May include drawing, graphing,
     or writing follow-up. (One or two groups of six
     children or three groups of four children with
     teacher circulating.)
2:00 Creative dramatics; experience chart, crafts activity
2:30 Story time; music; or language games
2:50 End of day

---

*The morning may end at 12:00, in which case kindergarten
children join the whole school's supervised lunch program.
If there is a separate kindergarten 12:30 lunch, a teacher
aide begins the afternoon with the children, in order to
give the teacher a contracted lunch period.

demic" depends on the school: In one, it may mean intellectual, experiential curriculum, while it may mean an alienated, rote approach in another. In either case, teachers have expressed a sense of "not having enough time." In practice, when some teachers have agreed that the two emphases, knowledge and socialization, should be integrated, they have planned together and felt less pressed for time.

The third type of schedule is a variation of the full-day one whereby the teacher works with the entire kindergarten group each morning and half or a quarter of the class each afternoon. The rationale is to provide more individual attention. In some settings, individual attention is devoted to skills building, in others to socialization, in still others to a combination of approaches, and others offer an extended experiential curriculum. Figure 2.5 depicts a sample schedule for what might be done with this setup.

In these varied ways, the longer kindergarten day provides an opportunity for teachers to plan for extended, significant development of meaningful content and applied skills in ways that coincide with children's natural pacing and development. It must be remembered, however, that these opportunities and present practices exist in a community climate where there is often pressure for teachers to do more than is natural, sooner than it is possible. Some of these concerns are discussed in the next chapter, which looks at the larger societal and developmental contexts in which the full-day kindergarten takes place.

3

Influences on
Human Learning

The full-day kindergarten is like a partly empty house that needs furnishing. Now that there is more time, we need to consider why and how to fill it so that the inhabitants experience a sense of harmony. We face the challenge of using the additional time for content from which children can construct meaning, skill building that is applied to content, and planning that integrates learning activities so that children can perceive the patterns and connections in their experiences.

This house does not stand alone. The kindergarten is influenced by society, by our understanding of what knowledge is worthwhile, and by how young children learn. This chapter will deal with each influence in turn and then consider the implications of these influences for the organization of a full-day kindergarten.

THE INFLUENCE OF SOCIETY

Human beings need to learn how to survive in society, to be able to make sense of their experiences, and to be able to have certain expectations met. Presumably, society supports an educational system that will make possible the survival and improvement of its community. The increasing numbers of full- and extended-day kindergartens, and talk about whether or not to extend half-day programs, reflect some societal influences.

When we look at the great diversity of political systems around the world and throughout history, we are confronted with the reality that there are many ways to organize human society, some better than others. We therefore need to be aware of how our society influences our assumptions about education for young children, including the views we hold about the nature of being human. With increased awareness, each of us may be in a better position to decide what is worthwhile education for human beings of kindergarten age and to respond to the following questions:

- What sort of human being do we want in this society?
- What knowledge is worthwhile?
- What can and should children learn?
- How can learning take place in humane ways?

Cultural Orientation to Time

As an example of cultural diversity and its impact on our lives, let us consider the differences between Eastern and Western cultures with regard to time. Western culture tends to value a future time orientation in which scientific knowledge, abstract thought, and indirect, vicarious experience are prominent. These characteristics are associated with the physical and social sciences. Eastern cultures differ in placing a greater emphasis on a present time orientation that includes intuitive knowing, particular results, concrete examples, and direct, immediate experience. These latter characteristics are associated with the arts and humanities (Northrop, 1946).

This is not to say that either culture excludes aspects of the other's valuing, but merely that there is a difference in the emphasis and degree of significance given to certain activities and aspects of human personality. While it is clear that all human beings are capable of developing the capacity for the full range of human experiencing, cultural differences mean that people who grow up in different societies will interpret their experiences with somewhat different emphases.

It also means that schools will have different priorities. As awareness has increased regarding the richness to be found in cultural diversity, some educators have become concerned that our schools offer too narrow a view of the world. They have recommended that schools need to offer a better balance among the varied ways of knowing (Eisner, 1985). For example, our schools have traditionally held that informational and scientific studies are more prestigious and take precedence over such "frills" as the arts. Budget allocations reflect these values quite dramatically. Since young children learn best through physical, aesthetic, and socioemotional activity, their schooling appears more concrete, sensorial, and playful — and therefore less "serious" — to the untrained eye. In the past, when budgets have been cut, early childhood education has been reduced.

Impact of Technology

Whether children come into a school where values emphasize a present time orientation or a future one, technological factors influence what they perceive there and how they perceive it. They have spent hours each week watching television. They have seen movies. Many have played computer games, traveled on airplanes, and been to Disney's fantasy worlds. They have been entertained by content that changes focus every few seconds, exploiting their excitement levels and pumping their adrenaline. They have been manipulated by sophisticated advertising techniques that grab their attention, influence their perception by creating particular "figures" out of "backgrounds," use multimedia approaches, and command attention with sensory volume. With increasingly complex technology, it is difficult for children to understand how things work in direct, concrete ways. Their schooling experience can be confusing by sheer contrast. It is often programmed by textbooks in which variables frequently are not carefully controlled. Time seems to flow more slowly, and physical movement and verbal initiatives are controlled.

Technology also has had a profound impact on the economy by changing the nature of employment and the way families function. Jobs have become increasingly informational rather than industrial (Naisbitt, 1982). This means that more people than ever before are spending more time studying in preparation for employment, rather than learning on the job. They also are having children when they are older than in preceding generations. Teenage pregnancies, however, are rising (Frost, 1986). More women than ever are employed outside the home. Many mothers who work outside the home are either in one-parent households or in families that depend upon the mother's wages. The majority of mothers with kindergarten-age children appear to be working outside the home.

At a time when so many more working-class and middle-class families need access to a full-day education for kindergarten children, it generally has been the wealthiest families who have been able to buy full-day kindergarten placements for their children in private schools. There are a few subsidized programs that provide a small percentage of poor children with after-school childcare or full-day programs.

With public schools increasingly extending the kindergarten day, however, there is a closer match developing between the needs of the community and the offerings of the schools. Even when school districts have debated whether or not to have full-day programs and have given parents the option of sending their children part time, only a handful of families have used that option. With a highly mobile society, a high divorce rate, frequent serial marriages, and uncertain childcare arrangements, the school may be one of the most secure places for young children.

Implications for Kindergarten Education

These societal influences — philosophical, technological, economic, and sociopolitical — relate in significant ways to what happens in schools. In a future-oriented society, there is a tendency to push abstract, cognitive accomplishments, even though this is not in the best interests of young children. At the same time, kindergarten curriculum content has been based on the traditional folklore reflecting the "here-and-now" (Mitchell, 1921) experiences of kindergarten children.

While it makes sense for teachers to start where children are and to help them move to their next logical developmental steps, the here-and-now of today is different from what it has been for many decades. For example, controversial research points out some differences between the aggressive play of kindergarten children who play with baby dolls (more aggressive and repetitive) and the aggressive play of children who play with more mature-looking "Barbie" dolls (less aggressive and more varied and adventurous) (Abraham & Lieberman, 1985). Other research indicates that young children have fears about war and nuclear bombs (Engel, 1984; Myers-Walls & Fry-Miller, 1984; Reifel, 1984a; Tizard, 1984). Still other research indicates that certain personality traits (perseverance and self-direction) appear to be common among those preschoolers who prefer microcomputers (Johnson, 1984).

The family context has changed, too. Many young children are living in single-parent households. Even where both parents are present, families often exist in isolation from other generations and with fewer siblings than in earlier generations, sisters and brothers who could serve as role models and caretakers. There is the increasing phenomenon of "latchkey" kindergarten children who return to an empty home after school.

What we are finding is that society provides children with very different here-and-now data than their parents received. They are closer to adult imagery, to adult violence, and to adult technology (Paley, 1984). The crux of this issue is that the content of their play symbols may be changing, but their developmental capacities remain those of kindergarten children.

Despite these dramatic changes in the here-and-now, textbook companies persist in persuading administrators and some kindergarten teachers they can offer some all-new K–8 textbook series that will take care of *all* the needs for teaching children social studies or values or science or English — or even thinking. Worthwhile kindergarten practice has moved beyond such a fragmented, limiting view of "knowledge as information alone," to considering "knowledge for understanding and cooperation" (Fox, 1984; see also Kamii & De Clark, 1984).

Kindergarten teachers find that they need to consider what children bring to school and help them classify their information, compare and contrast their data, and deal with their feelings. Indeed, school is the single agency in society that is designated to help children develop their minds. It must be remembered that thinking processes are supported or blocked by feelings. If we do not pay attention to feelings, we are setting the stage for academic failure. Regardless of how caring, creative, and sensitive a teacher may be, a child's sense of academic failure can have a devastating effect upon self-concept. It is crucial, therefore, to identify what defines us as human beings, what knowledge may be worth knowing, and how young children may come to know while retaining their sense of competence and caring for others as human beings.

THE INFLUENCE OF HUMAN KNOWLEDGE

While society has helped schools to define what knowledge is valued, we are finding that knowledge is no longer as absolute as we once believed. Even in physics, pioneering research in the study of subatomic particles indicates that understanding and knowledge about space is relative and not absolute (Zukav, 1980). In a parallel vein, author Robin Morgan (1982) suggests that time is a relative experience; for example, it is experienced differently by those who are politically empowered than by those who have less control over time and planning. People who feel powerless are less likely to make long-range plans because they have a sense that time is out of their control.

As this relativistic view of knowledge has grown, there has been an increased development of interdisciplinary teaching. Multicultural education reflects a need for interdisciplinary studies that include sociology, anthropology, geography, history, political science, and the arts. Global education ties political socialization and multicultural education with history, geography, and science as concerns develop about the nuclear arms race and its attendant fears, about peace studies, and about ecology. These interdisciplinary approaches increase our awareness that experience is a relative business. Once this is appreciated, the knowledge suggests egalitarian ways of viewing other human beings, regardless of gender, ethnicity, ability, race, or beliefs.

Human beings are unique in a number of ways that also bind them together in a sense of human unity. They can

Engage in complex social communication with language and other abstract symbols

Use tools inventively

Integrate their experiences creatively, in Guilford's (1959) and Torrance's (1962) sense of originality, fluency, elaboration, and flexible sensitivity

Engage in imaginative play (Vygotsky, 1978)

Be distinctly social and cooperative (Rensberger, 1984)

Follow a unique predisposition to behave ethically (Wilson, 1978)

Classifying and Connecting Knowledge

In the context of the full-day kindergarten movement, school people
and community members are searching for a relevant knowledge base upon
which to "furnish the rest of the kindergarten house." This period is a time
for reforming kindergarten education to take into account both the depth
offered by each discipline and the breadth that is possible through the interdisciplinary approach. A framework must be created to help teachers plan
for both depth and breadth.

As we consider how to select content and make plans for a full kindergarten day, we need to account for the processes by which children both
classify and connect experience. This book is organized to reflect established
bodies of school knowledge in such areas as the physical sciences, the social
sciences, mathematics, the arts, and reading and language. However, because kindergarten children organize their experiences in natural ways that
cut across these areas, perceptual models are given as well that suggest interdisciplinary ways in which we can connect various subject areas through
networks of activities.

Perceptual models are ways of approaching and understanding the
recurring patterns of related elements, the isomorphic images that we can
perceive in different disciplines. Teachers use perceptual models as a way
of sequencing activities that support children's natural tendency to make connections between their experiences. The perceptual approaches of these
models are experienced by children as they engage in activities in which they
construct their own connections. Activity can begin with the ways of knowing in any discipline and connect across time with other activities that reflect
the ways of knowing in other disciplines.

This *perceptual-models* framework and the *structure-of-disciplines* view
of knowledge are both compatible with Dewey's vision of the teacher as helping children move toward humanity's "fund of knowledge" (1933, p. 137)
in ways that are consistent with children's total capacities. Each approach
takes a different way of looking at humanity's "fund," but both conceive

of learning as being active. They value a setting where children engage in inquiry that matches their capacities and is consistent with a constructivist view of knowledge (Piaget & Inhelder, 1964).

STRUCTURE OF DISCIPLINES

The structure-of-disciplines movement of the past few decades has been an attempt to deal with understanding rather than only with information. Educators and subject matter specialists have tried to define the uniqueness of each area of knowledge in terms of its idealized domain, distinctive "key" concepts, unique methods of inquiry, and language (Bruner, 1961; Phenix, 1964). Thus, organized knowledge is a source for activities from which kindergarten children can learn.

As a separate-subjects view of knowledge, the structure-of-disciplines approach does not reflect fully the continuity of human experience. It presents children with a preconceived view of knowledge. Children are expected to act upon, process, and order events within the scope of existing disciplines. Although the advocates of separate disciplines would not spoon-feed it, they propose that the school provide children with a precut pie, with each discipline existing as a piece of that pie. One may detect occasional juices dripping into adjacent pieces, but the cuts have, after all, already been made, and the relative sizes are culturally determined.

This concept of knowledge stands outside of children, and this is a problem. While reality may or may not exist "out there," knowledge is an inside experience, the child's construction, the result of the child's receptivity and responsiveness. The process of learning is a personal struggle, the process of becoming.

PERCEPTUAL MODELS

Experience with a perceptual model in one discipline helps us to make new connections with a similar model in another discipline. This encourages new learning, whereby the "strange" becomes "familiar" (Dewey, 1933). The following are examples of perceptual models, some of which are familiar to all of us:

The whole is more than the sum of its parts (synergy)
Indirect progress
Cyclical change
Double bind
Dialectical processes (Fromberg, 1977)
Recursive loops (Hofstadter, 1980)
Fractals (McDermott, 1983; Gleick, 1985)
Scroll waves (Briscoe, 1984; Sullivan, 1985)

Figure 3.1 charts the intersection of four of these perceptual models with each of ten disciplines that have been taught in school. At each intersection are some activities and ways of working that children can use to build connections between separate disciplines.

Examples of how to use some of these perceptual models in planning content for the full-day kindergarten are discussed in chapters 5 through 9. You can sequence activities on the basis of the perceptual model that they represent. The major purpose of planning for such interdisciplinary activities is to help children make new connections that transcend separate subjects. Perceptual models reflect the nature of knowledge as a relative, interdisciplinary experience in a dynamic society.

Indeed, McLuhan (1963) has suggested that "models of perception" can be a framework for planning: "It follows that any existing 'subject' in our curricula can now be taught as a more or less minor group of models of perception favored in some past or at present. Taught in this way any 'subject' becomes an organic portion of almost any other 'subject'" (p. 66).

The perceptual model is part of the human potential for pattern recognition. It has greater generalizability than its representations, just as the finite structures of language relationships or genetic molecules or myths can generate infinite possibilities from a finite set of symbols. Perceptual models are paralleled by other transformational theories.* Perceptual models distill these transformational theories as children construct a pattern of underlying transformations within different disciplines. Since perceptual models cut across existing disciplines, it is possible that children can experience varied ways of knowing.

Children can apprehend perceptual models through the active use of tools, broadly defined. The use of tools, including applied skills, in ways that are consistent with children's development is integral to the planning framework. The teacher repeatedly introduces perceptual models that are embedded in different activities, using varied methods of inquiry. Thus, they are constructed by children across time.

The sequence of activities can begin from the ways of knowing in any discipline. As activities develop, the teacher can plan other activities reflecting the ways of knowing in other disciplines. The activities are connected

---

*Transformational theorists in various disciplines include Chomsky, 1972 (Linguistics); Minsky, 1967 (Computer Technology); Pfeiffer, 1962 (Genetic Research); Moore & Anderson, 1968 (Game Theory); Levi-Strauss, 1969a, 1969b (Anthropology); Steiner, 1970 (Topology); Jung, 1970 (Psychology); and McLuhan, 1963 (Communications Theory). The interdisciplinary confluence between visual art, music, and mathematics presented by Hofstadter (1980) as "recursive loops" is a compatible theory.

PERCEPTUAL MODELS

DISCIPLINES	CYCLICAL CHANGE	DIALECTICAL ACTIVITY	INDIRECT PROGRESS	SYNERGY
History	Interpret ongoing cultural evolution. Hear oral history.	Interpret conflicting events.	Interpret nonlinear events.	Interpret explosive events.
Geography	Map population shifts.	Map conflicting earth forces (tides, winds, and so forth).	Map indirect environmental influences.	Map environmental and cultural diversity and change.
Economics & Sociology	Survey food cycle, group relationships, and changing groups.	Survey action versus reaction; scarcity; group conflict; cultural interrelationships.	Play with short-term sacrifice. Role-play social leverage and values difference.	Experience socio-dramatic activity. Study and record roles and group memberships. Make cooperative products.
Political Science	Narrate political shifts and changes.	Narrate human conflicts and values; double binds; invert reality.	Imagine and narrate human conflict and values. Influence people in power.	Experience socio-dramatic activity. Role-play voting and outcomes. Vote.
Physics	Observe and record seasons and relate to planetary motion. Concretize change and radio astronomy.	Observe gravitation; loneliness of mass; interactions of forces; aerodynamics.	Combine forces for motion. Experience centrifugal force. Explore levers.	Explore physical actions and reactions.
Chemistry	Observe evaporation and condensation. Make electric circuits.	Observe and change solubility.	Identify substances.	Cook representative food products, e.g., popcorn, yeast dough, making butter.

(continued)

Figure 3.1 (continued)

PERCEPTUAL MODELS

DISCIPLINES	CYCLICAL CHANGE	DIALECTICAL ACTIVITY	INDIRECT PROGRESS	SYNERGY
Biology	Seasonal returns to sites of outdoor ed. trips. Grow plants and animals. Classify dinosaurs. Survey human growth.	Observe interaction of environment and life forms. Control variables.	Study nutrition of plants. Control variables.	Study growth and reproduction of plants and animals.
Mathematics	Classify varied objects. Measure time and changes.	Classify object differences. Measure polarities.	Measure physical progress.	Measure transformed changes.
Arts	Create present-time aesthetic experience. Make symbolic representations.	Play with counterpoint in music, dance, and visual arts.	Experience movement ed. exemplars, e.g., partners, group contradance.	Contrast melodies with choral and ensemble work. Collaborate in movement ed., visual arts, and dance.
Language	Listen to literature about mythic monsters and poetic cycles. Record past and present. Oral composition.	Select poetic forms and literature about oppositions. Do related composing.	Select poetic forms and literature about indirect progress. Compose.	Select poetic forms and literature about collaborative elements. Compose.

over time because they are based on a common perceptual model. The most important requirements are that activities involve children directly and that children have a chance to make connections, either immediately or later.

THE INFLUENCE OF KINDERGARTEN CHILDREN

In addition to considering a contemporary societal context and the nature of relevant knowledge, a modern curriculum for the full-day kindergarten — whether we call it an experiential, relative, interdisciplinary, constructivist, transformational, or perceptual-models curriculum — needs to consider the ways in which kindergarten children's right to an active, participatory education can be represented. It is relevant to consider how children learn what is worthwhile.

Kindergarten children learn through activity, exploring, playing, seeing patterns, and making connections. Their feelings of competence and their social experiences are as critical to their learning as are the availability of concrete materials and activities. Therefore, we need to attempt to assure success for children by respecting their ways of learning. Six ways in which kindergarten children learn the best are highlighted in this section. Examples of activities that use these ways of learning appear throughout subsequent chapters.

Inductive Experiences

One of the ways kindergarten children learn best is through direct, inductive experiences. When they have multiple, concrete physical or linguistic experiences, there is the possibility that they will perceive new patterns. Therefore, as teachers, our job is to provide contrasting experiences as we control variables. When we provide contrasting experiences, children are given an opportunity to perceive a new "figure" emerging from the contrast with a known "background." Children then have the chance to perceive the change and to extend their learning. It is simply easier to perceive something that is moving in this controlled way than something that is still and camouflaged.

Research into memory has shown that once we perceive something we never forget it (Luria, 1968; Piaget & Inhelder, 1973). In fact, as we grow, our perceptions become part of the networks of other perceptions and thoughts and become more accurately retrievable. Accounts of memory and connection making by Einstein (Sullivan, 1972) suggest that much of the imagery of the young child is an initial form of creativity.

Cognitive Dissonance

Another way kindergarten children learn is through *cognitive disso-nance* (Festinger, 1957; McNeil, 1984). When children expect something to happen and something else happens, there is an opportunity for cognitive dissonance to take place. Cognitive dissonance involves a three-stage process: predicting, transforming events through experiencing, and comparing. This is an essential learning process and the way in which critical thinking develops. Children restructure their expectations as a result of this ongoing analysis of the contrast between what they expect and what they find. They become better at differentiating what they may perceive and what is real.

Cognitive dissonance occurs first through concrete comparisons. An important difference between adults' thinking and children's thinking is that adults can manipulate abstract ideas and symbols and become more self-aware. Young children are much less able to stand outside of themselves (decenter) and see their behavior as others see it or to appreciate somebody else's ways of viewing a situation. As children develop increasing self-awareness, they are decentering themselves from their immediate, concrete environment.

Theories of development suggest that young children are much more centered than adults on the world of objects and what they can see, touch, and hear (Bruner, 1966; Piaget, 1965). They perceive the world in unique ways. As they classify their experiences, the decentering process is an occasion for growing self-awareness. An example is a statement such as "I *have been* the youngest, but I *am* the youngest no longer, and I *will become* the biggest" (Merleau-Ponty, 1964, p. 110).

It is important to note that self-awareness, the development of awareness of one's own thinking, is a dynamic, developmental process that is more likely to be dependable in preadolescents (Piaget, 1976). Before that time, children go through a series of transforming experiences that lead toward greater consciousness. These developmental phases include intuitive functioning without self-awareness or with incomplete awareness. Sometimes young children who appear to function and act adequately will contradict what they have done when asked to describe or explain their own actions or to direct others to do as they have done.

This process, known as metacognition, develops by degrees in a gradual process as we have experiences and get feedback from our environment. Activities that create cognitive dissonance for kindergarten children can contribute to this development. Metacognition and imagery are mental processes that help human beings to solve problems. They become coordinated through direct experiences.

As children begin to classify experience, it is possible that they will connect properties and variables in special ways that may be closed to adults as a result of acculturation. Where adults see a scientific phenomenon, a child might surrender to an aesthetic experience. During the ascendancy of this perceptual processing, young children are probably at the zenith of their absorbency, creativity, and flexibility in uniquely ordering the world. To lose this imagery is to diminish an individual's humanness and range of action. A lost fact or abstraction can be found, but the loss of flexibility is probably beyond salvage. Kindergarten teachers have a responsibility to help children maintain this flexibility of thought in a world marked by explosive change.

Social Interaction

A third way that kindergarten children learn well is through social interaction with other children. As they interact, children have the chance to observe different ways that other children solve problems. They can also disagree and exchange conflicting points of view. These contrasts between the way they behave and how other children behave, and between what they want and what other children want, are important ways in which they experience cognitive dissonance.

While young children may have difficulty "conserving" quantity in mathematics, they learn about the perceptual model of "double bind" emotionally as they deal with other children. They learn that hostility may be masked by a friendly exterior and that love may be delivered through clenched teeth. Children learn to "conserve" feelings in this sense before they learn to conserve quantity.

Children also explore different ways of satisfying their wants and needs and have the chance to develop ethical alternatives. The teacher's ability to plan activities and use unanticipated moments to explore ethical issues through skillful discussion techniques is pivotal.

Physical Experiences

Kindergarten children also learn well through physical experiences. When children move and manipulate the physical world, they begin to understand relationships between themselves and objects, and between objects. Concepts of space, time, change, causality, quantity, and, ultimately, quality develop first on a physical level. This is why physical knowledge has long been a focus for early science and mathematical study (Kamii & De Clark, 1984; Kamii & De Vries, 1978), and it is certainly a central way of knowing and using the arts.

As children engage in large-muscle activities, they perceive in kinesthetic and aesthetic ways many images and concepts for which they will later develop language, other symbols, and logic. Moreover, by exploring space physically, children come to appreciate and be aware of their own bodies in new ways. Space is another medium in which they can feel successful and strengthen their self-concepts.

Play

A fifth way that kindergarten children learn best is through play. When children play, they use their imaginations to try out perceptions and experiences. They can feel competent, powerful, and in control. It is through imaginative play that young children extend development and behave in advance of their years by subordinating themselves to rules, even flexible ones, thereby acting less impulsively (Vygotsky, 1978, p. 99). Morgan suggests that play, as part of being human, "is as basic a human need as food and water and air, in that it is perhaps what *makes* us alive, or at least human—this irrepressible capacity for creative play, this dogged, insatiable, tragicomic, both wild and disciplined need to *sing*" (1982, p. 277).

Through play, children merge the "East" and "West" in each of us. Play integrates the rational and intuitive aspects of our experience. It is a process by which young children achieve cognitive development by reconciling the aesthetic, physical, and socioemotional means of learning. Thus, play is the ultimate integrator of experience.

Competence

The final way that kindergarten children learn best is through a sense of competency. Children feel able to risk themselves and to try new things when they can anticipate the possibility of success. There is an emotional as well as a cognitive side to all experience. Children are willing to maintain or create tension both because they are curious and because they need to feel effective (White, 1959). They can feel satisfied by the process of being active, with or without a clear product.

When children create—and the teacher provides—activity ideas that can be done legitimately in divergent ways rather than only one way, there is a greater opportunity for children to feel competent. When there is only one possible way to do things or only one "correct" response, there is more likely to be competition, a sense of powerlessness, and more discord.

Children who practice skills can feel more powerful if they can use concrete materials that have built in self-correcting devices. When skills are applied to content areas, children have motives for practicing them in order to fulfill their curiosity and sense of competence. Skills are not ends in themselves. Skills are merely tools that serve the human needs to understand, create, and make friends.

REFLECTIONS

In order to provide an education in kindergarten that helps to develop caring, intelligent, cooperative, independent, curious, competent, responsible, and concerned human beings, successful kindergarten teachers have been taking into account these six ways in which kindergarten children learn. They have considered the integration of knowledge, remained open to the ways that children construct their worlds, and helped children apply skills to meaningful content in active, concrete, and careful ways. Exemplary teachers have done so with sensitivity, warmth, intelligence, and good humor.

The full-day kindergarten, an outgrowth of societal changes, is an opportunity to reform kindergarten education and to complete the work begun by enlightened half-day kindergarten program developers. It challenges us to use the time in an integrated, distinctive way that reflects our contemporary understanding of knowledge as a relative phenomenon which kindergarten children construct out of significant, concrete experiences. In the next chapter we will discuss how to organize and manage a full-day kindergarten classroom that reflects the influences that have been considered in this chapter.

4

Organizing a Full–Day Kindergarten

This chapter focuses on how the exemplary classrooms referred to in chapter 1 came to be organized, in light of the influences previously discussed. In order to understand these "decentralized" settings, it is useful to look at how teachers and children decide on their

Purposes — why they will plan and act
Choices — what they will be doing
Space — where they will be engaged
Pacing — when they will be participating
Social activity — how and with whom they will interact

We will look together at how these decisions can be made carefully, in ways that reflect how young children learn most naturally, relevantly, and appropriately. The tendency to make kindergarten a replica of first grade does not fill the bill. The kindergarten year is a significant time and experience, worthy for its own sake and not merely as a stepping-stone to later endeavors.

TRUTHS AND MYTHS IN CLASSROOM ORGANIZATION

The truths that guide our decisions about how to organize a uniquely relevant, appropriate, and natural kindergarten year need to be separated from a number of myths about classroom organization that have been part of kindergarten practice in some places. These myths may have grown out of the dearth of positive forms for kindergarten education, and we need to set them aside as we discuss more exemplary practices.

MYTH 1.   *There should be a period of time during each day that is devoted to reading (or mathematics) instruction and related activities, for everybody at the same time.* Those who maintain this position also tend to hold the corollary view that all children should have a "free play" period at the same time. Inasmuch as there are few independent readers in the kindergarten, independent reading for children who are outside the teacher's immediate instructional group is an option that has limited usefulness. The teacher would have to monitor children during reading-related activities when they need instruction, while trying at the same time to teach part of the class.

It makes better sense to attempt to teach a reading or mathematics group while the rest of the class is able to engage in more independent, self-directed activities, other than only reading- or mathematics-related work. For example, when a teacher is trying to teach reading to a small group without interruption, it makes sense for the other children to be self-directed in independent areas such as sociodramatic activity, observations in science education, conducting surveys, the arts, and educational games that reinforce learning. Kindergarten children can work in these kinds of activities with discontinuous teacher monitoring.

MYTH 2.   *If some children are playing board games, doing art projects, or engaging in sociodramatic activities, then children who are working with the teacher will feel deprived.* On the contrary, children working with the teacher have an opportunity to feel successful, to receive the teacher's direct, personal, caring attention, provided that the instructional activities are involving, appropriate, and relevant. Children in a well-organized classroom know that the full range of activities will be available for their use at some time. It is simply a matter of taking turns enjoying the teacher's direct attention, as well as working independently and with other children. Problems are more likely to occur when children are starved for self-direction and concrete materials, and/or feel pressurized and then erupt explosively.

MYTH 3.   *Reading groups should vary with ability but there can be whole-group instruction in mathematics.* Since it is clear that individuals vary in their grasp of mathematical concepts, this myth places a lesser value on mathematical learning. In a subtle way, it discriminates against those children who have difficulty in mathematics. This is especially likely to affect girls, since they tend to acquire more "math phobias" than boys do (Tobias, 1978). Also, schools usually offer more reading remediation than math remediation, so the smaller groupings for mathematics instruction would seem to make better sense in the first place. Especially with the recent national awareness of the need to improve mathematics education, it makes sense to offer more equal access to effective instruction by adapting to children's varied learning needs.

Moreover, whole-group instruction tends to be largely verbal and abstract. Kindergarten children, however, learn best when they are physically active, using concrete materials. Small-group collaborative work and plentiful participation strengthen mathematical learning.

MYTH 4.   *Pull-out programs serve mainly to fragment the school day.* Pull-out programs are those times in the school day when individuals or small groups of children leave the classroom in order to receive more individualized instruction in such areas as remedial reading, speech improvement, instrumental music, English as a second language, resource room work, and programs for gifted or talented students. Rather than attempting to reach all of the group during these times, for assignments or planning, these times can be viewed as opportunities for teachers to work more closely with the children who remain, to strengthen the instruction for individuals or small groups, to launch particularly messy activities that require a lot of direct teacher monitoring.

MYTH 5.   *Each child should have an assigned seat.* This assumes that the greatest part of the school day is spent (1) seated, (2) engaged in sedentary work such as paper-and-pencil tasks and workbooks, (3) being quiet, and (4) alone. Instead, each child should have a place for the storage of personal materials. Rather than an assigned seat, it is preferable for children to work in areas that have provisions for focused materials such as an art/special projects area, a writing area, a science/mathematics area, a sociodramatic area, a library area, a media area, an alone area, and a teacher's instructional area. In this way, the atmosphere is more like an amalgamated library/living room/family room/studio than that of a factory or a penal colony.

MYTH 6.   *The beginning of each school day should start in the same way, with the ritual recording of the weather, the calendar, and attendance, in order to give children a sense of security in routine.* When teachers consume as much as twenty to forty minutes on such repetitive procedures, children are placed in a bind. They want to be cooperative, and they know they are expected to appear attentive, although they may be bored. They learn that they are expected to be duplicitous in school.

There are numerous alternate ways to begin the day. A most meaningful way is to plan those activities that children might do during the day or hour ahead. (Additional alternatives will be found in subsequent chapters.) Indeed, sharing options and choosing beginning activities together is meaningful not only at the beginning of the day but perhaps again after lunch or other openings of large time blocks. It is a very important way of empowering children to participate in real decisions that affect their lives, as they share in choosing activities and pacing their work.

CHOICES

Kindergarten children are quite capable of making relevant choices from among activities at home and school. Indeed, when any human being chooses to do something, her level of attention and commitment is likely to be much higher than if a choice were not available.

This is not to say that "anything goes." Clearly, those materials and activities that exist in a classroom have been largely preselected by you, the teacher, beforehand. Even those activities or materials that children have brought to school, for use in school, have been filtered by you. If some of these contributions are less than ideal, you accept as much as you can in order to make the child feel welcomed and appreciated. At the same time, there are items that you may prefer to exclude on the basis of criteria shared with the parents and children ahead of time, for example, those materials that might be dangerous, violent, prurient, or developmentally unsuitable.

There are also *degrees* of choice that children understand because they have become conventions in your classroom. A real choice is an informed choice, an activity to which children are receptive and that they can pursue at a level of challenge or possible success. For example, you might say, "These are the activities with which we can begin the work period":

- *What.* What would you like to do to start your day?
- *How many.* We can have four people at the science area water table. Who else would like to join Deb?
- *Now or later.* Stephen, you had some writing to finish today. Would you like to begin with it now or do it later this morning?
- *Either/or.* Eden, you haven't been in the art center or in the socio-dramatic center for awhile now. Please choose either one or the other.
- *Now.* Mel, I will be starting the day with a base-three block game. You are ready for it now after doing so many games with base two. (Even at the level of "Now is the time," it is possible that if Mel had a pressing need to work in a different area, the teacher could respect his plans and feelings and include him in a base-three block game with another group at another specific time.)

When children have practice in choosing their activities, their attention tends to be more dependable. Moreover, from the first day, they have repeated practice in asking themselves the questions, "What will I do when I finish this?" "What will I do next?"

Where space in an area is limited, teachers have used various signals to limit participation. They have hung up a limited number of hooks on which children can place their photographs or name tags. Sometimes they have posted a number card with a matching number of marks so that a child who wants to enter an area can match the marks, one to one, against the number of children already there. Sometimes children place a mark next to their own name to indicate that they have been in an area.

Kindergarten children can carry on without continuous teacher supervision. The degree of choice for independent activity is earned. For example, if we were unable to monitor the ongoing work, we would not send a child who has trouble sharing to the carpentry bench. When children are more self-directed and independent, then we have more opportunities to teach small groups and individuals. The most important support for this system takes place when we take the time to circulate before and after each brief instructional time in order to keep in touch with the entire class as individuals and small groups working together.

SPACE, INDEPENDENCE, AND RESPONSIBILITY

How you organize the space in your classroom communicates how independent and responsible you really want children to be. It also communicates what kinds of activities you value and how children will spend their time.

For example, if the chairs and tables are lined up in one direction facing a chalkboard, it would seem that children are expected to focus on the teacher at the chalkboard or the materials on their individual desks, rather than in cooperative work with others. This placement also signals that a major activity will be to sit at assigned seats and work with paper and pencil for much of the day. This setup means that materials are placed in areas other than where they will be used, therefore, either there will be traffic created when children need to acquire materials independently of the teacher or there will be a monitor to distribute materials to passive recipients.

Exemplary programs arrange space differently so that materials are stored in the places where they will be used. This way, books are in the reading area, writing materials and children's individual writing notebooks are in a writing area, and art supplies are in an art area. Old newspapers are stored where potential messes are likely. Children work in the area where materials are stored. From time to time during the year, the teacher would change one area or another in order to highlight new concepts, materials, or experiences. Teachers consider that parts of the room used for active work should be kept at a distance from those parts of the room in which the children are expected to concentrate and to reflect.

Having materials accessible to children in the areas in which they will be using them means that the children can get them independently. The only time they would need to ask the teacher for help might be when materials run low unexpectedly or when unanticipated events suggest the need for things that are not present. When everybody needs to get a jacket from the wardrobe at the end of the day, teachers have invited individuals gradually — by initial letter of their name or particular kind of clothing — to select two or three friends with whom to get their clothing together.

There should be no designated "front" to the classroom, just as there should be no assigned seats or tables. Children store their personal materials in a number of ways other than in desks, such as

Cubbies
Clothing closets
Shopping bags hung from clothes hooks
Storage drawer cabinet
Shelves marked with children's names
Teacher-created "mailbox" system using empty ice cream cylinders or
    large cans nailed together
Shirt boxes
Empty commercial tea containers

Teachers use a variety of furniture to create spatial divisions, nooks, and areas defined by functions. Low bookshelves, screens, and the teacher's desk placed perpendicular to the wall immediately create areas in which children can feel part of a smaller group, focus on a particular activity, or even find a place to be alone. Consider the design of a classroom as a variation on L-shaped arrangements or configurations resembling perpendicular E's (i.e., set base to back), or combinations of the two.

Creating areas for limited uses means that you as a teacher need to present concretely some of the possible uses of the area. Occasionally you will need to "advertise" — announce in a graphic way — some activities. The area itself helps children to be more independent because it helps them answer the self-directing questions, "What will I do next?" and "Where will I put this when I finish?" A limited-use area should be labeled for everyone to see, such as "Art Studio," "Science," or "Writing." This also helps parents and other adults who enter the room to understand the range of worthwhile types of activities that take place.

When you are establishing an area for limited purposes, it is useful to ask yourself what you would need to use if you were a child in that area. It may well be that writing materials should be available in more than one "writing" area. As we shall discuss later, in addition to content, the needs for privacy, participation, and social activity are things to consider when placing furnishings and materials in your classroom.

A classic early childhood educator, Sheehy (1954), suggested that a good environment for learning held "invitations to learning." Building from this image, you can be a legitimate merchandiser of significant activities. Some advertising techniques that you can use include

Creating an aesthetically attractive setting
Contrasting a focal figure against an uncluttered ground
Using redundancy of product image and name
Changing the packaging, name, or location of a product or a service

Space should be comfortable as well as inviting. Since young children feel comfortable on the floor, you need to legitimize it for them. Arrange for the school, parents, or local businesses to provide mats or carpet remnants. Also consider having commercial carpet in the block-building area, in order to cut down on clatter. Other ways of making space inviting include providing a variety of seating arrangements beyond and including institutional chairs. Some classrooms include one or more soft armchairs or a couch that has been donated. Occasionally a small set of stairs for sprawling, a window seat, cushions, or a five-sided packing crate are available.

PACING AND ROUTINES

When children are engaged in different activities, or even when they are doing the same things, you can expect that different children will need different amounts of time to finish their tasks. Therefore, the built-in questions, "What will I do when I finish this?" and "What will I do next?" are basic if children are going to be independent and responsible. Of course, if you expect your children to pay attention to the activities in the first place, then they will need to perceive that what they will be doing is personally and educationally relevant and worthwhile.

As you circulate throughout the classroom, you will notice who is nearly finished and who may need more materials, a more varied activity, or additional tasks. When you anticipate children's attention spans, you can help individuals or groups to re-plan for their next activity or for a new phase, as they continue the current activity. In this way, by modeling the need to re-plan or to break down a task into subparts, you also reinforce the children's independent involvement. For children who may have problems with focus or who have special learning needs, you simply do this more frequently.

During a full kindergarten day, there might be whole-group planning times at the beginning of the morning and afternoon, and perhaps a shorter gathering around eleven o'clock. Then again, you will do frequent mini-planning with individuals and small groups throughout the day, as you circulate.

Successful full-day kindergarten teachers have found that it is critical to plan at least two long blocks of activity time each day during which children can engage in different degrees of choice and self-pacing. This encourages children to make longer-range plans and increases their relative sense of personal control and motivation for work. Some teachers begin such a time block with more sedentary activities and establish a signal, such as hoisting a flag or matching two pairs of clock hands, to show when larger-muscle areas such as the sociodramatic area are open.

Everyday Routines

Some of the activities in the full-day kindergarten classroom can be scheduled to occur at the same time each day, but others depend on the pace of groups or the needs of individual children. Successful teachers have found it best to anticipate these routine occurrences and develop strategies for handling them that are easily communicated to the children and minimize the demands on the teacher's attention.

CLEANUP TIME

From the first day of school, children can learn how to be responsible for replacing equipment or materials so that they can find them again and other people can use them. You can reinforce this responsibility by repeatedly asking children to ask themselves the question, "Where will I put this when I finish with it?" One teacher modeled replacing materials during the first days and would permit only "very capable" helpers to assist, explaining the need for keeping the materials and equipment in place for the next users. Replacing materials became a prestigious activity. You might outline the places on shelves where blocks can fit and the places on pegboards for woodworking tools or musical instruments. Then cleanup time also becomes a matching activity.

You can show consideration and respect for the children's need to concentrate by first circulating with the reminder, "Finish what you are doing because it will be cleanup time in a few minutes" and then following this with, "Now is the time to put away the materials." Remind those children first who have the biggest cleanup job and last of all those who have little more to do than finish reading a sentence. This way you are less likely to have children with little to clean up wandering aimlessly and getting into mischief.

This is also a good time to appreciate children's work and assess what help or instruction they may need. After most children have finished their work and before it is cleaned up, you can take a few moments for the whole group to focus on the different accomplishments of small groups and individuals, appreciating efforts and progress as well as results. You can encourage less risk-taking children to try new kinds of materials by having them see work in progress and projects in varying stages of completion.

SNACK

Just as many teachers respect children's need to pace themselves differently when they work at academic tasks, they respect different needs for food, privacy, rest, and toileting.

When it comes to snack, more and more full-day kindergarten teachers are setting out a snack table around mid-morning. Often children prepare and set out the snack with the teacher, and they can take their snack when they have need, much as they would do at home. This practice eliminates the time spent in transition from an activity period and permits children to move at their own pace in finishing activities as well as taking a snack. Since children learn this routine very quickly, there is not usually a problem of mass attack at the snack table. Children learn that it will be there for them as others vacate the chairs.

TOILETING

Toileting also should be self-directed rather than scheduled. At most, before beginning a story, the teacher might suggest that anybody needing to use the toilet might do so before the story, in order not to miss a part or interrupt the attention of the group. Similarly, five-year-olds should be encouraged to use the toilet before leaving on a trip outdoors.

EMERGENCY SIGNAL

There are times when you need the immediate attention of the entire group, especially when there is an emergency. When you have a shared signal, and use it only rarely, children are likely to respond right away.

In one setting, on the very first day of school, the teacher shared an emergency signal with her children. This signal was used only rarely for such occasions as fire drills or special scheduling reminders. She said, "When you see my arms up or anybody else's arms up (as in the 'halt' position), then look to see where I am and raise your arms for others to see. I will use this signal only when we have to do something very important right away or when there is an emergency."

Raising both arms has the effect of stopping activity and producing a quieter atmosphere, and using a body signal eliminates the problem of trying to find a piano, bell, or light switch, which may not even be at hand, such as when you are outdoors.

Schedule

The hours as well as the length of the full-day kindergarten need to be considered. In one school district, for example, the bus company dictated that the kindergarten should begin at 9:30 A.M. The teachers and principal protested because so many of the kindergarten children tend to wake up very early and have already been active for two or three hours before school begins. Then, by afternoon, they seem to need more time to be alone (Sheila Terens, personal communication, 1984). Although the bus company prevailed in this case, the school staff continues to appeal for the school day to start at 8:30 A.M. It makes sense to start the school day when children are their most active and social and to let them go home earlier.

It also is advisable to pace the day so that more active choices are alternated with more sedentary choices, after the initial activity period. Teachers have observed that children are able to concentrate better after active play than following quiet activity. It isn't wise to string several whole-group listening activities together any more than to overstimulate children with whole-group large-muscle activities one after another.

When children have options and can pace themselves, they manage to find their appropriate activity level. For example, in looking at children on a playground on a hot day, you will notice that children may start with activities in the center of the playground but will tend to move to peripheral, shadier areas as the afternoon wears on.

When you schedule long time blocks in which children can choose among varied activities, they will naturally develop the stimulation sequence that they need, just as Pat, one of our case examples in chapter 1, did. The longer kindergarten day makes such scheduling practical.

If you have taught a half-day kindergarten and met a second, different group in the afternoon, you may have felt the pressure of trying to "fit in" the varied program components as well as helping with boots and sweaters several times for each group. In the full-day kindergarten, this sense of pressure can be avoided and a more relaxed atmosphere promoted by scheduling longer time blocks for small-group and individual instruction and participation. Lunch, recreation, and rest and relaxation also need to be planned in consistent ways that sustain the wholesome pacing of stimulation throughout the day.

LUNCH

Your school may have food available for children at lunchtime or simply offer milk or juice for sale. It is important for someone to escort the children to lunch. During the first week of a full-day schedule, this could be done by you in order to provide a smooth transition. At the same time it is helpful if the regular lunchroom aide can come to the classroom ten minutes before the children leave for lunch, to escort them. This should be sufficiently important to the principal and teachers in a school for them to find a way to make it happen, even though flexible scheduling and minor budget adjustments may seem daunting at first.

Consider also that, if your school was not built to accommodate kindergarten children in the lunchroom, you may need to check the height of the cafeteria counters to make sure that young children can see what food is available and to manage their trays (Joyce McGinn, personal communication, 1984). Also, cafeteria lunch service normally will take a bit longer for kindergarten children than for the general population.

An alternative to the cafeteria arrangement in any school is to have children take turns bringing and serving food family style at their tables, when lunch is available in the school. If children bring lunch from home, they might take turns serving milk or juice and setting the table, even if only with napkins. It is preferable for children to sit at smaller tables rather than at tables for twenty. This encourages conversation and a sense of belonging.

RECREATION

Following lunch, and before rest, many schools have a recreational period in the school yard or gymnasium, depending on the weather. For kindergarten children, it makes sense to use an area containing equipment that fits their size and is suited to their capacities.

Some schools provide tricycles, climbing apparatus, and large hollow blocks, both indoors and outdoors. A sand box, a garden, balls, hoops, ropes, and other equipment for large-muscle use have been provided. One school provided phonograph music for free-form dancing during indoor lunchtimes. Some interesting choreography resulted in a group of kindergarten boys and girls. In still another setting, from time to time the gym teacher or an aide would lead group games, ball-and-rope games, or "New Games" (Fleuegelman, 1976).

When there is enough constructive activity available and several adults who can circulate, converse with children, and appreciate their efforts, children are likely to be constructive and civilized. It is worthwhile to train lunchroom aides to use positively worded suggestions and instructions and to speak to nearby children rather than those at a distance. If constructive activities are not present, children will seek stimulation with each other, sometimes in asocial ways.

It is worth asking yourself what children will be doing that they perceive as relevant and stimulating. If you find yourself in a school with a tradition of requiring children to stand in line formation for any length of time, consider finding another teacher ally who can help you plan and install more appropriate alternatives. Then children can return to class ready to concentrate and focus their energies constructively. It is this sort of activity— wondering about what is happening and acting on your values—that makes you a professional.

REST AND RELAXATION

Even though teachers and children find ways to pace themselves with ongoing active and sedentary pastimes during the full day, teachers find that it is important to plan ahead and pause for rest, relaxation, and quiet recreation. Let us look for a moment at five-year-olds at home. After lunch, what do they usually do? It is rare to find a five-year-old taking a regular afternoon nap at home. With rare exceptions, most toddlers give up a regular afternoon nap between two and four years of age.

Consider also how a family deals with inter-age planning when there may be a baby, toddler, kindergarten child, and older children at home. Clearly, whoever needs a nap takes a nap. Whoever does not need a nap is either involved in independent activity, playing near an adult in the home, or doing things with an adult or another child. If somebody is taking a nap, the others at home would either move to another area or keep down the sound level or sudden noises, in order to avoid waking the sleeper.

These observations may seem quite ordinary; nonetheless, teachers sometimes find themselves engaged in lengthy debates about rest time, naps, and discipline problems that arise during this time after lunch. In schools where caring people have thought about these matters, there is usually a flexible rest time after lunch. You, the teacher, also need time to yourself. In some settings, there is an area of the classroom where mats are placed for the occasional children who may have fallen asleep after the others have put away their mats. Often the rest time for full-day kindergarten children is about twenty minutes in duration.

In the Lawrence (New York) Early Childhood Center, children lie on their mats in a dimmed room and listen to recorded music. One week might be Mr. Mozart's week, and the next might be Mr. Beethoven's. You can see children lying down, sometimes with a stuffed toy, listening and keeping time to the piece. In other schools, children might sit or lie reading a book, playing quiet board or card games with one other child, or working on a puzzle.

Different individuals have different needs for quiet and privacy, so provision should be made for meeting these needs throughout much of the day.

PRIVACY, PARTICIPATION, AND SOCIAL ACTIVITY

The school setting is, at best, contrived. Because of this, it is especially important that you carefully consider providing for private experiences in the full-day kindergarten, as well as for social participation. In order to humanize the experience, you will need to create a caring, comfortable, and physically involving environment.

The need of human beings for privacy some of the time and social participation at other times is a personal need. Each human being needs time alone. A child at home with one or two siblings often has a favorite place to be alone. Whether this is in an armchair, in a space behind a couch, underneath a table, or in a bathroom, it is important that it is there.

In your kindergarten, too, you will need to create places where a child can feel alone, when he or she feels the need. Montessori encouraged children to retire to a mat, taking with them something to learn from, as a signal to others that they wished to be alone. Other teachers have used

Crannies in the reading area
Carrels (sometimes created by cartons) facing a wall
A listening center with earphones, facing a divider
A pup tent or tipi in the classroom
A carpet square under a table
A cushion in a corner
A blanket-lined packing crate

Teachers discuss with the group the courtesies of privacy for individuals who are using these or similar facilities.

In quite as conscious a way, you will need to plan for social interaction that is constructive and for activities that lend themselves naturally to cooperative work. Learning is strengthened by social interaction. Piaget (1965, 1976) reiterates the importance of dialogue with peers where contrasting views and "cognitive conflict" become a source for cognitive feedback.

Spontaneous social interaction creates opportunities for repetition of ideas and techniques that children need to learn. Indeed, the oral repetition for children that takes place in cooperative learning situations increases information storage and extends memory (Johnson, Johnson, Holubec, & Roy, 1984; Slavin, 1983). Teachers in exemplary full-day kindergarten settings plan significant, independent, small-group learning opportunities for children.

There are also a number of occasions during the school day when participation in whole-group activity is reasonable. Periodic planning periods for the whole group have been mentioned already. Among other occasions for the whole group to be together are

Story time, at least once each day
Celebrations
Special resources (e.g., film) or visitors
Discussions of group process issues
Plays and performances
Music and movement education
Sports
Sharing work
Lunch
Rest time

In some classrooms, snack time is a whole-group activity, with the teacher participating in conversations. In other classrooms, snack is provided for children at a small table during an activity period so that children and their teacher can meet and help themselves at a natural break time.

You will find additional ways of providing for privacy, participation, and cooperative work throughout this book.

A professional teacher in the full-day kindergarten spends the majority of time working with small groups and individuals. Teachers will spend most of their time instructing and circulating. In well-organized, effective classrooms, teachers spend more time on instruction and less time on procedural distractions (Barnes & Edwards, 1984).

Organization and content blend to create the quality of learning experiences that children have in school. In helping children to feel powerful within the classroom organization, teachers will help them to do what they perceive as relevant and stimulating. In the chapters that follow, there are numerous activities that teachers can use within the full-day kindergarten structure that has been presented here.

PART II

The Interactive Content of the Full-Day Kindergarten

5

The Social Study
of Social Science

This chapter looks at how children can learn about their social world in ways that promote understanding and cooperation. The chapter opens with a discussion of the significance of sociodramatic activity as a major social learning medium and tool in the kindergarten. The remainder of the chapter is devoted to an analysis of two main approaches to the teaching of social studies: the structure-of-disciplines approach and the interdisciplinary approach.

The structure-of-disciplines approach as a basis for organizing instruction is applied individually to the ways of working in five of the social science disciplines: history, geography, economics, sociology, and political socialization. This discussion includes numerous activities that can be used in the kindergarten classroom.

Next we will examine two interdisciplinary approaches to teaching social studies. The first takes a look at the unique area of multicultural education, where the knowledge base is still in its formative years. The second discusses another perspective, the perceptual model of cyclical change. We will see how it can be used to integrate knowledge and activities across disciplines, thereby bringing great breadth to the social study of social science.

THE SOCIODRAMATIC AREA

Sociodramatic activity is a valuable, legitimate medium that helps kindergarten children develop in a variety of ways. By engaging in imaginative play with others, children come to appreciate that other human beings have feelings and ideas that may be the same as or different from their own.

When they represent themselves, however incompletely, in other roles, children are mapping relationships and working out personal moves and alternatives for which mathematical sociologists could produce matrices. Children are experiencing on the social, aesthetic, and physical levels what eventually will become cognitive awarenesses, as they continue to develop and make new connections.

As in all human interaction, "reversible thinking" begins to grow as children come to recognize the legitimacy and possible relevance of other persons' views and feelings. Children, originally centering their perceptions on their own views, strengthen their perceptions of others as they continue the process of decentering through sociodramatic activity. As we observe their interactions we will be able to assess some of their social science understanding and needs as well as their behavioral skills.

In this respect, fantasy and imagination play important parts in extending cognitive development. This kind of activity is ideally suited to the kindergarten child's level of development. Fantasy and imagery are early forms of symbolic representation that stimulate and prepare children to interpret and use humanity's full range of symbolic forms, such as written language, mathematics, and the arts.

Setting Up the Sociodramatic Area

Children come to school with a base of experiences on which they can build imaginative social plays. You as a teacher bring to the children opportunities and provisions for extending these experiences by introducing tangential activities, new "figures" that children might perceive and use. You can focus attention on social studies by creating a defined space for sociodramatic activities. It is worthwhile to ask why you might choose to provide certain equipment and materials and then consider how they could be used.

The equipment and materials in a sociodramatic area can serve various functions for children in today's world. It is a useful practice for each teacher to make a yearly reevaluation of the material elements in the school. Sociodramatic play has been invested traditionally with the major task of supporting the incidental learning of young children. Some adults have narrowly defined this learning in terms of bits of factual accretions and conversational skills; however, there are further-reaching implications for children's experiences with sociodramatic play.

When teachers talk about starting to provide instruction for children at their developmental levels, there is a tendency to refer unquestioningly to the "here-and-now" experience of children. This appears to be a reasonable principle; however, as we discussed in chapter 3, the "here-and-now" of today's young child has changed dramatically since Lucy Sprague Mitchell

(1921) coined the term, and it continues to change. Judging from the material provisions given in many schools, we might conclude that there has been only the barest recognition given to these changes. For example, while not all kindergartens provide for a sociodramatic area, the housekeeping corner and the block corner, when they are present, are relatively stable and predictable, as unquestioned assumptions. Yet a closer look will tell us that children's play in the housekeeping corner will tend to reflect their relatively specific base of experience in some *specific* sort of home. By contrast, their experience base in construction activities, which is reflected in block corner play, is relatively *unspecific*. It is axiomatic that that which is specific provides clearly *convergent* guidelines for its use whereas that which is unspecific suggests more *divergent* interpretations.

With the changing roles of women and men in our society, especially in relations to each other and their work, the traditional housekeeping corner and block corner appear to be contradictions at the least and repressive tutors in the extreme. When we look at children's play in these areas, it is apparent that sex-role stereotyping is often present. Children break into groups of boys playing mainly with the blocks and girls playing mainly at housekeeping. Although there is visiting between areas from time to time as part of the play, and an occasional girl will venture into building, or an occasional boy into parenting, the larger picture remains segregated.

Research shows that children's language in the housekeeping area is severely restricted (Cazden, 1971). It may be that the rituals and routines are sufficiently repetitious and limit expanded possibilities, especially when the same children repeatedly meet one another. The very furnishings, being highly specific, appear to sustain traditional images and close off one of the major purposes of early education — the maintenance of openness to new connections and alternative possibilities.

In contrast, block play, building with nonspecific materials, stimulates symbolic representation, divergent imagery, and comfort with spatial relationships. Girls are willing to play with blocks, particularly when the teacher is present. Boys are more likely to reject typical housekeeping tasks. Researchers corroborate that traditionally female roles have already been categorized as less desirable in the early years (Maccoby & Jacklin, 1974).

This is not a surprising finding when you review the popular cultural images of women and men, strongly communicated by television, books, and adults who are the repository of generations of shaping. Women are presented as people who have passive, convergent, and trivial pastimes, while men have active, divergent, and creatively adventurous pastimes. Very early, teachers need to participate actively in avoiding the subtle ceilings that are placed on the aspirations of girls as well as on members of other groups who have been culturally underrepresented or mistreated. When school experience affects aspiration levels it also touches the very marrow of an individual's self-concept and general feelings of success, guilt, and anxiety.

There is a growing redefinition of the role of women in the family and the larger community. This reflects an increasing commitment to the ethical issues of preventing a caste system within a society that intends to be democratic. With this in mind, consider the possibility that a large investment in a separate housekeeping center, filled with specific equipment, is unjustified. Particularly now, when school districts are doubling the numbers of classrooms as they move from half days to full days in the kindergarten, there are reasons for spending limited funds in ways that reflect modern values.

The sociodramatic area provides an excellent alternative to the housekeeping or doll corner. In it, there would be a place for blocks, a variety of dolls, and nonspecific at-home symbols, alongside puppets, props representing retail shops, hospitals, other community experiences, and travel opportunities that empower children to include and move beyond a limited piece of here-and-now experience. The emphasis in this area is on the integration of sociodramatic contents and skills. By extending dramatic play beyond housekeeping, all children may comfortably participate.

Activities in the Sociodramatic Area

At different times in different classrooms, kindergarten children engage in a range of sociodramatic play other than housekeeping. A look at these varied activities suggests several sorts of provisions for socialization. Children play at

> Going for an automobile, a bus, truck, railroad, or covered wagon trip, and traveling to many places for vacation, business, or curiosity
> Moving from their home, using a moving van
> Going to an airport and flying in, or piloting, an airplane; going for a space trip in general or to the moon or other planets
> Taking a boat trip and engaging in harbor play, oil rig work, and fishing fleet activity
> Going to an emergency on a fire engine, in an ambulance, on a boat under flood conditions, in a police car, or on a horse
> Visiting the hospital, police station, jail, fire station, post office, telephone company, ranch, farm, beach, or desert
> Going to the bank, library, movies, theater, garage and fixit shop, or construction site
> Going to the printing shop, factory, restaurant, toy store, candy store, bakery, supermarket, shoe store, department store, or bicycle shop

Children play not only at going and coming, but at arriving at, participating in, and operating the environments that they have created. Children display power in humorous ways as they act out television commercials and substitute their own frequently uncomplimentary words and phrases. In addition to playing with the sounds of words themselves, children are displaying skepticism about propaganda and advertisements that seems to grow more readily when they have had contacts with older role models. Therefore, consider planning for inter-age projects from time to time, keeping in mind that for kindergarten children, activity is often episodic in that there may or may not be a clearly defined beginning or ending.

It is clear that you would need more than a single year to use as many topics as have been mentioned here or the many others that could be conceived. One group of children would be unlikely to generate this much variety in any significant depth. Also, children in different locales would be inclined toward different commitments.

PROPS.   The following things serve children as props in their sociodramatic play:

Puppet frame, purchased or made out of a cardboard carton; puppets
Wooden screen
Two-dimensional façade of a wheeled vehicle
Floor blocks and other blocks used as dishes, foods, nonstandard measures, microphones, tickets, weapons, splints, gems, and furniture as well as furnishings for different interior and outdoor settings
Cut-out cardboard "television" screen
Wooden or cardboard cartons of varying sizes used as vehicles, hospital bed, coffin, lake, valise, and tray
Ropes and strings
Real and toy telephones
Variety of caps, hats, belts, badges, buttons, ribbons, vests, boots, shoes, scarves, and other articles of clothing for costumes
Sticks, twigs, broom handles, and rubber or plastic piping, used as a magic wand, stethoscope, fire hose, fishing pole, sword, saw, axe, and orchestra conductor's baton
Disembodied wheel from a broken toy or shopping cart, circle of cardboard, or commercial toy as steering wheels
Pulley system with ropes and boxes or baskets that extend across a section of the room

In addition to these imaginative uses of everyday objects, children can use commercial toy accessories such as miniature trucks, cars, airplanes, animals, dolls, and wooden people. Be aware as you include wooden people that there are those that suggest careers. Ideally, these should represent both men and women and different ethnicities in an equitable way.

Resources and imagination will limit the specific large equipment and props that you can have. If anything, be careful about overstocking to the point of inhibiting activity or movement. Sometimes less material can lead to more imagination. One kind of screen or frame can serve as a retail store, a ticket booth, and a cashier's counter. You may find puppetry and a super-market too much to handle in the same space or you may find a way to fit in both activities. How many options and when you make them available are important administrative decisions that you can discuss with children.

PUPPET PLAY.   Provision for puppet play is an important element in a sociodramatic area. Hidden behind the puppet character, more reticent individuals can enter the stream of social interaction. Kindergarten children can use puppets that they have made alongside or instead of commercial puppets. They have made puppets from some of the following materials:

Paper bags
Oaktag or paper plates stapled to sticks
Styrofoam balls with buttons held on by pins
Stuffed toys with capes draped over them
Stuffed stockings
Balloon "heads"
Woodwork constructions
Papier-mâché.

As children feel the security of hiding behind the puppet, they can save face when the puppet is reprimanded. An entire commercial "self-concept" kit (Dinkmeyer & Dinkmeyer, 1982) uses puppets as a major vehicle for discussing socialization issues. When children use puppets, their voices change. Stutterers will occasionally speak more fluently, and children often identify comfortably with the puppet character.

Puppets alone do not create dialogue; they are only a vehicle for dia-logue. Children need ideas and a positive focus in order to use puppets in a constructive way. While ideas will come from their experiences, they will need your help from time to time if puppetry is to develop beyond a punch-ing show or peek-a-boo humor. You can help by addressing the puppet directly.

FLANNEL BOARD.   A flannel board with felt forms to manipulate is a variant of puppet play. Children can act out their fantasies, reproduce parts of stories that they have heard, or alter sequences of stories. *Ask Mr.*

Bear (Flack), in which a child asks each animal to suggest a birthday present for his mother, and other simple cumulative tales are easily adapted and seem perfect for this medium. You might provide some uncut felt from which children might construct their own characters or props. Inasmuch as a certain amount of cutting, sewing, and possibly gluing could be part of these activities, a crafts shelf should be nearby.

BLOCKS. Large floor blocks are stored in the sociodramatic area as an integral part of that area and its activities. When this is done, various props and costumes, which may increase verbal interaction, can be integrated with the block play, and boys and girls are more likely to work together. In this way, all of the children can build skills in spatial relationships. (The uses of blocks are discussed also in chapter 7.)

OTHER PLAYTHINGS. Such materials as Lego, Tinker Toys, and Erector Sets should be nearby. It is easier to manage and retrieve the many pieces of these toys when children use a cloth mat on which they can play with each of the sets. Most kindergarten children prefer to use these materials on the floor, and mats also can serve as effective containment for the playing ground. Each set can be stored with its own mat.

These toys can be used by two or three children at a time, or by an individual, together with floor blocks, miniature animals, or other figures. The toys also can be used to make representations of figures and miniature furniture. As long as their purposes have a constructive focus, the children's new associations should be encouraged and appreciated.

From time to time, children may want to include the class guinea pig in the sociodramatic area. They also can construct and use their own electric circuitry to light the puppetry area and other projects. When science materials are nearby, children may come to see new relationships and divergent ways of using materials.

SYMBOLIC REPRESENTATIONS. Children's writing and other expressive forms often grow out of sociodramatic projects. Children welcome labels and picture symbols on their constructions and projects. They have created shopping lists, receipts, and tickets. One child was happy to wear a dust mop on her back, representing a tail, and a sign on her shirt that read "rabbit."

Sometimes children feel impelled to repeat their episodic play, at which times it becomes ritualized. The play then lends itself to written records, audiotaping, and photographed records. Teachers and children can "save" cooperative constructions by photographing and drawing them. Saving children's work in these ways signals to them that you appreciate and value their cooperative ventures. It is also a useful way to communicate with parents about your program.

OUTDOORS AND INDOORS.   In the full-day kindergarten, teachers schedule a balance between classroom activity and the large-muscle activities that are possible outdoors or in a gymnasium. These latter areas are outfitted with such things as large hollow blocks, a climbing apparatus, and tricycles. Sometimes there are tunnels, huge parachutes, inflated trampolines, ropes, pulleys, balls, large wagons, and hoops, all of which are useful and enjoyable equipment.

The outdoors and the gymnasium are important socialization resources. Experienced teachers circulate to help children extend the imaginative possibilities of their play and to encourage increased physical development. Among other things, they

Engage in episodic role playing with children

Raise questions about alternative social solutions

Stimulate questions and contrasts that grow from aesthetic, mathematical, or scientific perspectives

Introduce vocabulary

Bring together children who need one another

Appreciate cooperative efforts.

When packing crates, real discarded boats, automobile tires, hollow blocks, and wagons are available, the sociodramatic activities continue. Most important, outdoors or in the gymnasium, they can be much louder and larger in scope. While facilities vary, it is particularly helpful when there is an easy flow between indoors and outdoors.

The Teacher's Role in the Sociodramatic Area

Smilansky (1968) has shown that teachers can intervene successfully in children's sociodramatic play without unduly influencing its content. A combination of the teacher's help in learning play techniques and the children's direct, school-enriched experiences is demonstrably more effective than one or the other exposure alone. Smilansky observes that the early childhood teachers initially resisted intervening in children's sociodramatic play. Although the same teachers felt comfortable in stimulating their own offsprings' play at home, their philosophical preparation for teaching inhibited such activity with the children in their schools. However, Piaget's position, that "creative imagination" improves with stimulation and experience (1962, p. 289), is in harmony with Smilansky's findings. Modeling and stimulating cooperative and problem-solving social interaction is far better than a laissez-faire atmosphere or training children to say the "right" thing. In short, teachers and researchers have found that it is all right to play with children in their classes. Everybody learns.

ADD A MATERIAL.   When an activity has been well developed, perhaps repeated, it may be useful for the teacher to add a material to help extend the activity. Teachers also can add signs such as "stop," "no parking," or "gas station," or they can supply play money, bags, boxes, string, a box marked "cash register," and even drawing materials.

REMOVE A MATERIAL.   Occasionally it makes sense to remove a material from the activity, such as when children ignore the presence of a thermometer or have had access to the cardboard television screen for more than a month. If it is relevant to bring back a removed material after a few weeks or months, the children often perceive it in a fresh light and create new adventures. Sometimes the removal of a particular doll, truck, box of Lincoln Logs, or wagon can be synonymous with the removal of a conflict. It may help an individual who is fixated to move on and try other materials.

When you remove or move one or more items, you may create needed space into which children can expand other activities, or in which they may see other equipment in fresh ways. When you change the number of children permitted in an area, the activity may improve because there may be more opportunities available. Some teachers place numbers and/or markers over some areas so that children can check independently whether or not there is space for them to participate. Of course, the group should discuss this procedure together beforehand.

REDIRECT OR ADD AN IDEA.   You might redirect or add an idea by a direct suggestion such as, "Try to find out what happens if you add more beans to the bag." "How can you make a train of people on the slide?" Some teachers have developed a kind of artful "verbal harmony" that they use to accompany children's work. For example, when a block building falls, the teacher might say, "That's what happens. So, we'll just build it up again. Sometimes you don't expect that one block will change the balance but it does. Now, what other ways could you do it?"

Children might find a new direction through a well-timed question: "What other way could you go?" "How could they solve their problem without hitting?" "What things about a person make you want to be her friend?" One kindergarten teacher (Paley, 1984), who was distressed by violent "superhero" play, struggled with ways to redirect it and found that one way was to take the highly aggressive fantasy and accept it by postponing it, with the children's cooperation, to a later group role-playing time. Then she could supervise the activity, first by inviting children's oral dictation as she wrote on an experience chart, and then with role playing. This combination of composing and role playing with teacher involvement generated fluidity and elaboration.

STEP INTO A ROLE.   You can also elect to step into a role during sociodramatic activity in order to extend the action or expand language. You can suggest a problem to be resolved by adding comments such as the following:

"Uh-oh, I see a truck coming."
"Look out, the hose is about to break."
"How many centimeters is that?"
"That dog looks so ill, he might need hospitalization."
"I just lost my watch and it's floating all over our space vehicle. How might we retrieve it?"

In addition, you can take a role in order to avoid or avert stereotypical actions.

BRING CHILDREN TOGETHER.   Another significant way in which you can intervene in children's social activity is to bring children together. You can encourage a child to join an activity by focusing on a task to be done: "They need your help in order to attach the hook." You can suggest that a group invite another player: "This store seems to need a cashier as well as sales persons and stock clerks. George looks as if he's just finished painting. Perhaps he would want to make change." If you notice that three children are ready for more stimulation after some individual, sedentary activity, you could suggest directly that they work together at the flannel board, or with the puppets they have made.

While you may be anxious to enrich children's experiences through social activity, it is also important to respect children's rights to privacy as well as to recognize individual styles of working. In addition, the intrinsic structure of some activities suggests that they are pursued best in an alone area.

Experienced teachers respect the developmental significance of parallel play, when children may use materials side-by-side with other children. Not only do children have a chance to concentrate, focus their energies, pace themselves, and extend their scholarly skills, they have a chance to observe others as alternate models. It is only when the same child persists in this exclusive pattern day after day that you need to intervene. You might bring other children to sit near him and share the materials, or develop activities that require cooperative effort. Rocking boats, extra-long clay rollers that need more than one person, and various games and surveys lend themselves to joint efforts. Kindergarten children can play checkers and some chess, with predictably bendable rules. Children can take turns jumping rope.

In short, you can find many ways to bring children together in the sociodramatic center, to give them a balance of experiences. Much social learning will take place in this area, as it will in many spaces inside and outside of the classroom. The sections that follow discuss additional active ways of working with children in enriching their social knowledge.

THE STRUCTURE-OF-DISCIPLINES APPROACH TO SOCIAL STUDIES

From whichever avenue you enter the social studies, it is essential that meaningful social experiences remain the destination. The structure-of-disciplines approach, broadly conceived, is one direction that you can take, and it is the one we will discuss in this section.

It is the contention throughout this book that children construct a strong base of information, knowledge, attitudes, skills, and social wisdom when they are directly and actively involved in an interactive and responsive environment. Teachers expose and bring activities to children. Both the children and teachers are active participants who can influence what takes place.

For example, when children study holidays, the emphasis needs to be placed on the roots of celebrations, which arise as responses to human struggles for safety, sustenance, freedom, and justice. In their unique ways, kindergarten children can appreciate these emotional and social factors. After all, the issues of struggle, impediments to freedom, power relationships, frustration, and overcoming problems are all part of a child's experience in ways that parallel those of individuals and groups in different cultures. Children can apprehend these phenomena aesthetically as well as emotionally and socially. Through such meaningful practices, it is possible to integrate the children's personally rich after-school reality, however painful or inspiring, into the school curriculum.

When teachers maintain the social dimension in children's studies of their world, they help children to approach new situations with an appropriately tentative attitude. Our approach to the five social sciences discussed in this section focuses on the *ways of working* in each discipline that can help kindergarten children increase their understanding of the social sciences in concrete ways.

Understanding History through the Interpretation of Events

Historians agree that a tentative attitude is basic to their interpretation of past and current events (Genovese, 1974; Meyerhoff, 1959). It is important for students to approach history with the understanding that alternative interpretations are valuable. As kindergarten children grow in their ability to decenter themselves, it is easier for them to appreciate shifting perspectives. Whenever possible, it is important that they use original sources on which to build their own interpretations. Original sources include photographs, art work and artifacts, oral history, and diaries that can be read to them. Other independent views can be shared and contrasted, through discussions. Activities such as those in Figure 5.1 stimulate diverse interpretations of as well as critical thinking about history.

There are many ways that you can order and interpret human experience. These personal constructions are as direct in their way as are block buildings that children construct, and they ultimately influence children's social interaction. When children hear or see how others have handled situations, they may follow these models.

Notice that the chronology of events and time lines and the "facts" about history are open to interpretation. Historians develop consensus about probable facts. By focusing upon the process of interpreting events and practicing the ways of working used by historians, young children have the opportunity to be active in ways that are compatible with their development.

Understanding Geography through Mapping

If the interpretation of events is a tool for studying history, mapping is a tool for studying geography. Just as the use of tools that are physical instruments suggests active uses, so do the ways of working in a discipline suggest active ways of learning more about it. In this section we will focus on the human aspects of geography, and we will see how mapping and other activities lead toward an understanding of the interdependence of human beings and their environments. (Additional related activities are found in the later section on multicultural education.)

For those tools that require skill in symbolizing, kindergarten children need different kinds of practice than for tools that are more clearly extensions of the hand. Maps are such symbolic representations that can extend the understanding of young children, but they need systematic help in learning to use these tools and inquiry skills. We will use as an example a discussion that was observed in a kindergarten classroom* as children greeted a visitor from India:

> TEACHER: Do you know where this visitor comes from?
> CHILDREN: Yes! India!
> TEACHER: How did you know?

---

*Adapted from dialogue with Sunitee Dutt (1961), University of Dehli, after she visited Gertrude Luttgen and a kindergarten group in Minneapolis.

Figure 5.1:   Activities to Stimulate Critical Thinking

-Read to the children different biographies about the same
  person, such as Mary McLeod Bethune by both Anderson and
  Greenfield.
-Have children dictate or tape record their own
  biographies and compare them.
-Read stories written by different authors on the same
  topics, such as new babies or friends.
-Present more than one edition of a particular story or
  tell a story from the point of view of a different
  character (Cullinan, Karrer, & Pillar, 1981).
-Listen to different singers render the same song, for
  example, "City of New Orleans," by Steve Goodman, sung
  by Judy Collins, Arlo Guthrie, and Willie Nelson.
  Discuss why different children vote for or rank the
  selections differently.
-Poll children about a presidential election or other
  controversial event.
-Use pictures, puppets, or flannel-board figures that
  interact in ways suggesting varied interpretations.
-Role play different interpretations of values-based
  pictures (Shaftel & Shaftel, 1967).
-View several brief motion pictures that show varied human
  patterns of life.
-Use a diorama with figures that move in relation to it
  (Lavatelli, 1970). These materials involve changing
  perspectives and stimulate the beginnings of
  reversibile thinking.
-View different photographs of the same subject, then
  draw about, write about, tape record, or personally
  photograph similar subjects and share their different
  renderings.
-Elicit analogies and compare the different outcomes.
  See discussion later in this chapter and in chapter 2
  for other uses of analogy.
-Highlight the multiple interpretations of driftwood,
  art forms, mystery boxes, and incomplete data.

CHILD 1: My grandmother lived in India for a long time. [To visitor] Did you
  know her?

DR. D: I don't think so.

TEACHER: Let's find the place where she came from. [Brings globe to the
  group; Dr. D shows children the place in India from which she came.]

TEACHER: [pointing] What does the blue mean?

CHILDREN: Water.

TEACHER: What does the green mean?

CHILDREN: Land.

TEACHER: How do you suppose Dr. D came all the way here? What might she
  have used?

CHILD 1: Maybe she came by boat.

TEACHER: You think that's possible? Let's see. [They trace some alternate routes.]

CHILD 2: Maybe she came by car.

TEACHER: Let's see if she could really come by car. [Children note water part of the globe.] Let's ask her how she came.

DR. D: By airplane.

CHILDREN: I was on an airplane. . . . Me too. . . . I went . . . [sharing experiences.]

TEACHER: She could have come around this way, moving east, or the other way, moving west. Let's find out which way she came. [Dr. D points out the route.]

CHILDREN: How long did it take you?

DR. D: Thirty-two hours.

It is clear that these children have acquired some beginning understanding of and skills in using the globe. First let us imagine the steps they may have taken in acquiring the knowledge they do have. Then let us use the gaps in the children's thinking to suggest the next steps they might take.

PREPARATORY ACTIVITIES

Beginning geography activities can include (1) sorting by color, size, and shape; (2) imagery building; (3) creating physical representations; (4) matching objects and patterns; (5) exploring spatial relations through body movement; (6) learning about land forms; and (7) telling stories.

SORTING BY COLOR, SIZE, AND SHAPE.   At first, children can try sorting objects of two colors into two separate boxes; then they can sort by shape or size. Each variable becomes a new "figure" that is contrasted against a known "background." This prepares children to understand how color, size, and shape are used symbolically in maps.

IMAGERY BUILDING.   Objects can be placed in boxes and bags so the children can feel but not see them. Additional properties can be added gradually as the children get better at projecting their imaginations toward the unseen. In addition to building toward mapping land forms, this sensory play is a step in building toward future conceptions of unseen phenomena such as atoms.

CREATING PHYSICAL REPRESENTATIONS.   Children enjoy bringing home a map of their own hand, outlined with crayon on paper or impressed into plaster of paris attached to a paper plate. They are fascinated by watching their friends' silhouettes become larger and smaller shadows as the teacher moves a light nearer and farther away. They can be asked to decide whether they want a tiny silhouette, a real-sized image, or a giant-sized image of themselves.

These activities build a foundation for the concept of scale in architecture and map making. Children's play with pegs and peg-city accessories, miniature animals, dolls of varying sizes, play houses, wooden puzzles, Playskool Village, Lego, Lincoln Logs, Tinker Toys, and large building blocks also contributes toward this development of the concept of scale. The teacher can take photographs of children, or they can bring their own from home. When they use sets of the same objects and series of pictures in various sizes, they also are strengthening their concept of relative scale.

When they replace woodworking tools on a pegboard, children can learn to use the outlined shape of the tool to find its resting place, just as they can do with shelves that hold large building blocks. The children use these blocks on the floor to make physical representations of their dramatic fantasies.

Children can explore simple symmetry and patterns by playing with mirrors, by splattering paint on paper and folding over the paper, or by doing vegetable and sponge printing with water-base paints. One teacher, having seen children's pleasure in "Simple Simon" and "Do as I Do" kinds of activities, plays a complex version of Woody Guthrie's song, "Put Your Finger in the Air," and has begun a series of simple cards on which she draws stick-figure representations for children to act out.

An especially enjoyable representational activity is to offer each child the opportunity to lie down on the back of a large sheet of discarded wallpaper and have her or his body outlined by the teacher. Then, according to ability, each child can "map" the terrain within her or his own boundaries, using large felt-tipped pens, yarn, and other textured materials. For some children, this may be one of the first times that they have started an activity on one day and completed it over the next few days.

Children can be shown a Montessori-inspired "rough-smooth" globe that differentiates land and water. When they then compare it to a colored globe, they translate tactile information to the visual sense.

MATCHING OBJECTS AND PATTERNS.   The teacher can set out a box of colored cubes and cards with square patterns that are the same colors. The cards progress from simple patterns using a few colored squares to complex patterns using many colored squares. The children place each cube on the corresponding square on the card. After some practice, children can construct the patterns of cubes directly on a cloth and use the cards as a reference.

EXPLORING SPATIAL RELATIONS THROUGH BODY MOVEMENT.   The teacher accompanies children with a drum as they explore different spaces and directions with their bodies. They can use hoops, boxes, furniture, ropes, and a wire-and-cloth tunnel as accessories to the exploration.

LEARNING ABOUT LAND FORMS.   In one class, some of the children traveled with their teacher to collect possible collage materials outdoors in the autumn, and they had a long discussion about reaching some seed pods across a small stream. After discussing alternate ways of crossing and ruling out a log that looked too brittle, they walked to a small wooden bridge. They talked about its construction and other bridges they had seen. Somebody mentioned a tunnel that had a toll also. The next day the teacher set out in the library corner mounted pictures of bridges and various views of tunnels, from her own collection, and related picture books. One child connected the idea of animal burrows and began another line of study, comparing how animals and people solve similar and different problems in varied ways. They visited sites that represented varied land forms at other times. In these ways, children build an image of the relationship between land and water surfaces, and different elevations.

TELLING STORIES.   This interest in bridges and tunnels was not pure happenstance. The teacher had planned in advance to stimulate the stream-crossing discussion as part of the collage-and-outdoors-in-the-fall activity. She was delighted with the various connections children made as well as their large and small block representations and dramatizations. As the children role played the *Three Billy Goats Gruff* with large hollow blocks, they added still more support and direction to this growing awareness of land forms.

Other books that the teacher read to the children that year included McCloskey's *Blueberries for Sal* and *One Morning in Maine*. These stories are woven into hilly terrain and the style of life of an island, as well as wholesome family relationships. She also read them MacDonald's *The Little Island*, a story of a cat's aloneness experienced as a purely existential moment.

NEXT STEPS

Once children have engaged in preparatory mapping activities, they can go on to more complex matters. Ongoing activities for the kindergarten children in our example would be the following areas: (1) classification; (2) mapping family trees; (3) seriation; (4) creating physical representations and exploring spatial relations; (5) imagery building; (6) using maps; (7) exploring directionality and relative thinking; and (8) learning about land forms.

CLASSIFICATION.   Have each child in a small group place a sheet of paper on the ground in areas such as a construction site, beach, business street, and grassy plot. They can note what is under their pieces of paper and collect samples in separate bags. When they return to school, they compare notes and the teacher can record their findings on a large pad of paper. Throughout the several weeks during which these data are collected, the teacher can read the children such books as Beim's *Eric on the Desert*, Credle's *Down Down the Mountain*, Lipkind's *Russet and the Two Reds* (set in the city), and Tresselt's *I Saw the Sea Come In*. Later on, children may enjoy matching objects to photographs of locales in which they might have been found.

MAPPING FAMILY TREES.   Many of the children can "map" their family trees during the latter part of the year, copying the labels for such family members as mother, brother, and uncle from teacher-made cards in a "Breakthrough to Literacy" project folder (see chapter 9 for details). Older school children can visit and help the kindergarten children to copy names onto their family trees.

SERIATION.   The children can continue to play out increasingly numerous seriations with pictures and objects. Children who have sorted two objects by size can then go on to order three and more. Chapter 7 provides examples.

CREATING PHYSICAL REPRESENTATIONS AND EXPLORING SPATIAL RELATIONS.   Children continue their use of blocks and woodworking materials in increasingly complex ways. Some teachers report five-year-olds using blocks and other materials to represent and dramatize their firsthand study of harbors (Imhoff, 1959; Mitchell, 1934; Spodek, 1962). Other concrete activities that support the children's growing abilities to deal with representation include dioramas, sandbox play, and work with clay.

The Elementary Science Study's Colored Cubes are used with colored loops to extend children's concepts of spatial relations. They learn to develop and plan towns as they use these materials, and some have experienced great pleasure when they have set their own rules for building and then asked other children and adults to guess their rules. (For example, one rule was that only houses of a different color than the loop may be built within the area of the loop.)

Our sample class was fortunate to have a mobile three-dimensional model of the planets available for observation and manipulation. While the concept of ordinary earth-bound space grows slowly, this kind of concrete exposure merely adds a referent for the children. Problem solving in space can be extended by the use of three-dimensional wood puzzles.

IMAGERY BUILDING.   The teacher can help children to project their thinking by using picture matrices, such as those suggested by Lavatelli (1970), and block matrices, such as those suggested by Elementary Science Study, using Colored Cubes. Through the year, children can progress to the use of six-by-six matrices. For example, the teacher can set out alternating color, size, or shape patterns, or their combinations. Small groups of children or individuals can play various games with the matrices. "What's Missing?" is one such game; another involves reversing two elements and finding which ones have been reversed.

In still another variation, children set problems for each other and the teacher. It is intellectually and personally valuable for children to set problems for adults to solve. Using task cards that have stick-figure/picture directions made by their teacher, children can create designs on geoboards. (Geoboards, made in various shapes, are boards with pegs arrayed at regular intervals to form a grid. Rubber bands are stretched across the pegs in varied patterns.) They may also work in pairs, back to back, and compare the patterns that result. These comparisons can become moments of cognitive dissonance. When children have repeated experiences with concrete and pictorial systems, they strengthen their ability to deal with varied symbolic systems.

USING MAPS.   As skills grow, the teacher can give some children outline maps of their room. The children's tasks will vary in complexity as different pairs of children set out to find a missing item or a hidden object, using pictorial "treasure map" instructions.

EXPLORING DIRECTIONALITY AND RELATIVE THINKING.   During the kindergarten year, children can refine their own left and right orientation skills in functional ways, including body movement games. The classroom walls can be labelled north, south, east, and west, and the teacher can use these terms regularly.

When children practice setting the table for special occasions such as Thanksgiving, they can discuss the spatial relations among the utensils. In one classroom, some children were puzzled when other children on the opposite side of the table questioned their placement of eating utensils. The teacher allowed ample time for the children to play out the walking around the table needed to experience changes in hand and wall orientation. For example, children were told to sit at the table and notice which of their hands was nearest the spoon. They then folded the fingers of that hand, walked to the other side of the table, and compared their hand with the new place setting.

LEARNING ABOUT LAND FORMS.   In our sample class, within the week that the visitor came from India, the teacher hung some strikingly colorful aerial photographs of varied terrains, islands, and locales. She also set out some maps near the globe on which they had located India.

Understanding Economics and Sociology through the Concept of Interdependence

By viewing economics as the study of *scarcity*, the disparity between what we want and the resources available to fulfill these wants, we can see that people are placed into relationships with each other and their environments. Sociology as the study of human groups focuses on the relationships involved in group behavior.

Scarcity enters into sociology in terms of personal needs, just as scarcity exists in economics in terms of material needs. Since the concept of *interdependence* is common to both disciplines, they are treated together here. Some appropriate activities for the kindergarten are presented in the following sections. They have in common some ways of working in economics and sociology — among them the use of contrasts and descriptions that sometimes lend themselves to surveys.

GOING ON A FIELD TRIP.   "Engineered" visits to local construction sites touch on many issues relating to interdependence. Teachers can ask the construction workers to carry family pictures and possibly pictures of fishing trips, bowling nights, or other outings with friends. In this way, children can see the varied group memberships of the construction workers.

Children can also observe the workers' dependence upon each other for hoisting, dumping, building, signaling, and measuring. With repeated visits, children are able to see the progress of the building and hear about such problems as plumbers finishing in time for the painters to begin.

TELLING STORIES.   In one classroom, kindergarten children heard the story *Benjie on His Own* by Lexau. They wondered about how their lives would be different if they were a member of a different family in which their nurturant grandmother had become hospitalized.

CONTRASTING DATA.   The interdependence of people and their environments and the influence of locale on employment, social opportunities, and group interactions may be understood best when children can perceive a contrast with their own experience. Teachers can help invert children's sense of reality by asking how their lives would be different if they lived in a house rather than an apartment, or on a farm rather than in the city. Teachers can help them to find answers to these questions and to raise their own questions by gathering lots of contrasting data. Visiting, meeting people, seeing films, contrasting books, listening to recordings, and building their own models and representations are among relevant experiences for kindergarten children. Answers found by contrasting direct experience, rather than by memorizing bodies of verbal information, are likely to remain more closely intertwined with children's experiences.

In a similar manner children build understanding about living communities. They can compare a series of aquarium or terrarium containers that are influenced by different conditions of light, heat, air, water, and nutriments. When resources are limited, several groups can cooperate in creating the planned variations, by using surplus materials scavenged from homes, businesses, and even the school cafeteria. For example, many uses can be found for commercial-size food jars.

EXPLORING POSITIVE AND NEGATIVE FEEDBACK.   When teachers help children to invert their sense of reality, it builds comfort with seeing more than one viewpoint. Children learn through such contrasts and through positive or negative feedback in their daily contacts with other people.

Experiences that further this dialectical development, which is an aspect of economic and social functioning, also influence children's ability to deal with reversibility and relative thinking. Good debaters, for example, see opposing positions. A useful inquiry tool is the question pair:

- How is this event (object, feeling, place, evaluation, attitude) like that event?
- How is this event (object, feeling, place, evaluation, attitude) different from that event?

Children can be asked to pretend that they are visiting a country that does not use money. They can imagine what the people in that country could use instead of money and what kinds of problems would arise as people tried to use this substitute. This discussion could follow shared shopping expeditions outside and inside the school, where children can use money and can discuss the exchange with the teacher. Pairs of children or small groups might come up with ideas separately before sharing their suggestions with a larger group. This activity helps children to focus on, retrieve, and relate material.

USING INDUCTION.   Inductive learning takes place primarily when systematic contrasts are built into children's activities. When teachers carefully provide clear contrasts, children have a chance to perceive a new "figure" because it appears in contrast with a known "background." Such figures wear different "costumes" in relation to the different questions and purposes of the activities.

For example, when a group observes the supermarket receiving a delivery of produce from a truck, they also acquire background information for comparing marketing patterns in a book or film of an Asian community committed to water transportation. Their observations may lead to a study of the food chain, economic comparisons, or comparing the interactions between people and their environments.

As long as children have many samples of direct data, they can extend their thinking inductively. These connections take place over time. Children need time and the opportunity to leave and return to data so that the bits of experience can be fully absorbed. Kindergarten children build an understanding of economics and sociology through the concept of interdependence as they engage in a variety of activities. Some of these activities also represent the particular perceptual models of indirect progress and synergy (see Figure 3.1) as they intersect with economic and sociological concerns. Sample activities are presented in the next two sections.

APPRECIATING INDIRECT PROGRESS.   Economic policy decisions frequently reflect short-range sacrifices in favor of longer-range progress, much as do playing strategies in checkers or chess. Children learn to sacrifice a playing piece in order to gain a better position. In addition, they become increasingly proficient in considering alternate moves.

Many other games that children play provide practice in indirect progress, a perceptual model. The extended exposure to indirect progress in varied forms provides children with a stronger network of associations and ways of knowing than if they had only a single way to view economic sacrifices. For example, Tangrams, detailed in chapter 7, is a classic game that entails the breaking of set expectations. Knock Hockey is a large-muscle game that uses triangulated action as children knock a disc of wood against the sides of the board in order to bypass obstructions. Three-dimensional wood puzzles also require planning several steps ahead. Many five-year-olds are able to play these games.

When children save together for a common purpose, rather than immediately consuming their property, they are collaborating to exchange short-term for long-term benefits. Sales of baked goods, potholders, needlework, and wood crafts are some activities that can encourage longer-range planning.

COOPERATION AMONG THE PARTS: SYNERGY.   Cooperation among the parts underlies a good deal of economic and social life. In economics,

effective mass production requires cooperation among people. One kindergarten group compared their mass-production assembly line of Easter baskets
to individual production and were able to see how the joint effort was more
productive (Robison & Spodek, 1965). The book *Two Is a Team*, by Beim
and Beim, is about cooperation between a black child and a white child.

The study of family life illuminates cooperation, and kindergarten
children have engaged in the following studies of families, among others:

Different roles and functions within each child's own family
Different kinds of families
Families in different cultures
Different climatic conditions and terrains and how they support family
    life and survival in different ways

Films, stories, pictures, trips, and visitors add data upon which children
can build contrasting views of alternative ways in which human groups live
and work with each other. Through these resources, families at a distance
in time and space become a kind of here-and-now experience. In the full-
day kindergarten classroom, teachers plan for the most direct experiences
possible, so that children can build their own personal associations.

Dramatic play and more focused simulations occur when children role
play with props. This is another way to expose children to synergy from a
social standpoint. (In chapter 6, synergy is used in the study of chemistry.)
As children identify with their roles and the problems that their characters
face, their sensitivities to other people deepen.

Extended blocks of time during the full-day kindergarten make it possible for teachers and children to engage in in-depth study in these natural
ways. Beyond knowledge objectives, children and their teacher deal with
feelings and values as they interact.

Understanding Political Socialization as the Result of Imagination

Political action is an outgrowth of values. There is agreement among
educators, psychologists, and political scientists that political awareness
grows with self-awareness, through the socialization process and cognitive
development (Hess, 1968; Hess & Torney, 1967; Lasswell, 1958; May, 1972;
Peters, 1967; Sorauf, 1965). While children achieve true conceptual awareness of political phenomena beyond the early childhood years, the early years
"are not only formative but for the most part enduring" (Jennings & Niemi,
1968, p. 467). Thus, while political awareness becomes measurable beyond
the early childhood years, it does not surface full-grown and rootless.

The child's peer group, family, school, and community relations serve as initial exposures to the core of politics, which is power and its use. Laws and rules, authority figures, political leaders, and government institutions are among the forms through which children may perceive the use of power.

Social forms precede cognitive forms in power relationships. Children directly experience rules and limitations as "given" and behavior as "good" or "bad" as it conforms to the rules. We would expect kindergarten children to have difficulty separating an individual authority figure from that person's institutional role (Hess & Torney, 1967). As children mature, the idealization of adult political figures gives way to the notion of fallibility. It is this very distinction between appearance and reality that teachers can help children to perceive in the kindergarten.

The "double bind," which is part of the dialectical perceptual model (see Figure 3.1) in which appearance and reality contravene one another, includes politics and takes many forms outside of politics. (For example, the dialectical perceptual model also is reflected in history and other disciplines.) Through many concrete experiences and their accompanying verbal exchanges, children participate in the long process of distinguishing between intent and action, between the officeholder and the office. This understanding, and critical thinking in general, grows when you engage in discussions that welcome different views and offer experiences in which first appearances prove to be inadequate, including activities that stimulate cognitive dissonance.

Children need to work in an atmosphere where varied suggestions are aired and attempted; where they are encouraged to predict, guess, set problems, and try alternative routes to solving problems. Teachers add to this learning when they comment on children's intentions and express appreciation for their motives.

When children are asked for their opinions and to make choices, they have a chance to become aware of themselves: "I am expected to have an opinion" and "I am considered capable of making a choice." Whether or not a child expresses his perception, it is useful for adults to remember that it was a young child who clearly saw that the emperor wore no clothes. By these different routes, early concerns on the aesthetic and personal level grow toward conceptual and universal issues.

The main focus of political education at the kindergarten level is action rather than knowledge, emotional attachments, or attitudes for their own sake. Kindergarten children can engage in a variety of activities that help build their political skills.

SENSE OF POWER.   One school that houses all of the K–4 children in the community has successfully used inter-age student advisory councils that include kindergarten children (Raywid and Shaheen, 1983). The governance is based upon Kohlberg's "just community" concept and focuses on "civic ethics" and "fairness." Leaders or class officers need to have responsibilities, which the group and the teacher work out together and respect. Voting for the kinds of games or materials to order, the place to visit first on a trip, whether to go outdoors or to continue an exciting indoor activity, or what theme will dominate a party may be a way for children to develop a further sense of what "majority rule" means.

SENSE OF REALITY.   Teachers can ask, "What would happen if there were no police (governor, judge) in a particular situation?" "What would happen if we selected a president in a different way?" This sort of dialectical questioning can provide contrasts that sharpen children's understanding of conditions as they actually exist. The inversion of reality can take on a humorous cast while sharpening children's awareness of reality or demonstrating their grasp of it. The four-year-old who could not read to the older folks because he could not find his reading glasses is one example (Chukovsky, 1963). You and your group might consider a newborn baby brushing his teeth.

SENSE OF EFFICACY.   Children need to build a sense of efficacy in relation to government. If they see things that concern them, such as graffiti, they can dictate a letter to the mayor and offer advice concerning ways of coping with it. When such a letter draws an answer from an elected official, children have a chance to feel effective. Sending petitions to the principal or school lunch director are other possible activities.

To develop this sense of efficacy further, a teacher might help children to become aware of ways in which they have used their influence to sway the teacher to change a decision. Perhaps when children have experiences through which they have been able to influence visible political or authority symbols, they may feel encouraged to extend their participation in political matters later on.

CRITICAL THINKING.   Kindergarten children often put together images from adult concerns that come to them on the level of mythology, and in this way they pick up a good deal about political matters. They notice major adult elections as they look at television and hear adults repeating the same names and issues. Parents add to this mass of imagery when they bring their children to polling places each year and arrange for them to watch the voting process. Teachers add to these experiences when they talk with children about the names of candidates, political parties, and the kinds of issues that are present. Children have certainly asked about war, about nuclear bombs, and about pollution.

Literary critic Northrop Frye suggests that, "in a modern democracy a citizen participates in society mainly through his imagination" (1970, p. 104). Children learn to separate what is real from propaganda or mythology only after they have been exposed to a variety of humanly authentic imagery. When adults legitimize variety rather than a single viewpoint or a single right answer, children have a better chance to sort out the real from the imaginary.

Some activities that help children to perceive varied points of view and forms in which human beings organize their experiences include the critical thinking activities in Figure 5.1 above. Another activity that lends itself to this kind of "discrepancy analysis" (or cognitive dissonance) is a "shoe box" (or any other container) activity adapted from Donna Barnes (personal communication, 1981; also Taba, Durkin, Fraenkel, & McNaughton, 1971). This activity, shown in Figure 5.2, generates divergent and creative responses that help participants to see the objects in fresh ways and from different points of view.

Children willingly cooperate in those activities that are simple, concrete, physical, social, and encourage divergent thinking. They can discuss stories, television programs, and practices in their community that reflect career aspirations, sex-role stereotypes, and minority-group roles. While there is a growing body of literature for children that attempts to reverse

Figure 5.2: Teacher's Plan for Classification Activity for Critical Thinking

---

Purposes: Encourage comparison of classifications. Create possibility for cognitive dissonance. Encourage cooperative small group work.
Materials: Containers, such as shoe boxes or cereal cylinders; 15 to 36 varied objects in each container, including old objects or replicas that have sensorial contrasts.
Organization: Small groups or pairs of children work together for 10 to 20 minutes as the teacher circulates.
Procedures: Encourage children to decide what to do with the objects. There is no right or wrong way to decide. Ask questions and make suggestions:
  –Look at, pass around, feel, smell, tap each object.
  –Make up a name for each object you use. How might you want to organize the objects in relation to one another in space?
  –What sorts of things were you coming up with as ideas of things to do with what you found in your box?
  –Compare your classifications with those of other groups.

---

such stereotypes and values, teachers have found plenty of need to discuss such issues. When children compare and discuss their findings with one another and generally engage in peer-mediated instruction, they have a chance to gain insights into reciprocal roles.

It is relevant to plan activities that can help children develop critical thinking. As the perceptual model of dialectical activity is apprehended through varied activities, such as those suggested here and in subsequent chapters, critical thinking can develop.

MULTICULTURAL EDUCATION: A UNIQUE INTERDISCIPLINARY APPROACH

Each of us prefers to believe that we are egalitarian and fair. Because of the society and times in which we grew up, however, various attitudes, values, and expectations have come to control us without our having as much awareness as we might like. For example, Harrison (1974) observed that a group of teachers and an administrator who resisted self-examination and change of sex-stereotyped behavior did so because they already viewed themselves as providers of an open and liberated setting. As teachers, we need to make a particular effort to become conscious of our values and to move beyond consciousness to action. Multicultural education provides us with a perfect opportunity for this.

As we consider in this section the possibilities for multicultural education as an interdisciplinary approach to social studies, we must do so with the understanding that this is a relatively new area in education. This means that the knowledge base for multicultural studies is still very much in its infancy and that teachers may be learning almost as much as the children they are teaching, not simply in the area of factual information but also in the understanding of the meaning and workings of culture in human lives. It is simultaneously a body of knowledge, attitudes, and behavioral strategies. As a body of knowledge, it resembles a synoptic discipline; as a combination of applied attitudes and behavioral strategies, it cuts across disciplines.

Under the umbrella of multicultural education are many areas for concern, drawn from history, geography, sociology, anthropology, economics, and the arts. Some programs include attitudes, values, and skills in living with other people. Specific concerns involve cultural pluralism, global education, career education, and preventing or undoing stereotypes about culture, ethnicity, gender, age, and disability. Perhaps the central purpose of multicultural education is to foster understanding of the diversity of human groups and to cultivate appreciation for the uniqueness of each person as well as the needs that all human beings share.

When teachers plan activities, it is worthwhile to distinguish between the surface and the deeper structures of a culture. Educators Williams and De Gaetano (1985, p. 57) suggest that we differentiate among the three levels: "what" things are visible in a culture, "how" members of the culture behave, and "why" their values direct the variety of their behavior. Too often, schools have offered activities primarily in the "what" area, with attention paid occasionally to "how"; "why" is frequently neglected altogether. While kindergarten children inferentially understand the values level of "why," it is important for teachers to consider that the variety of human behavior within a given culture is a function of the values that people display when they choose to respond to, ignore, praise, or sanction a given action. Teachers who provide activities that display contrasts may help children to appreciate deeper values.

It is important to expose young children to the variety within a culture only after they have had activities that reveal some of the commonalities. When teachers use relative rather than absolute language, such exposure takes on more profound meaning. For example, instead of suggesting that *all* people from Hispanic cultures share an extended kinship structure that includes godparents, or that all elderly people retire from useful work, one educator (Morris, 1983, p. 81) suggests that it makes sense to use terms such as some or many.

In order to help kindergarten children to sort the similarities and differences between other cultures and categories of people, we need to provide activities that begin with a data base that they can relate to their own experiences. This is why many kindergartens engage in a study called "Myself." Some components of self-study that children can engage in are presented in Figure 5.3.

When children have considered the roles and functions of members of their own families, such as their family customs and the ways in which their families celebrate holidays, they can begin comparing other families and cultures. Photographs of families in different parts of the world and of children in other environments who are engaged in activities can form the basis for a contrast that stimulates discussion questions. Here are some examples:

- How does a new baby change the culture of the home?
- Where do people sleep? On what do they sleep? When do they sleep? For how long do they sleep? (Adapted from Muessig & Rogers, 1965, p. 87.)

Figure 5.3: Activities for Self-Study

-Create a book about each child, sometimes with one or
  more photographs or drawings of the child and his or her
  family.
-Make a map of the child by outlining the child's body
  on paper and have the child fill in the parts with paint
  and/or collage materials.
-Draw a timeline of major events in the child's life.
-Take a group survey of nonstandard measures of body parts,
  such as height, arm length, hand span, and so forth.
-Take a group survey of teeth lost. This activity can be
  tied to working with a dentist or school nurse who can
  help children compare the similarities and differences
  in human teeth (adapted from Grant, 1977, p. 148).
-Conduct a group survey of family sizes, people who live
  in the child's house, or of different generations.
-Create a board game using photographs relating to one
  child or several children in the classroom (adapted from
  Williams and De Gaetano, 1985, pp. 96-97).
-Put together a book of the child's favorite things, using
  illustrations and/or collages.
-Put together a book of things the child hates, using
  illustrations and/or collages.
-Create a book of funny or frightening dreams, illustrated.
-Create a collage of "What I want to be"; or "wishes."
-Draw an individual family tree.
-Decorate an immigration map of the world, with personal
  markers indicating the locations from which families
  came. This map is nice to have at a family breakfast
  for which children participate in preparations. Parents
  and other relatives can attend. A related activity can
  be an immigration museum consisting of family keepsakes
  from other times and places, such as a foreign passport,
  citizenship papers, old photographs, a special spoon or
  bowl, and even a braid of hair.

- What are some things that all people need besides sleep?
- What are the different ways that people find shelter? Celebrate
  holidays? Dress?
- What are different head coverings? (See Williams & De Gaetano,
  1985, pp. 77–78; and Grant, 1977, p. 160, for head wrapping ideas.)
  Making hats, as well as using hats that represent different cultures
  and occupations in sociodramatic play, is a popular kindergarten
  activity.
- Where did various foods or customs come from originally?
- What titles can we create for these photographs? (Arrange for pairs
  of children to create titles and then share them. The different results

are a basis for discussing and clarifying perceptions. This is a possible instance where cognitive dissonance can take place.)

Many kindergartens provide for a variety of music, songs, dances, and games that originate in different cultures. Children can be encouraged to taste and categorize foods from different regions. They can celebrate a variety of holidays, taking into account the context and traditions of holiday practices, as well as the surface symbols.

Young children often acquire multicultural information, attitudes, values, and skills in their daily lives. Teachers find that they can intervene by highlighting aspects of children's exposures, by contrasting and comparing, and by helping children to classify data without the pressure of a single "correct" answer. They encourage children to raise questions and to make their own connections.

Countering Sex-Role Stereotypes

A calm surface presented by a person may hide an underlying storm of anger and aggression, but we tend not to probe calm surfaces. Since most teachers of young children have been women, handling aggression is a particularly subtle issue. As women, they are the repository of society's constraints upon women's assertiveness, currently in a beginning process of change, due in part to research findings as well as economic and political developments. While some researchers have found that boys tend to be more aggressive than girls and receive more scolding and restraints from teachers (Maccoby & Jacklin, 1974), others have found that boys also receive more attention than girls (Serbin, 1978).

In order to encourage children's desire to explore and be creative, to be independent and assertive, teachers must notice and communicate their appreciation of these characteristics in girls as well as boys. Researchers have found that teachers who give only directions and favorable comments to girls may encourage conformity to less adventurous behavior (Fagot, 1975; Lieberman, 1977; Paley, 1984). There are techniques, however, that teachers have used to reverse these unintended outcomes. Guttentag (1978), for example, found that both girls and boys changed their sex-role perceptions after only six weeks of an intensive intervention curriculum that emphasized career opportunities for girls and that contradicted stereotypes about job roles.

Increasingly, materials for children have become more egalitarian and gender free. Consider the hidden messages or missing messages in books you read to children. Be sure that career opportunities for all children are kept open and assertiveness and adventure are depicted equally as possibilities for girls and boys. We want to keep open and enlarge children's great expectations for their lives while they are in the kindergarten.

Countering Racial Prejudices

There is agreement among many researchers that children's self-concepts develop parallel to their understanding of language (Clark & Clark, 1939; Goodman, 1964). In our society, black children learn to perceive themselves as black somewhere between three and six years of age (Clark & Clark, 1939). Children who are not black are believed to perceive these differences around the age of four years (Goodman, 1964).

One kindergarten teacher who worked with predominantly black children was incensed when a child pointed around the table stating, "You're light, you're dark," and everybody wanted to be light. When a child, in anger, called another "black," the teacher wondered why that constituted an insult. If anything, should they not be proud to be themselves? When one of the children called the teacher "white," the others, quite disturbed, shushed the child saying, "Oh, no, teacher isn't white," in a tone indicating that this significant person in their lives could not possibly be such a terrible thing. These incidents indicate an unfortunate disparity of feeling on a most vital subject — the children's images of themselves.

Sociologists have found situations where the "lower-class parent aligns himself with the child *against the teacher* on grounds of class antagonism" (Davis & Dollard, 1940, p. 42). They also learned that the child often "finds that neither his parents nor his teachers expect a person in his social position to go far in school" (p. 286). You might substitute the terms *race* or *ethnicity* for social position, with some degree of accuracy. In turn, these attitudes can be used as an excuse for nonachievement (Horney, 1939).

Although black children come to school from a variety of economic backgrounds, there has been more economic hardship among people of color than others. And the perceptions of both black and white teachers need examination. It does not do for us to dilute or deny differences; on the contrary, they must be accepted and appreciated. Otherwise, "if an individual has low personal self-esteem, he may project this onto his racial group" (Porter, 1971, p. 183). There is no substitute for a sense of competence and acceptance.

Attending to Bilingual and Bicultural Children

The bilingual and bicultural child may feel particularly isolated in school. Current programs are attempting to support the retention of cultural heritage, notably in parts of the country where there are relatively large Spanish-speaking, Native American, or Asian-American communities.

Particular controversy around the bilingual aspects of educational programs reflects a collision between the "melting pot" and the "pluralistic"
views of the mission that society assigns to schools. Current public funding
for subject matter instruction in the Spanish language, alongside instruction
in English language skills, is a break from the tradition of the melting pot,
where pluralistic approaches in the past had been privately funded.

Bilingual education can strengthen children's self-concepts as they see
themselves progress in the subject-matter areas in their own native language
while simultaneously acquiring English language skills. Kindergarten children seem to be quite adept at functioning with two languages and often
acquire a second language within the school year.

Just as teachers plan for critical thinking and a sense of success with
questions and activities that lend themselves to more than a single correct
answer or interpretation, they can ease the problem of code switching for
children who come from different cultures by building in divergent language
materials. One such material for initial writing into reading is the *Breakthrough to Literacy* "sentence maker" that is detailed in chapter 9. The
reading and writing are based upon the children's own spoken language
structure or dialect. Therefore, children do not face the problem of translating the syntax of typical printed material in this early approach. Bilingual
and bidialectal children have a greater chance to feel competent and successful with this kind of material.

Using Inclusionary Materials and Language

The project of Resources on Educational Equity for the Disabled found
that "the combined impact of real experience with the use of symbolic
materials can make children more aware of the many options that exist for
people regardless of sex or disabling condition" (Women's Action Alliance,
1982, p. 1). It is useful to analyze books, toys, and other materials in order
to provide educational experiences that avoid racism, sexism, ageism, and
handicapism. Children need direct and indirect contact with feeling, thinking people who may be in a wheelchair or who may be elderly yet lead
productive, sensitive, and caring lives. Career models and role models need
to be available that show both sexes and a range of ages, abilities, pigmenta-
tions, and cultural backgrounds.

Consider developing a bulletin-board montage of elderly people who
are working or have just discovered new talents (Grant, 1977). Similar
activities might include people who have a disability and work at interesting
careers or women and men in nontraditional careers.

Avoid excessive use of gender as a category. Children can get their
jackets from the wardrobe by color of clothing, birthday month, or any other
characteristic besides gender. Good alternatives to words that are gender

specific include such terms as everybody, people, class, thinkers, and friends. Instead of "Atta boy/girl," use "Thoughtful job," "That's progress," and "You're really thinking/concentrating."

CYCLICAL CHANGE:
A BROAD INTERDISCIPLINARY APPROACH

The holidays and seasons have formed part of the common cultural experience of kindergarten children across the country. The weather is another apparently safe topic in the universal culture with which schools deal. I propose that the culture-free, competition-free equalizing of weather or of what is happening out of doors, and the sterilized ritual study of holidays ought to become more controversial, or at least be considered more seriously.

In this section we will deal first with several points of view about the weather and holidays. On the basis of the perceptual model of cyclical change, we will explore a variety of concrete activities that reflect the ways of working in different disciplines. Continuing within the framework of that model, we will then look at what children can learn about time, growth, and temperature as they use a variety of methods of study.

Young children first begin to perceive cyclical change directly through their eating and sleeping schedules and through seasonal changes. Since change is a constant factor in life, activities themselves may build toward an understanding of cyclical change, even if only part of a cycle of change is reflected in the activity. Kindergarten children have shown themselves capable of building toward this understanding inductively when they work in playful ways with concrete situations, in such instances as

> Role playing and creative dramatics
> Building with blocks, sand, mud, and clay
> Oral history
> Examining artifacts and replicas from different times and places

The perceptual model, by suggesting the possible connections between concrete, diverse experiences, also suggests alternative ways of sequencing activities. Using this approach, different children engaging in different activities at different times can have equivalent experiences.

Weather

There is sufficient reason to reassess the school's preoccupation with weather, if only to break out of a morning ritual of "Today is Monday. It is cloudy and raining. We will have indoor lunch. . . . " There is a time when educators must reconsider those activities that are taken for granted and accepted because they are the way things have always been done, that is, because they are the folklore of the school.

Usually weather has been viewed as a science study in schools — a study of the rain cycle, the related study of seasons, and of growing things. However, weather conditions represent social as well as scientific issues. Teachers and children have studied social aspects of the weather in the context of its impact on food supplies, transportation routes, and the possibility of settlement. Studying weather is one way to understand cyclical change.

It is worthwhile to look at weather as part of, rather than the focus for, the study of cyclical change. Looking at cyclical change as a basis for connecting subjects can provide a broader range of options and activities for teachers and children. As we saw in Figure 3.1, there is a natural flow of imagery that connects the perceptual model of cyclical change across disciplines. This imagery unites the weather, life cycles, animal migrations, holidays, cultural evolution, ecology, outdoor education, measurement, poetry, and economic issues such as the food cycle. Even dinosaur study can become related to the young child's preoccupation with mythic monsters as part of her emerging conscience development.

Teachers and kindergarten children also can develop surveys based upon the cyclical changes that children observe. They can measure whether there were days without rain in a week or in a month.

Holidays

Since most of our holidays are dictated by the calendar, it is easy to remain seduced by a kind of ritual pagan calendar worship. The possibilities become so much richer when, instead of the paper cutouts punctuated by scissors and paste, the holiday study focuses on the cyclical changes inherent in the study of the "social" in social studies, such as human efforts or struggles and successful revolutions worth celebrating.

Ellen Ray, a Hofstra University graduate early childhood education intern, has engaged in role playing and creative dramatics activities with kindergarten children that have provided a truly social study of various holidays. For example, they have celebrated Martin Luther King's birthday by role playing Rosa Parks's initiation of the Montgomery bus boycott; they have observed St. Patrick's Day by dramatizing the potato famine; and they have expanded the feast of Thanksgiving by acting out the story of the peaceful strivings of the Iroquois nation. A social scientist at Hofstra University, Donna Barnes, has worked out some concrete activities around the Thanksgiving theme that reflect the role of colonial women.

Superficially, the study of holidays does differ from the study of outdoor education or the weather. On a deeper level, however, holidays illustrate the changes of passing-through struggles in human lives.

Time

Time is an important element in cyclical change. It is also a constraint for teachers because young children are still learning to sort out time distinctions and sequences of events. Analogy as well as concrete experiences can help children deal with the distant in time.

Various representations of time can be used with kindergarten children. A *time line* can be hung on the wall, containing children's baby pictures beside pictures taken of them when they began kindergarten in September. After a few weeks, the chart can be stored until May, when another set of even more recent photographs can be added. Children will notice changes, such as in hair length and sleeve length. Krauss's *The Growing Story* is one book with which children can identify in this context, but it generally is more meaningful to introduce a book to children *after* they have had the related experiences. Some children experience a sense of cognitive surprise when they see their teacher's personal photographic time line. Kindergarten teachers have used a variation of the time line by taking photographs to create a sequence of events during trips and various other group projects, including parties. Tape recordings of group events are other kinds of records that can contribute to a sense of temporal order. These kinds of visual and auditory records stimulate the development of children's self-awareness.

The various rites of passage in early childhood help children to become more aware of themselves. Beginning and finishing kindergarten are such events. Learning to ride a bicycle, receiving a first umbrella (see Yashima's *The Umbrella*), and acquiring a library card (see Felt's *Rosa-Too-Little*) are such benchmarks.

The understanding of the duration of immediate time is enhanced when children wait patiently for pudding to cook, cookies to bake, a film to end, or a story to begin. They can take a survey of heart rate by tallying the number of beats in ten seconds both before and after running for one minute, or they can count the number of birds at a bird feeder during a three-minute interval. Such activities deepen their sense of time on a personal level.

Children can use clocks with second hands, mechanical timers, metronomes, and such nonstandard measures of time as water wheels. Sometimes children are quite ingenious about suggesting ways of recording changes. In addition, they can keep records through communal or individual "books of changes" at their own levels of representation.

Growth

Human beings of all ages wonder what will happen when they grow older. For young children, visiting a family with an infant and talking to elderly people are important supplements in an age of nuclear families.

Kindergarten children welcome the presence in school of babies and senior citizen volunteers. The stories told by older people, other people who have interesting and unusual careers, and parents of babies form an oral history and provide vivid experiences for children to use in creating a data base and making connections.

Science-related activities that deal with animal and plant growth parallel these concerns. Children acquire useful data about social behavior through the analogies to be found in observing animal and insect behavior and their social communities. Children can reinforce their social studies by comparisons with the cyclical changes in plant growth also. (Chapter 6 provides related examples.)

There are also books for young children that deal with growth, generations, reproduction, birth, and death. A most sensitively written book that deals with warm family relationships, different generations, the loss of a significant family member, and a rite of passage in an aesthetically beautiful way is Miles's *Annie and the Old One.*

The notions of death and extinction are important human concerns. Considering the limits of kindergarten children's grasp of time, it is a constant wonder to notice them wrapped up in dinosaur lore. It is hard to say whether dinosaurs have more appeal because of their lengthy and varied labels, which have prestige in the child culture, or because of their attraction as images of powerful monsters.

Some children have brought to school fossils that their families acquired on vacation trips. One group of kindergarten children collected "future fossils" outdoors (Wynne Shilling, personal communication, 1985). Then their teacher asked them to classify and predict which items would be likely to last and which would not last. They believed that rocks, metal bottle caps, and leaves would last (leaves were included because they had seen the dried remnants of a fern in a fossil at an earlier time). They believed that plastic and glass would not last because "they break easily." Nor did they believe that cigarette butts and rags would last. Using plaster of paris, they first made impressions of the "longest lasting" items and then later created imprints of the "would not last" items in a second layer.

Making plaster-of-paris handprints or footprints and making other prints with sponges, vegetables, and then words all build toward the fossil concept. Early exposure to these objects lays a base for later ties to geological changes and the interactions between living beings and their environment.

Temperature

Temperature change, reflecting the days and seasons, is cyclical. It is important to plan ahead for varied activities that explore these cycles, but unplanned opportunities may also present themselves: The rare excitement of an unexpected snowfall can be turned into a spontaneous aesthetic event that children can appreciate either from indoors or as an outdoor tactile immersion. Woven through each day are such fleeting moments that hold the potential for deeper meaning when you take the time to appreciate them with children. For example, children can become aware of the physical impact of wind as the weather changes. As breezes occur, they also can appreciate aesthetically the changing appearance of the precisely balanced mobiles that they have built.

The Use of Analogies

We can help children to notice that one cyclical change leads to another, and since our discussion has come around again to snow and wind, we will use weather activities to illustrate two kinds of analogies.

DIRECT ANALOGY.   Ask the children to imagine that the weather today is just the opposite of current conditions. Then continue:

- What would you (the children in Puerto Rico; in Jamaica) be doing?
- What do those clouds look like? Remind you of? What else?
- How is a rainy day like a jail?
- What animal is like a rainy day?
- Why is a laugh like a rainy day?
- What kind of weather is like a song? A dance? Like you?
- What makes you feel like a sunshine sky? Thunder and lightning?

PERSONAL ANALOGY.   Children can be encouraged to use their imagination to project themselves into familiar experiences in new ways. A good example of this technique is the following activity, adapted from Gordon and Poze (1968, 1972): Ask the children to imagine they are spiders trying to spin a web on a rainy, stormy day. As they try to feel what the spider feels, ask them:

- As a spider, what does the storm do to you?
- How do you feel about it?
- What other things might you do? Feel? Wish?

Notice that aspects of the perceptual model of cyclical change appear in particular concrete activities that kindergarten children have experienced. These experiences cut across separate subjects. The activities are within the teaching range and help children integrate learning in personalized ways. This will help children and their teachers feel successful and comfortable.

When kindergarten children learn together about the social world in the various ways that reflect disciplines, and when they make connections that cut across disciplines, they have a chance to feel competent and successful in their activities. Through these active ways of learning, critical thinking skills are integrated with content-based activities to achieve the major purpose of social studies, which is to build understanding and cooperation. The longer kindergarten day can provide the time. The teacher can create the opportunity.

6

Action-Centered
Science Education

Scientists view the various branches of science as attempts to study and understand the physical processes that touch upon human experience and imagination. Yet the sciences are often taught as if they were a set of facts and bits of information that are designed to be memorized. In this chapter, the study of the sciences is presented in the context of experiential happenings and potential understanding.

In keeping with this approach, ways of knowing in the disciplines of physics, biology, and chemistry are discussed, in order to provide examples of ways to plan selected activities. Children learn concepts as they participate in these activities. Since activities, when you develop them with children over time, suggest ties to other disciplines, vistas are offered into how you might plan from an interdisciplinary viewpoint.

You can also work in a variety of ways to communicate to parents, teachers, and administrators the significance of kindergarten science activities. Some of the things you might do are

Send home collaborative class books of science findings for which the children have made illustrations or for which you have taken photographs of the children at work.

Present science work on classroom and hallway bulletin boards.

Along with other teachers, participate in science fairs where children can display their photographs, models, drawings, experience charts, and audiotapes.

Create classroom newsletters, participate in schoolwide newsletters to parents and the school board, and contribute slides for schoolwide presentation to these groups.

THE SCIENCE AREA

Whether you plan to set up a separate science area or integrate science and mathematics materials, consider beginning to provide for a science area that might include the following:

Some things from the physical world, such as magnets, water, and
  pulleys or other simple machines
Some things from the living world, such as plants, cuttings, seedlings,
  insects, and animal life
Items to compare, classify, or sequence
Some things to manipulate and use playfully
Tools for measurement, such as rulers, timers, and a stethoscope
A table, chairs enough for 6–8 children, and storage shelves that set off
  the area
Writing materials
A sign to identify the area as a science area

These kinds of provisions can be replaced, revised, retired, and renewed on a regular basis, as needed.

UNDERSTANDING PHYSICS THROUGH THE INTERACTION OF FORCES

Physics has been defined as the science that measures how objects move through space and time (Toulmin, 1960). One scientist suggests that "imagination . . . is physics come alive," and that "discovery is actually the act of creation" (Zukav, 1980, pp. 10, 89).

If you begin to see physics in this dynamic, relative way, there are many ways that you can help make a concept become a concrete experience for young children. Even though you begin to plan at the point of your own "fund" of knowledge, as you work with your children their actions will suggest ways of implementing the underlying concepts. In this way, each interaction between you, your children, and the experiences will be a unique fingerprint in time.

For example, let's look at the case of a kindergarten group where a five-year-old, Kay, showed others in the group a "trick" with magnets (Fromberg, 1965). Kay laughingly showed how her magnet could attract a piece of paper and then gleefully explained: "It can't pick up the paper without the nail but it can pick it up with the nail." Since time was limited, the teacher planned to follow this new path the next day. She brought various nonmagnetic materials. Kay shared her "trick." The teacher then asked, "Can you *guess* which materials could be used for such a trick?" Among the carefully selected materials were copper discs. Children variously predicted whether or not each material could be attracted by the magnet before attempting to use it as an intermediate body. When a number of children felt sure that the copper could be attracted, the teacher took the time to explore their thinking before continuing with her advance plan to classify metals based upon their magnetic properties.

When you build on children's active contributions, continuity of learning is a kind of negotiated result. As you look at the concept of the *interaction of forces* in nature, it is possible to see how you might help tie activities together in this negotiated way. If you relate this concept of the interaction of natural forces to the interdependency of living beings, you can see a clear base for interdisciplinary activity that builds from a unifying conceptual framework.

Interdependency and Interrelationship

Craig (1958), a science educator, proposes *interrelationship* as a major concept in science. Some subsidiary forces that reflect the interaction of forces concept in nature would be gravitation, magnetism, air pressure, and centrifugal force. Figure 6.1 shows a conceptual planning map for using these forces to organize instruction. These forces can be translated into concrete activities and materials for young children.*

You do not need to plan activities that focus only on any single force and pursue it to the ends of human knowledge, nor do you need to make explicit to children the interaction of these forces, regardless of children's receptivity. Plan concrete experiences as you go along, taking into account children's reactions. Bear in mind that, were any other group of children to begin with the same set of materials, the actual experience would most likely be different.

Now let us look together at some actual kindergarten experiences with gravitation, magnetism, air pressure, and centrifugal force. These examples are drawn from my observations of a single kindergarten class over the period of a school year.

---

*Note that air pressure or magnetism at this level might be part of chemistry. When considering "conceptual literacy" or perceptual models for kindergarten children, however, there is an emphasis on helping children to become exposed to the underlying pattern.

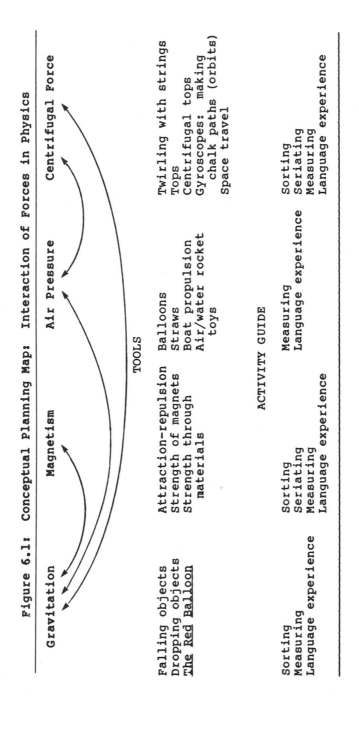

Figure 6.1: Conceptual Planning Map: Interaction of Forces in Physics

Gravitation	Magnetism	Air Pressure	Centrifugal Force
		TOOLS	
	Attraction-repulsion	Balloons	Twirling with strings
Falling objects	Strength of magnets	Straws	Tops
Dropping objects	Strength through	Boat propulsion	Centrifugal tops
The Red Balloon	materials	Air/water rocket	Gyroscopes: making
		toys	chalk paths (orbits)
			Space travel
		ACTIVITY GUIDE	
Sorting	Sorting	Measuring	Sorting
Measuring	Seriating	Language experience	Seriating
Language experience	Measuring		Measuring
	Language experience		Language experience

GRAVITATION

Since gravitation was a common experience for these children, their teacher planned some activities that might help them become more aware of this force. She planned to focus upon contrasting up and down and finding out why objects stop moving up. At about the same time, the children had watched a popular television program at home in which the hero was flying in a basket suspended by a balloon. They also had heard Lamorisse's story, *The Red Balloon*. The teacher drew upon these experiences by preparing lesson materials that included helium-filled balloons along with paper cups, strings, ordinary balloons, rubber balls of various density, yarn balls, and shuttlecocks.

After briefly talking with the children about the story characters, particularly the child Pascal, their teacher asked them how they could solve the problem of getting the paper cup off the ground. When the children tried and saw that one helium-filled balloon was inadequate, they made guesses concerning how many would work and repeated the process after adding extra balloons. Following the children's exclamations of "Ready! Aim! Blast off! Any minute!" and "Pascal, come down!" the teacher asked them to suggest ways of bringing down the cup.

> CHILD 1: Hey, we could put the wood in.
> TEACHER: What would that do?
> TEACHER: [After several children have placed a block in the cup.] What happens now? . . . If Pascal is up too high, how do you think he might come down?
> CHILD 2: Weight.
> CHILD 1: How about a ladder?
> CHILD 3: If he had a pin, he could pop it.
> TEACHER: What would happen to the balloon?
> CHILD 4: The air would come out. . . .*

Notice that the teacher accepted each suggestion. She was in no rush to feed them a single "right" answer that would end the speculation. Instead, she asked them to describe the possible consequences of their actions. The teacher used the terms *gravity* and *force* casually, as they spoke. In this way, she began to build a pattern of guessing, observing, repeating, describing, and explaining that allowed the children to deal with a basic outlook of the physical scientist: defining the limitations within which a particular natural phenomenon could or could not occur.

---

*Different children are represented by the use of the same number designation in the different episodes that are reported. However, within each episode, the same child's contribution is indicated by the same number.

In an ancillary activity later in the week, the teacher asked the children to dictate statements concerning their prior group meetings, so that they could share them with a youngster who was absent. Some of the responses follow:

CHILD 1: The balloons and the cups went around the room.
CHILD 2: 'Cause they had helium in them.
CHILD 3: They lifted the cup up.
CHILD 4: Four balloons.
CHILD 5: We counted to four.
TEACHER: We had balls, too. What kind of balls?
CHILD 6: Little balls.
CHILD 7: [Moving hands.] They were shaped like this.
CHILD 8: Like a capsule.
TEACHER: [Reads back what is written.]
CHILD 4: They went up, up, up, up, up.
TEACHER: What made them come down?
CHILD 8: The air came out.
CHILD 7: Gravity.
CHILD 5: Because they have no motors.
CHILD 6: They don't have propellers or wings.
TEACHER: A bird can have wings and he can come down. Why does he come down?
CHILD 1: There's nothing to keep it up.

By recording the children's statements for the absent child, the teacher was able to gain some understanding of what the children perceived. As they continued to be receptive to these exposures, the children added to their information and began to apply it. In contrast with these earlier experiences, notice the wider scope of their comments five weeks later, during an activity period. (They are looking at pictures of space travel on a bulletin board.)

CHILD 1: That's a rocket!
CHILD 2: My friend has a cardboard rocket that goes round and round.
CHILD 1: Hey, that rocket's upside down.
CHILD 2: I'm not crazy. The rocket is upside down.
CHILD 3: He's flying.
CHILD 4: He's standing on his head because there's no gravity.
CHILD 5: There's no gravity in space.
CHILD 6: If you get very far away the gravity can't pull the rocket down.
TEACHER: What if you were up in space where Meg said there's no gravity? How could she be kept from flying around?
CHILD 7: She wears a gravity belt.
CHILD 5: If she didn't have one she would be flying around.

TEACHER: What if she were flying?

CHILD 2: Just like upsy-daisy.

TEACHER: What if she tried to pick up her mommy?

CHILD 8: She could pick up her mommy.

CHILD 3: . . . because there's no gravity.

MAGNETISM

The teacher selected the force of magnetism as another focus for activities since it contrasted with gravitation. Another consideration was that children can see and feel the effects of this force directly, possibly strengthening their concept of force.

The teacher worked with two groups of four and five children at adjacent tables. She had set out the materials with enough magnets for most of the children. She limited group size so that there would be a maximum opportunity for children to use the materials. Also, in this way, she could be in touch with both groups. At other times, she worked with eight children as one group in order to stimulate discussion.

She provided magnets of different sizes, shapes, and strengths and a variety of magnetic and nonmagnetic articles. The teacher suggested that they guess into which pile each article might be placed. She encouraged the children to separate the objects into piles of those that the magnet attracted and those that were not attracted. After they finished sorting the objects, the children listed for each other the articles in their respective piles.

When the teacher asked them what the attracted materials were made of, some children variously mentioned metal and iron. However, after several different magnets were used unsuccessfully to attract a metal ring, children were left with a new classification to ponder until a later activity. New words such as *repel* and *attract* became part of the children's vocabulary in a functional way.

Another classification activity with the magnets was to differentiate them by size and strength. The teacher asked the children to notice which magnet the object was attracted to first when she moved magnets of different sizes toward an equidistant object on the table. She asked them to guess which magnet would be stronger each time the activity was repeated. After this procedure was repeated several times, the children concluded that a smaller magnet *might* be stronger than a larger magnet.

In another activity to measure the relative strength of magnets, the group used paper clips. They saw which magnets could attract more and fewer paper clips, and they represented their findings graphically on a survey chart.

Approximately two months later, the children applied these experiences to a situation with a gyroscope, in an attempt to change its direction of movement.

CHILD 1: I don't think the magnet will do anything.

CHILD 2: [Indicating the gyroscope.] I don't think it will spin. The inside will but not . . .

CHILD 3: [As child has brought a magnet.] Nothing happens. I'm going to use all the magnets.

CHILD 4: 'Cause it's going too fast.

CHILD 1: Maybe it's not metal or something.

CHILD 5: Maybe it's not iron, not iron, not iron . . .

CHILD 6: You sure it isn't the broken one?

They certainly were able to use their knowledge of magnets independently in this new situation. Independent work with the magnets as well as discussions with the teacher both contributed to this facility in applying their knowledge.

Kay's "trick" of attracting paper, described earlier, was turned into another session the following day. Children tested the magnet's power to attract through materials that were not themselves attracted. The teacher encouraged children to predict with each additional material, to test each guess in turn, and to describe and compare each occurrence.

They did several tests to see how many pieces of cardboard could be "attracted" to the magnet through the use of a paper clip. Children held their breaths in suspense at the veritable drama that ensued as each piece of cardboard was added. They found that seven pieces was the maximum number through which a paper clip might be attracted by any of their magnets. A child who noticed that the paper clip had been attracted but that it did not go "zip" stimulated the group to think about the relative strength of the force. While to an adult it may seem to take a long time to find out about seven pieces of cardboard, one at a time, the children derive a direct, aesthetic satisfaction from such an experience.

AIR PRESSURE

Children can see and feel the force of air pressure directly. When the teacher planned the viewing of an astronaut's rocket launch, which relied upon jet propulsion, she felt that children who had been exposed first to the use of air as a propelling force might bring more associations to that later experience. She thought about what materials could offer experiences with air pressure. For example, she decided against using pressurized cans because children could not feel the pressure build up. Since they had used plastic bottles and squeezed air out of them at other times, she added model rockets designed for children to use outdoors because they require a combination of water and air pressure for their propulsion. The children could pour the water, attach the parts of the model rocket by themselves, and then feel the air pressure build up as they pumped.

Initially, the teacher encouraged the children to select balloons, blow them up, and play with them in whatever ways they chose. Some children blew them up and asked the teacher to seal them. They would pat and throw the balloons up and down and follow them around the room. Other children, who had difficulty blowing them up, tried to fill them with water. Still other children blew them up and let the balloons loose to enjoy the sight of them deflating and the sound of the air escaping. This last play became popular, and children also placed the deflating balloon against their cheeks. One child said to nobody in particular, "Can't see air, but you can hear air."

The teacher planned activities with balloons, drinking straws, and toy boats. She asked the children to tear off an end of the paper covering the straw, to suck at the straw and describe what happened, and then to blow out and notice what happened. The children had a grand time and compared this activity with others they had had.

CHILD 1: It stuck on.
CHILD 2: Kind of like a magnet.
CHILD 1: When I blow up paper it's like a balloon.
CHILD 2: He was the pump.

She asked the children to predict in which direction an untied balloon would move if it were released. The children pointed in a variety of directions and later described and compared the actual course. They repeated the procedure several times, and the teacher remarked, as she had done before, "Now you have to do things several times to see where they're going." In this way she was trying to make them aware of the need for repetition and tentativeness as a way of studying natural phenomena.

Then they discussed the plastic boats. A hole was drilled in the rear of each boat and a glass dropper, from which the rubber cap had been removed, was set through the hole so that an end of the dropper would be below the water line. The teacher attached a balloon to the opposite end of the dropper that sat in the boat, and rubber bands held the apparatus together.

Children blew up the balloons in the boats through the dropper, set the boats in a large water-filled tub, and gleefully watched the boats being propelled by the air that was escaping from the balloons. As they repeated their activity, they talked together about jet propulsion:

CHILD 1: What would happen if it had two balloons?

CHILDREN: It would go faster.

TEACHER: What if we put three balloons?

CHILD 3: [A child who rarely spoke; smiling.] It would go faster.

CHILD 4: Round and round.

CHILD 1: Let's do it.

CHILD 2: If they were on the sides it would go . . . [Makes a zigzag motion.]

CHILDREN: [Laugh.]

TEACHER: That would be good to try. Hal thinks it will stay pretty still, wouldn't go in any direction.

CHILD 3: That's the problem. We really don't know.

The children seemed involved and comfortable in expressing conjectures and extending the discussions. Yet, through the discussions and introduction of new materials, they were allowed to be active and to inflate their balloons. This was similar to their ongoing use of magnets. The physical involvement with materials appeared to help them keep their thinking focused. They were simultaneously able to manipulate materials and to expand ideas.

CENTRIFUGAL FORCE

An understanding of orbits in nature requires some idea of centrifugal force. Therefore, the teacher planned classroom experiences in which children could feel and see the effect of centrifugal force. To equal lengths of string, they attached a spool, cardboard square, small plastic toy, cork, or other small object, and created a twirling motion by hand at the top of the string. As they did, they saw each object swing around and spin away from the hand. Her plan included the considerations shown in Figure 6.2. The following dialogue shows how the kindergarten children and their teacher interacted as they explored this force by predicting, observing, comparing, and attempting to explain their findings.

Figure 6.2: Teacher's Plan for Centrifugal Force Activity

Purposes: Predict. Observe. Compare.
Use the term centrifugal force. Differentiate
centrifugal force from other forces.
Materials: Wooden spools, cardboard squares, and other
small objects suspended from strings; wooden tops; and
meter stick.
Organization: 8-12 children at a time work with teacher.
Procedures: Compare the weight of spools, cardboard, and
other small objects.
Twirl each object suspended from a string.
Use a meter stick.

Predicting Stage

> TEACHER: Look at what we have here.
> CHILD 1: A merry-go-round.
> CHILD 2: [Holding strings apart.] If it would stick out like this it would look more like a merry-go-round.
> TEACHER: Is there any way we could make it go out?
> CHILD 3: Sticks.
> CHILD 4: Glue it out.
> CHILD 2: You can push it around.
> CHILD 5: Like blow it.
> CHILD 1: You could twirl it.

Observation and Comparison Stage

> CHILD 6: It's going faster.
> CHILD 2: I saw the string going with it.
> TEACHER: Is the cardboard under my hand?
> CHILD 1: At the sides.
> TEACHER: [With a meter stick.] How far off the ground is it?
> CHILD 6: Eighteen.
> TEACHER: Yes, just about. Let's see if it goes down closer to the ground.
> CHILD 7: No, higher.
> CHILD 5: Lower.
> TEACHER: Let's measure and see.
> CHILD 1: Twenty-four.
> TEACHER: Is twenty-four more than eighteen?
> CHILDREN: [Nod.]
> CHILD 4: 'Cause your arm is higher.
> TEACHER: Let's measure if it goes higher without an arm moving. [They repeat the procedure until all are satisfied that they are repeatedly seeing the same thing.]

Explaining Stage

> TEACHER: What might make it go up?
> CHILD 1: Air.
> CHILD 8: Your hand.
> TEACHER: Does it go out by itself?
> CHILD 8: When you twirl it the air holds it up.
> TEACHER: Is it moving faster or slower?
> CHILD 4: No, faster.
> TEACHER: When it goes faster, what else is happening?
> CHILD 2: It's going outer.
> TEACHER: What makes it go out?
> CHILDREN 2 & 4: Air.
> TEACHER: Remember, when we drop things, what's the force?
> CHILD 3: Gravity.

TEACHER: [Mentions forces of magnetism and air.] The force that makes the spool go out is centrifugal force. This is the center, and the force that's moving it out is centrifugal.

Notice the integrity of the children throughout these interactions. Children are saying what they actually see. They are not simply trying to guess what the teacher might expect or what a single "right" answer might be.

They followed a similar procedure after the teacher had added some transparent tops to the materials that children used during work periods. These "centrifugal" tops contained colored water, colored oil, and grains that separated into three rings when they were twirled. They were used enthusiastically by the children, some of whom acquired great skill at keeping numerous tops twirling simultaneously.

Meeting half the class for a discussion, the teacher distributed these tops so that three or four children shared each top. The children identified materials in the tops and then compared the materials with regard to weight and color:

TEACHER: Look at the tops and see what's in them.
CHILD 1: [Describes.] Beads . . .
CHILD 2: Red beads . . .
CHILD 3: White, green, and orange.
CHILD 4: White, green, and orange.
TEACHER: What's the color of the oil in yours? [The teacher repeats the question as she moves between groups.]
CHILD 5: Green.
TEACHER: And the water?
CHILD 6: Red.
TEACHER: Which would be the heaviest?
CHILD 4: The beads.
TEACHER: Which would be the lightest?
CHILDREN: [Spin their transparent tops and describe the colors on the outside ring, the inside, and the middle ring. They compare color with weight.]
TEACHER: What do you suppose makes it move out?
CHILD 5: Centrifugal force.
TEACHER: [Brings a different-colored top to each group and they repeat the twirling.] Do the beads always go to the outside?
CHILD 3: [Seemingly confident.] They don't!
TEACHER: Try again. . . . What colors are the beads?
CHILD 3: White.
CHILDREN: [Twirl the tops again. The children have been twirling or turning or looking at them throughout the entire discussion.]
TEACHER: What color is on the outside?
CHILDREN 3 & 4: [Smiling and wide-eyed.] The white!

These interchanges suggest that the children were becoming more careful observers. They seemed able to challenge the observations of others and to offer explanations for events, based upon prior activities in the classroom. Their numerous earlier experiences with differentiating relative weight were essential to this activity. Over the next weeks the teacher planned several other related activities:

1. They observed the rotation of a sphere by using clay spheres rotated on pencils in the presence of a flashlight. The teacher's purpose was to build toward the concept of an orbit around the earth in an imminent space flight. The children were able to compare these activities with the transparent tops. They were also able to attribute the ending of the spinning to the force of gravity. One youngster said, "Gravity pushed it down, but what pushed it up?" This child seemed to have a beginning feeling about the interaction of forces. It would be difficult to conclude, however, that children ever directly applied centrifugal force to answer this youngster's question. They were able only to verbalize that centrifugal force was operative in centrifugal separation, a concrete observation.
2. Children heard the story *Follow the Sunset*, by Schneider and Schneider, while a globe lit by a filmstrip projection lamp was nearby. A globe had always been present in the classroom, and the children had often referred to it. The teacher's purpose was to highlight the notion that the earth moves continuously. This activity preceded a look at a large model of the sun and planets in motion.
3. They used chalk to follow the path of a gyroscope spinning on the floor.
4. Children launched their own toy rockets outdoors.
5. They watched a space launch on television.

Children were beginning to apply some of their learning and to try out their growing vocabulary, sometimes more accurately than others. They brought in newspaper clippings about the spaceship's orbit and discussed why the path was not straight up. The children were able to relate the path to the "round" earth. The youngsters communicated excitement. They were receptive to activities that dealt with the interaction of opposing forces such as gravitation and magnetism, centrifugal force and gravitation, and air propulsion and gravitation.

Measurement

In dealing with the physical world, we often deal with quantities. In their study, the children discussed in the previous section repeated their manipulations of concrete materials and measured changes when possible.

For example, the meter stick was used repeatedly when children studied centrifugal force. The use of this tool was possible only because they had had prior experiences in the classroom measuring and seeing numbers written. They also frequently used rulers at the woodworking bench.

The children had also heard their teacher use terms that described the relative position of phenomena, such as *bigger than, smaller than, heavier than, stronger than, lower than, shorter than, above, up straight*, and so forth. They discussed angles in connection with the earth's axis as well as in their rhythmic movement and dance activities. Continuing with this same class as an example, let's look at some other experiences kindergarten children can have with measurement.

MEASURING TIME AND DISTANCE

These children measured time. They quickly noticed that counting was inadequate for timing the fall of objects, because individuals counted at different rates. The teacher obtained a one-minute timer with a clock face; however, the children were confused by the representation of a whole minute in the space of half the area of the circle. Further search in photography shops uncovered a three-minute timer that had a clock face marked into seconds and minutes. The teacher left these timers on a shelf, without comment. Several children who noticed one recognized it as some sort of "clock without hands." One youngster said, "Hey, I know what that is! It's a countdown on rockets."

The children began to use the timers to time their cooking play, to find out how long their tops would spin and their rockets would fly, and to measure the length of time it took for a boat to sail a given distance.

When the children used the timer with their own jet-propelled boats, they talked a good deal about the "countdown"; however, the timekeeper had been counting *up*. That is, while several children seriously and patiently waited, the timekeeper was starting the timer at zero and counting *up* to the zero and the three-minute mark, which were identical. After three repetitions, during which the timekeeper was counting off seconds by tens, he announced, "Blast off," promptly pocketed the timer, and enjoyed the boat race.

The children clearly were not able yet to coordinate their interest in the boats with the timer. Therefore, in an attempt to extend the children's experience with the timer beyond the "countdown" and "countup" phase, the teacher planned a short session in which they used the timer and the meter stick. The children's comments during this discussion revealed that several of them needed to clarify vocabulary and concepts about length of time as duration and length of meter stick as distance or height.

At the teacher's request, the children suggested various ways that they could make the boats sail. The children mentioned pushing, blowing, and fanning the boats, in addition to jet propulsion. They predicted and measured how far the boats would move and how long it would take when the methods of blowing, fanning with cardboard, and jet propulsion were used.

Then they compared which method took the longest and the shortest time to move the boats the greatest distance. As each procedure was repeated, the teacher wrote their findings on a chart so that they could compare times and distances. The children were physically involved and attentive as they coordinated their manipulations of materials and their discussions of events.

Depth of Study

The study of the interaction of forces in the physical world can be spread over half or all of the school year, depending on the density of activity to which your children seem receptive. When children engage in related activities, rather than isolated one-time events, they can integrate new perceptions in individually meaningful ways. Depth in this sense refers to the personal involvement and the meaning level of a series of experiences that extend over time.

For example, look at erosion as an illustration of the interaction of forces. You can speak of and observe the interaction of air, temperature, water, soil, wind, rock, and humanmade structures. You can notice the relationships among forests, fires, rainfall, climatic conditions, and land forms, tying in human use of land as another interactive element. You can observe eroded sites; directly witness erosion during and immediately following rain or a thaw; and compare pictures taken before and after land development for construction, pictures before and after fires, and pictures before erosion compared with a later seashore or riverbank visit. You can see films, slides, and filmstrips. You can read about mud slides and avalanches and adventure stories, including the most adventurous ones, the real-life ones in the daily newspaper. You can create structures in the classroom or on school grounds and play at eroding them. Film technology and even tape-recorded dramatization are certainly possible substitutes for the real thing. For example, the child growing up on an Iowa plain may not have direct access to mountainous terrain; the teacher should therefore plan a series of related experiences that reflect the interaction of human beings and nature in their own locale.

Measuring tools may differ. Instead of measuring water erosion, the plains child might measure wind or drought damage. Nonetheless, the interplay of different tools and varied data can provide a comparable quality and quantity of experience. Here again, the nature and purpose of experience is to use knowledge to gain understanding and cultivate coopera-tion, with absorption of information being a by-product, not the end, of learning.

UNDERSTANDING BIOLOGY THROUGH CLASSIFICATION

As we teach kindergarten children, we need to remind ourselves that they will perceive best those things that they can see, feel, touch, taste, and smell. We need to keep in mind also that humans can perceive things most clearly when two conditions are present: (1) movement and (2) contrast. Among these conditions, we might consider that a *contrast* is *structural*, for example, an unknown figure set against a known background, where the unknown figure represents a single new variable. By the same token, we might consider that *movement* is *functional*.

For example, when there is a sufficient contrast between the figure and ground structures, children can perceive the interrelation of these structures as movement. For biologists, function and structure are undergoing con-tinual change and self-regulation because they are both processes: "What are called structures are slow processes of long duration, functions are quick processes of short duration" (Bertalanffy, 1960). Making these processes explicit for ourselves can help us to plan the activities and conditions in which kindergarten children can perceive and learn. Children can learn about biology when they can experience contrasts between figure and ground, between slower and quicker phenomena.

Among the major concepts in biology are cyclical change, adaptation, and variety; these are broad categories that lend themselves to many types of activities, and indeed, numerous volumes have been written on the sub-ject. The purpose of this section is to share some of the approaches and activities that represent these categories, in the form of experiences to which kindergarten children have been receptive. Figure 6.3 provides a conceptual planning map for using the concepts in biology instruction. It is clear that we have an overwhelming array of activities from which to choose. Several criteria that can be used in deciding which activities to pursue are presented in Figure 6.4.

Plants

Plants in the classroom provide a periodic activity that represents ele-ments of cyclical change and variety for children. It is useful to provide more than one sample of each of several types of plants, such as cactus, moss, green leafy plants, geraniums, elodea in the aquarium, peas, and bulbs. Beyond

Figure 6.3:   Conceptual Planning Map In Biology

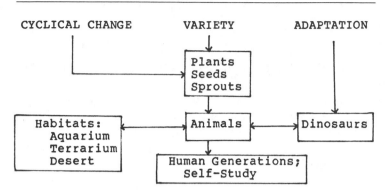

Figure 6.4:   Criteria for Selecting Biology Activities

-**Gregariousness.** Which activities represent the most
  gregarious processes or concepts? More gregarious
  activities are the most likely to help children to
  suggest and generate possible ties with other related
  activities.
-**Appeal.** Which activities are the most exciting and
  attractive to pursue? For example, it is ridiculous to
  initiate a study of snakes or mealworms if they make your
  stomach dance. Hatching chicks, peeper frogs, or fish
  provide equivalent opportunities for studying growth
  concepts.
-**Resource Availability.** For which activities do you have
  the most ideas, materials, and resources?
-**Children's Receptivity.** In which directions have your
  children shown greatest interest and capacity? To what
  activities do you estimate they will be most receptive?
-**Opportunity for Participation.** Are there opportunities
  for different children to engage with different degrees
  of involvement and commitment?
-**Representativeness.** Which activities most clearly
  represent an underlying perceptual model or part of a
  perceptual model?

labeling the plants, there are various actions that you and your children might take:

Vary locations in relation to light sources.

Measure the amount of water that different plants require each week.

Vary water quantities.

Vary temperature.

Record actions that you take.

Measure plant growth with direct, continuous, nonstandard measures such as yarn or paper strips, and record on a chart and in individual science/mathematics notebooks as relevant.

Cyclical change is easily represented in activities with seeds. One of the most popular activities over time is an autumn trip to a pumpkin farm, scooping out the pumpkin seeds, drying them, sometimes eating them, and cooking the pumpkin itself. Some teachers have saved some of the pumpkin seeds until the following springtime and helped the children to plant them in used milk containers. It is advisable to plant seeds in several containers, for this practice both increases the likelihood that something will grow and provides an opportunity to vary some of the growth conditions.

Other activities with seeds involve collecting a variety of seeds, some of which can be obtained from fruits and vegetables used for snack time. These can include fleshy fruits such as apples, pears, melons, oranges, pomegranates, grapes, and pineapples; other, drier fruits, such as avocados, peas, cucumbers, squash, and tomatoes; and vegetables such as peppers, sprouts, and corn. Potatoes, rice, and lima beans are other types of seeds that you might collect. The following are some ways you might use them.

Classify seeds according to one variable at a time, such as texture (rough/smooth), color, shape, or size.

Create collage patterns with seeds. Children can write or dictate descriptions of the products.

For peas, predict the number of seeds in a handful of pods, shell them, and list how many peas you find in your set of pods, the largest number and the smallest number in a single pod, and the most frequent number.

When you cut open the fruits and vegetables, note any symmetrical patterns and chart which seeds were or were not aligned symmetrically.

Find a collection of other objects that look like seeds and ask children, "What might these be?" "How do we know they are seeds?" "How do we know that they are not seeds?" You might plant the various samples, attaching a sample to a stick with transparent tape so that it stands in the soil where you planted the sample. Accept all responses.

Sprouts grow very quickly from such seeds as alfalfa, mung beans, sunflower seeds, and peas, as do plant cuttings such as carrot tops, turnip tops, and sprouting sweet potatoes. Several other growth conditions can be varied, such as

Medium. Seeds can be grown in water, dry soil, and damp soil, as well as on paper towel or a sponge.

Distance. Plant seeds close together and farther apart.

Depth. Vary how deeply the seeds are planted.

Direction. Using two transparent containers, plant several seeds in the usual way, but turn one container on its side and turn another upside down.

Moisture. Vary the amount and frequency of watering.

State. See what happens if you plant half of a seed or a frozen green pea.

Measure the sprouts and predict and compare the growth of different varieties and growth under different conditions. Record the results on a chart. Even a single variable can be enough; for example, the children might measure the growth of peas in moistened soil after one week, and then again after two weeks.

Whichever of these activities you decide to use with your children, do keep in mind that the major purpose is to keep open the questions, the wonder, the imagination, and the excitement, rather than to provide a predigested set of statements for children to hear and repeat.

Animals

Children enjoy animals in the classroom, and there is much important learning connected with the play, care, observation, comparison, classification, measurement, and description that take place. Animals create an opportunity for children to develop feelings of responsibility, caring, and reverence for life.

Hamsters, gerbils, and rabbits can be kept in kindergartens successfully, with families taking turns in caring for these pets over the weekend. Children can learn about feeding habits, water consumption, elimination, growth, reproduction, illness, unique behaviors, and even death. They can survey what a particular insect or animal will or will not eat. Measuring the girth and the length of a young animal every two weeks for about two months is another exciting survey activity. Two or three months is ample time to study a single animal. If resources are limited in your school, perhaps you can exchange animals and findings with another class.

Local ponds in the springtime can be a source for tadpoles that grow into peeper frogs. These can be raised easily on crumbs and fish food in an aquarium. Children take great pleasure in watching them develop into peeper frogs, after which time they need to live out of the water. Children can develop their own booklets of drawings and will raise many significant questions when they are exposed to these dramatic events.

Alternative activities can include raising mealworms from a local pet shop or incubating chicken eggs with equipment available from the local 4-H club. Children predict, observe, classify, compare, measure, write, draw pictures, model in clay, and talk about their experiences with animals. It is particularly useful when children communicate their experiences and findings with other children and adults who were not present.

The study of contrasting life forms can highlight an understanding of *adaptation* to different environments. Studying fish in classroom aquariums is another way of learning about adaptation, cyclical change, and variety. It is most useful to have more than one aquarium, in order to be able to compare events resulting from different variables. One well-tested and adaptable environment includes guppies, snails, plants, and pebbles. When the water needs to be changed, the replacement supply should be left at room temperature for a day before use.

Children can classify elements in the aquarium according to their own criteria, including

> Living things (plants, animals); and nonliving things (water, a liquid, and pebbles, a solid); once-living things that are no longer alive (waste products)
> Large and small objects
> Slow-moving and fast-moving things
> Animals that have fins or shells

The environment can be controlled for such variables as the location or absence of plants. Children can predict and then count with pegs or numbers, depending upon their skills, the number of times in a minute that a fish flaps its gills for breathing. They then can compare their findings with the breathing rates of other classroom pets, as well as humans.

A terrarium in the kindergarten is another environment that permits children to study adaptation and change in plants and animals. Soil, rocks, various plants, earthworms, and moisture are a sufficient beginning for study and comparison with the aquarium environment, with many of the same processes being applied. Moreover, the observation of water condensation is particularly apparent in the terrarium habitat. A related activity could be comparing changes at different spots in the school yard throughout the year (Russell, 1973).

Animals in the Classroom is an Elementary Science Study publication that describes the establishment of a desert habitat and classroom study of the kangaroo rat, the pocket mouse, and the desert iguana, a type of lizard whose scientific name, *Dipsosaurus dorsalis*, kindergarten children love to use. This habitat provides a fascinating contrast with the terrarium and the aquarium. You will find a list of other exciting classroom-tested science topics of particular interest to kindergarten children in the bibliography, put out by Elementary Science Study.

In addition, kindergarten children enjoy the study of dinosaurs, whether you call this study history or biology. In the biological sense, dinosaur study illuminates the concepts of cyclical change, adaptation, and variety. Kindergarten children are certainly motivated highly enough in studying dinosaurs to differentiate and label them with rather complex names, such as pterodactyl, brontosaurus, and trachodon. They enjoy classifying the different limb structures, teeth, and running capacities of vegetarian as opposed to flesh-eating dinosaurs. One knowledgeable kindergarten group even voted for their favorite dinosaur. Children's fascination with dinosaurs is an example of how emotional and aesthetic concerns influence motives for cognitive attention. Kindergarten children can deal with the subject of dinosaurs playfully and for purposes of classification, only within the context of their own developmental level.

Humans

Focusing on different generations of people can also help kindergarten children to reinforce the elements of cyclical change. It may work out well in your classroom to ask parents to send baby pictures of the children. As the school year wears on, you will have many reasons to record class events and photograph the children. Whether some of the children create "A Book about Myself," using these photographs, or you decide to develop a bulletin board chart, there are interesting comparisons to make.

You can invite a parent to bring in a baby early in the school year, then at midyear, and at the end of the year, so that the children can create a chart of the baby's growth. Perhaps you can weigh her, measure her length with nonstandard as well as standard measures, list the food she adds to her diet, and notice the behaviors she develops over time.

You might compare varied sorts of care that parents give their offspring and observe differences between classroom animals and humans. For example, children might notice differences in gestation. Do be prepared for their possible curiosity about where fertilization occurs. It makes sense to be ready rather than to offer unsolicited or inadequate information. This attitude is also useful when dealing with questions about death.

While dealing with intergenerational study, consider inviting a well-prepared elderly resource person who might bring photographs and stories about how things used to be. The best preparation for this is for you and the resource person to plan the activity together. Perhaps you could consider this visit to be part of your social studies program, since this information is social as well as biological. This case is a good example of the futility of trying to draw strict lines between disciplines.

Children also enjoy learning more about their physical selves and what they can do. There are many measurement activities, using nonstandard methods, that relate to the children's own selves and can be enjoyable cooperative mathematics activities. Here are a few ideas to suggest to the children that have been adapted from "Science 5/13" (Richards et al., 1976a; 1976b), rich sources for activities:

> Measure your height, weight, and girth.
> Measure the length between your knee and the ground.
> Measure the length of your cubit (elbow to middle fingertip).
> Compare lengths of your upper and lower arm and leg.
> Determine your hand span (using yarn or string).
> Compare the length of your left and right feet.
> Count how many beads, pegs, or other objects you can pick up in your right hand. What about your left hand?
> How much water can you displace in a transparent container with each hand in turn immersed to the wrist? (Mark water line with tape before and after immersion.)
> Tally your wrist pulse or heartbeat, briefly using a stethoscope.
> Compare the different hair colors of people in the classroom.
> What colors can you see at the greatest distance?
> What colors can you see in the dark? What difference does sunlight make?
> What can you see when you look at a ruler in a transparent jar full of water?
> What can you see through jello?
> What can you see when you look at a leaf or newsprint through a magnifying glass? Through a drop of water? Through a drop of oil? Through (how many) layers of plastic wrap?
> Compare and sort out transparent and opaque objects. Which objects are easier to see? Where?

How can you change the way things look with mirrors? (This activity
might tie in with earlier explorations of symmetrical patterns of
seeds in such fruits as apples and pears.)
What can you see with a periscope?

The teacher can also help the children create a graph of the relative distribu-
tion of eye color among the children in the class, using a standard-sized index
card for each child, as shown in Figure 6.5.

Other sensory studies of children's own capacities include smelling and
hearing. Children enjoy identifying different smells such as soap, perfume,
vinegar, dry cheese, and so forth. They enjoy identifying sounds of objects
when they are dropped, such as a coin, comb, rubber toy, plastic spoon,
and so forth. They also feel powerful when they can guess that another child
is pouring water, rubbing sandpaper, or blowing bubbles through a straw.
It is intriguing to wonder and compare whether it is easiest to hear when
an action is taking place to the right, left, front, or rear of you.

A standard Montessori material consists of covered cylinders that are
filled with gradations of grains. Children can seriate by size as they shake
the cylinders, listen, and project an image of the grains, guessing, for example, whether they are sand grains or pea-sized grains. Of course, as with
any seriation activity, it helps when you begin with a single contrast and
then add new variables gradually.

As children look at and compare body coverings for their own selves

Figure 6.5: Graph Survey of Children's Eye Colors

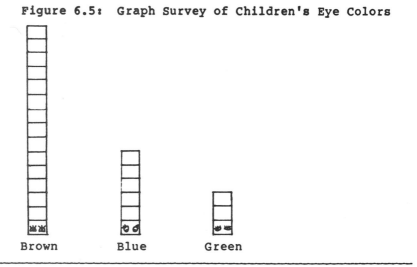

Brown   Blue   Green

as well as for birds, classroom pets, and other animals, they can consider different ways that living beings keep themselves warm or cool. This may even lead to exploring the school's heating and cooling systems, tracing pipes or other conduits. Some people may say that we are too far from classical biology, but it is my belief that understanding in its broadest and most useful sense is achieved best through such networking and exploring of connections.

UNDERSTANDING CHEMISTRY THROUGH SYNERGY

Chemistry really concerns cooperation among the component elements of matter in such a way that chemical processes often seem to become more than the sum of their parts. This is known as *synergy*. For young children, cooking is a familiar activity in which they can see transformations of the parts into new forms, whether apples become apple sauce, dry corn becomes popcorn or sprouted corn, or heavy cream becomes whipped cream and eventually butter. Of course, sensitive teachers will try to tie such experiences in synergy to other activities. A visit to a dairy where children can see cows at milking time is an exciting first step in following the food chain, which will lead ultimately to a market, where they can buy cream. In some families, butter may not even be a usual food item, so making their own butter for a school snack with crackers can have extra meaning for the children. Here again, we are crossing strict disciplinary boundaries, to touch briefly on economics.

These activities also lend themselves well to recording with photographs, audio tape, and experience charts. Teachers and kindergarten children can develop recipe charts that integrate pictures and words and become part of a reading readiness program. They can also develop stick-figure directions on task cards for use in the science area.

Figure 6.6 shows a conceptual planning map for chemistry instruction through the use of synergy. It includes cooking activities, usual in kindergarten practice, and extends to other more or less chemistry-related activities. (Refer back to Figure 3.1 for the connection between chemistry and other disciplines.)

The Evaporation/Condensation Cycle

Particularly when we approach the study of the behavior of particles that we cannot see unaided, we need to integrate the study of chemical properties with concrete activities. Children are intrigued by the evaporation/condensation cycle. As with the study of cyclical change in biology and social science, children's experience with only a part of the cycle will help

Figure 6.6: Conceptual Planning Map for Chemistry Instruction

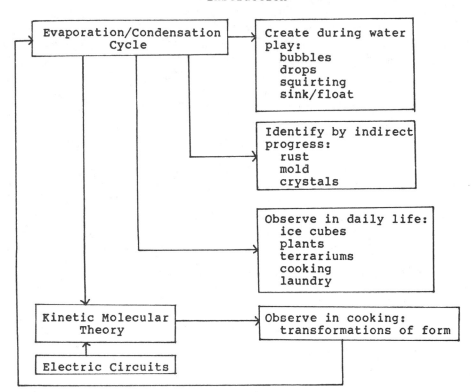

them to build toward broader understanding. Also, as in all investigative activities, it is useful to develop and use open-ended questions:

- What do you see? (This is worthy of lots of time.)
- What do you suppose will happen if . . . ?
- What happened when . . . ?
- When might it not happen that way?
- How might we find out?

WATER PLAY

Since water is the most familiar form in the evaporation/condensation cycle, water play is a good, concrete place to begin. Ice cubes are fun for young children. Consider having some available at the snack table for children to use from time to time. When it seems to fit, after children have had many occasions to savor the ice, you might discuss when the ice seems to melt most quickly or lasts the longest. You might even have occasion to try different coverings on the ice cube container, such as a cloth towel, aluminum foil, styrofoam, or a high-pile fabric, in order to see which material keeps the ice frozen longer.

If you have a snowfall in your area, take the opportunity to look carefully at the snow outdoors; bring some indoors and try to find different ways of keeping the snow frozen longer or of melting it. If you heat the snow or ice in a pot, consider using heat-proof glass with a cover so that you can see the steam and the condensation form. Even if you do not have a glass pot, you can always open the pot to look at the steam, which looks "cloudy," and then see the "rain" form on the cover and the sides of the pot when it cools.

As part of your plant studies, you might consider if there are some places in the room where moisture lasts longer and other places where evaporation is faster, such as on the radiator or in direct sunlight. Consider placing transparent containers of the same size, containing the same amounts of water, in these places as well as in a closet or near an outside door. You might consider putting salt and sugar in some containers, to see if they make any difference. Do take the opportunity to see what happens after all of the water has evaporated in the salted or sugared containers. In all such activities, predict and compare.

The terrarium is an ideal environment to look at when you consider the moisture cycle. You can even place a transparent plastic bag over a seedling long enough to see condensation form. If the occasion arises at birthday parties, you might ask the children to describe what they see as they look at the candles. Just observing is an adequate activity, as long as you accept what you hear from children.

Clothing does become wet in school from time to time, and there are occasions when children might launder sociodramatic play clothing. If there is a reasonable moment, ideally not planned grandly ahead of time, you might take the time to consider with the small group involved in the activity which fabrics seem to dry more quickly. It would be good to have cotton, nylon, silk, corduroy, wool, and plastic items handy for such an event.

This activity can lead to a written chart that has a sample of each labeled item, in the order of drying time. You can record statements such as "The silk dried faster than the cotton shirt," "The nylon was the first to dry," and "The wool sweater took the longest to dry." Other language-related activity could include asking children to describe how various wet and dry objects feel, so that a small group can share a list (Richards et al., 1976a, p. 84).

Making bubbles with water is another favorite activity. Richards et al. (1976a, pp. 65–66) recommend asking the children, "How many ways can you make water bubble?" The children's suggestions might include clapping hands under water, moving a large cloth, blowing through a pipe, blowing through a drinking straw, and blowing up a balloon and letting out the air under water.

Another idea that the Elementary Science Study offers in *Drops, Streams, and Containers* (1971a) is for children to compare the bubbles that they create with soap, vinegar, oil, or milk. Children have compared density, smell, color, and viscosity of corn syrup, vegetable oil, and water, and have observed what happened when objects moved through different liquids (Sprung, Froschl, & Campbell, 1985). Kindergarten children also enjoy playing with the "grabbiness" property (surface tension) of water as they fill a cup beyond the top — one suspenseful drop at a time. For other activities, also see Bird (1978) and Kamii and DeVries (1978).

Other water play activities that might be classified more readily as physical rather than chemical knowledge are worth mentioning in this context. Certainly, seeing which objects sink or float is an involving activity. It is most useful when children predict whether or not an object will sink or float, try the object, and become puzzled to find their prediction unfulfilled. For example, young children tend to expect that larger objects will sink. When a larger object floats or a smaller object sinks, they experience a moment of cognitive dissonance, which jars their learning, just as it did with magnet sizes.

Sometimes children discover on their own how to alter the surface area of an object so that it will float or sink. While you can provide a variety of objects for this classification activity, ask children to suggest others. It is most useful to record children's findings *after* plenty of exploration. You might either list the objects that float and those that sink or develop a cooperative collage or drawings of the sunken and floating objects.

Other water play activities include squirting water into a tub, using containers of different shape, size, and size of opening. Observations can include the following:

Notice which openings water squirts out of more quickly.
Determine how high the container needs to be before the stream either becomes wiggly or turns into droplets.
Notice what differences you see when you use funnels, straws, eye droppers, and syringes.
Watch what happens when two streams meet as they fall.
Using a balance scale, weigh different liquids such as water, juices, oil, and milk (Elementary Science Study, 1971a).

While we have moved some way from the beginnings of the discussion about the evaporation/condensation cycle, it is worth mentioning one other role of water that you might study, that is, water as an aspect of the weather. You can compare quality of precipitation, such as heavy or light rain, drizzles, or snow. Together with the children you can count the seconds between lightning and thunder; this helps to allay fears a bit at the same time that children are exposed to the concept of relative frequency.

TEMPERATURE

Children need to understand the notion of density somewhat if they are ultimately to understand temperature. Concepts of density grow from their daily experiences with balance scales and water play.

The child who has time to study a straw sinking into a thick milkshake and says, "Oh, look; like quicksand," is learning about density just as she did when she viewed a film that showed a person struggling in quicksand. Experiences with foods, plant textures, the bathtub, and blowing soap bubbles are related, as are rush-hour train trips, packed elevators, and popular buffet tables.

Kindergarten children can survey and seriate food and plant densities using straws and lenses. They can survey traffic density and crowd density at different places and times and chart it. Their observations of heating and cooling processes further contribute to building a notion of density. One of the most time-honored activities is to heat in a pan of water a bottle whose opening is covered with an attached balloon. As the water heats, children become excited to see the balloon expand; when the bottle is placed in a pan of ice cubes, they watch the balloon shrink. This demonstration is a dramatic example of the *molecular-kinetic theory*. In effect, heat speeds the movement of molecules and causes them to expand away from each other, whereas cooling slows the movement of molecules while compressing them.

Bear in mind that kindergarten children can gain more when they actually do things physically that grow out of their inquiries, rather than merely observing a demonstration. A worthwhile activity is worth repeating for others, as they become receptive. At the same time, not everybody needs to have participated in each activity.

Children have many random exposures to temperature changes. When you plan contrasts and help them focus their observations, they have a chance to construct order and make sense of their random experiences.

Because temperature is a more abstract and changeable condition to measure than something like length, it is helpful to use nonstandard representations and analogy. An example of nonstandard representation would be marking a large thermometer by color designations such as red for hot, yellow for medium, and blue for cold. Varying the sizes of the thermometers is another way to do this.

When you introduce a personal analogy, children have a chance to learn about temperature personally and aesthetically: "When you get into bed at night and the sheets are cold, what does your body do?" "When you get into bed and it is a hot, sticky night, what does your body do?" The mercury in the thermometer thus becomes more accessible to the young child, as children empathize their way toward understanding.

Electric Circuits

Kindergarten children's earlier experiences with magnets can help them to appreciate the concept of forces in electricity. They are quite comfortable setting up electric circuits that work to operate a light or bell. Children can assemble the circuit themselves when they have clamps that can be squeezed open and shut easily in order to attach the wires, light, switch, and battery. These inexpensive materials are available in hardware stores. Some teachers have created electrical matching games, where pushing two matching switches is sufficient to ring a bell. Kindergarten children can trace the circuitry on the back of the game and change the facing cards to create new games.

The concept of closing and opening circuits for the transfer of energy is a fruitful one. Children can draw pictures and write experience charts with their teachers about the activity. They can use the light as a stop and go sign in their sociodramatic play. Parents and other adults in the school are usually pleased to see children using such sophisticated-looking material.

Although kindergarten children do not grasp the underlying concept of unseen electrons in an adult sense, they are receptive to these activities inasmuch as they can feel successful. This is an opportunity to help all children, regardless of gender, to feel comfortable as they handle technological materials.

The Whole Is More Than the Sum of Its Parts

Besides cooking, there are other chemical transformations that you can look at through concrete classroom activities. There was mention earlier about looking at the results of evaporating liquids that contained salt or sugar. Evaporation, as well as electrical conduction, is one of a number of means for identifying materials indirectly. Crystallization is a sophisticated chemical process that children may encounter in their later studies. Their work in building with blocks, playing with mirrors, stringing beads, building patterns in their art work, and classifying objects and changes can build toward an understanding of these concepts.

There are other chemical changes that children will notice around them, such as rust, decay, and mold. It is relevant for them to question these changes and to see what happens over time, as well as when conditions are varied. Here are some examples:

- If you sandpaper rust off your bicycle, will it rust again?
- Does wood rust? How can we find out what rusts?
- Will objects rust in a plastic bag? On a shelf indoors? On an outdoor window sill? Before/after they are painted? When they are refrigerated, frozen, or heated? When they are buried in soil?
- What happens if you change the environment of rusty objects? [Adapted from *Changes*, Elementary Science Study, 1976c.]

Similar questions can come up when your Halloween pumpkin molds, when children notice that bread dries and crumbles and crackers become soggy and taste stale, and when molds of different colors appear on foods.

INTERDISCIPLINARY VARIATION AND INDIVIDUALIZATION

In all of these activities that emphasize the physical, biological, and chemical sciences, the main work for us in the kindergarten is to create experiences in which children can be physically active, questioning, and touched by awe. As Zukav (1980, p. 9) states, "Every lesson is the first lesson."

Acting and wondering together are at the heart of the study of science for kindergarten children and their teachers. Talk comes at the end rather than the beginning, and some things just never need words. There are books written for young children that deal with "science" topics. If you do use any of them, you will want to apply your best criteria for selecting literature for children and will save the books until after children have had the experiences.

Activities provide the possibilities for children to perceive the kernel models that extend beyond a particular datum of experience. A particular activity, in itself, conveys no magic; a particular tool, in itself, carries no insight. It is the children, through experiencing inductive possibilities, who can construct their own perceptions and their own insights.

If it is your initial responsibility as a teacher to plan concrete activities, it is your ongoing responsibility to appreciate children's unique ways of making connections, being flexible, and expressing their receptivity to activities. This understanding of how the children experience things can then become the basis for planning future work.

In the sciences, as in all areas of study, there is certainly plenty that each adult does not know and about which scientists today still wonder. When your teaching raises many new questions with children, you are helping to keep them open to exploring the unknown and preparing them to find excitement in the challenges that they will inherit. As a case in point, let us take an interdisciplinary look at black holes.

Black holes in space are a source of wonder to adult scientists. They are intriguing because it is exotic to consider a mass of such density that its gravitational force makes it "invisible" (Sullivan, 1974). Kindergarten children can have concrete interdisciplinary experiences that relate to the dialectical perceptual model and contribute to their later understanding of black holes. These dialectical processes include repulsion-attraction, conservation of angular momentum, and reversibility.

REPULSION-ATTRACTION.   One activity through which to expose kindergarten children to this concept is through the use of magnets. Take a large, blunt-tipped embroidery needle and draw it repeatedly in a single direction along a magnet, thereby magnetizing it. Children can easily observe the needle's new two-sided powers, just as they will have done with the original magnets. If children magnetize a second needle in the same way, both times holding onto the eye part, then they may observe opposing ends more easily, since the eyes of both needles will have the same polarity. When one of the needles is suspended from a string, it will turn away or move closer in relation to the turning of the hand-held needle. Since the major purpose of this activity is to note the repulsion-attraction properties, children's imaginations remain open to future work with electromagnets and engines, as well as to long-range understanding of subatomic particle behavior.

CONSERVATION OF ANGULAR MOMENTUM.   There are many ways that children can learn about the "conservation of angular momentum," which is represented by a star spinning more rapidly after it contracts. Children come by this knowledge intuitively as they turn and spin in their dances and games. Ballet dancers and figure skaters make use of this principle.

Vehicles are streamlined to make them more efficient. When children look at automobile, railroad train, and airplane designs through the years, the changes are apparent. While there are few children who will grow up to be as inventive as the Wright brothers, there are many children who play with kites as they did, making their own kites in school, and experimenting with different designs in their early education.* Children appreciate the

---

*Kite-making is usually considered part of the art program in kindergarten, often in the month of March, coinciding with talk about the wind. Too often, all children in a class are asked to create a paper tail using uniform paper shapes that the teacher had pre-cut so that children could have identical materials. In order to provide genuinely aesthetic experiences in art and truly physical knowledge experiences in science, however, teachers should offer children varied materials and suggest that children try out different shapes and the use of three-dimensional as well as two-dimensional forms. Kindergarten children need to be encouraged to predict, try out, and compare different combinations of variables.

relative movement and efficiency of angles and aerodynamics from the aesthetic standpoint of design and body movement before they are ready to understand the technology.

REVERSIBILITY.   The process of crystals dissolving in solutions and then reconstituting during evaporation can be illustrated easily by adding coarse salt to water and then either heating the water or leaving it for natural evaporation to occur. These contrasts are an important inquiry tool that raises children's consciousness about controlled variables. Simple types of square dances and games in which children divide, regroup, and then reconstitute original patterns also represent a similar perceptual model in quite a different form.

While these activities are far removed from subatomic fusion, they can contribute concretely toward long-range understanding. Whether or not you plan a square-dance type of game with black holes in mind does not change the child's experience of a pleasurable, social, physical, aesthetic, and perceptual pastime.

All too often, activities in school that involve art forms and concrete experiences with natural phenomena have been categorized as "frills." In times of fiscal austerity, funding for these ways of learning can fall prey to the financial guilt felt among uninformed lay groups who understand only the linear thinking and abstract information contained in traditional textbooks. However, richness and variety of experience and coming at things from varied perspectives are principles that support human, functional learning.

When we plan activities for kindergarten children that are based upon an appreciation for the unique ways in which workers in the domains of physics, biology, and chemistry study the world, we find that the division between domains becomes secondary. What is primary are the active, concrete experiences that wrap themselves around data from many perspectives. Children learn through aesthetic, social, physical, and cognitive means. They learn and apply language skills, art skills, and mathematical skills in their study of the sciences. The ways of working in the disciplines, the processes of inquiry, become content for kindergarten children. In the course of their activity in the full-day kindergarten, children acquire both pure information and knowledge that lead to understanding and cooperation.

7

Cooperative Mathematics

Mathematics is a discipline that is usually regarded as a tool or a skill. Children can learn mathematics as they apply it to the study of many disciplines; however, it is often taught as if it were an end in itself. In this chapter, mathematics is presented so that it can be used as an applied body of constructions and activities.

One of the big problems in the full-day kindergarten is finding a way to teach mathematics that will satisfy parents that teachers are doing serious business, and at the same time minimize or eliminate parental questions about the use of workbooks and ditto sheets as the core of the program. As I emphasize throughout this book, early education can be a public relations nightmare because learning develops through physical, social, and aesthetic means. In order to communicate the seriousness of our purpose, we as teachers must plan to present our program so that other educators and parents can understand that we are engaged in mathematics education through a variety of forms.

To this end, it is useful to establish a mathematics area that includes many of the seven components we will discuss in the following section.

THE MATHEMATICS AREA

Physical Setup

There should be a physical space set aside and labeled as a mathematics area. It should contain

Concrete materials (see list that follows)
Mats upon which to use each set of concrete materials, in order to define
work space for many small pieces in a set

Storage space

Writing materials

Standard measures such as a cup, ruler, meter stick, and tape measure

Two tables and six to eight chairs

Floor space as an alternative area for manipulation of materials

Concrete materials often include the following:

Beads and laces

Pegs and peg boards (rubber bands and sometimes geoboards)

Parquetry blocks

Balance scale with accessories such as labeled boxes of buttons, pine cones, wooden cubes, washers, and so on

Sand/water table and accessories:
   — Containers (ideally, the containers are transparent and include different shapes that hold the same volume)
   — Measuring cups and spoons of varying sizes
   — Funnels, tubes of varying length and diameter, squirting bottles, occasionally a rotary beater
   — Sponges and cloths

Unifix blocks

Sequential pattern cards such as the ones from Developmental Learning Materials (suggestion: to keep the cards in sequence, punch holes in them and secure them in a ring binder)

Stern arithmetic blocks

Commercial and teacher-made games such as board games and card games

Less usual concrete materials that are worth having, even if you build your stock by adding a few each year, would include

Attribute Blocks and People Pieces (Elementary Science Study), or their generic equivalents

Cuisenaire rods

Nonstandard measures such as drinking straws, yarn, and strings of differing thickness and texture

Centimeter graph paper

Dienes's Multibase Arithmetic Blocks, beginning with base two

Tool tote trays for holding together related materials so that they can be moved easily to a place where children will use them, whether to a table, a mat on the floor, or outdoors

Aids in Teaching Mathematics

MATHEMATICS NOTEBOOKS.   Each child should have a personal mathematics notebook, labeled as such, with the child's name. These notebooks are stored in the mathematics area, next to writing materials. The notebook can begin as a set of blank, unlined pages with an oaktag or construction-paper cover.

Content might include drawings, photographs, and attached lengths of yarn, straws, or paper with labels. Many kindergarten children can copy a single word or a single line of text early in the school year, and most of them can do this before the year ends. A folder of word cards containing words that are related to a particular topic may be stored in the area. Examples include plant and measurement words, family-size words, and so forth. Do keep in mind that mathematics is an applied tool.

MATHEMATICS HOMEWORK.   Each child should be encouraged to bring home a zip-lock plastic bag, labeled "Math Homework," each week. The purpose of this bag, in addition to providing children with a worthwhile activity, is to involve parents. Develop ideas cooperatively with other kindergarten teachers and use them optionally. You might send home different homework with different children. Send parents photocopied homework instructions. Some homework samples are:

> Dear Parent,
> We have used the piece of yarn in this bag to measure some objects in school. Please help your child find things at home that are the same length as the yarn. Please send two objects from home to school that are the same length as the yarn.

The same technique can be used in studies of family size over generations, and the result is often a truly engrossing kindergarten social science research project. Again, send letters home to the parents to enlist their cooperation, such as the following:

> Dear Parents,
> We are making a survey of families at school. Please have your child make a mark for each brother and sister that you have.
>   Mother's brothers and sisters: _____
>   Father's brothers and sisters: _____

> Dear Parents,
> We are comparing generations of families at school. Please have your child make a mark for each brother and sister of his/her grandparents.

Maternal grandmother's brothers and sisters: _____
Maternal grandfather's brothers and sisters: _____
Paternal grandmother's brothers and sisters: _____
Paternal grandfather's brothers and sisters: _____

Begin with the data from the children's immediate families, graphing the results of the survey and then describing the findings. Then you can graph and describe the results of the parents' families and then the grandparents' families. Did the sizes of families in different generations in your class change or remain about the same? Children might also create an individual family comparison as well as a group study of generations. What patterns exist in different families?

In these kinds of surveys, you are applying mathematics to social science research. You are also integrating writing skills by describing your findings.

Do be sensitive to the possibility that you may have a parent who is unable to read or is otherwise uncomfortable with messages from school. Be sure to talk about the homework task with the child or children beforehand and read the precise message to them at school before they take home their homework bag.

BULLETIN BOARDS AND DISPLAYS.   The findings of your class's studies and homework surveys can be represented in graphic forms and displayed on classroom and hallway bulletin boards or display cases, as well as in children's mathematics notebooks. For example, you might label a hallway display, "Kindergarten Math Study in February," and present a concrete format in which one or more groups of children have engaged.

TEACHER'S TASK CARD FILE.   Keep a personal card file of cooperative mathematics activity ideas. When you have one idea on each card, it is easy to add new ideas and to sequence activities.

CAMERA.   Photograph children when they are engaged in cooperative mathematics with concrete materials or as they record findings in their notebooks. Share these prints and slides with parents at meetings or on bulletin boards and hallway displays.

While funding is sometimes difficult, most school districts have a system where teachers can request small grants for special projects. Parents' associations are another source for funds. You may even find that your building principal has some discretionary funds that you can use for buying and developing film. Try asking around. You can also ask the school district's public relations representative to come into your classroom to take photographs when you have accumulated several surveys and children can demonstrate some of their activities.

REPORT TO PARENTS.   Let parents know what you are doing in mathematics education at meetings, parent conferences, and with occasional notes. Consider setting yourself a daily goal of some convenient number of children to whose parents you can send a brief note that tells them something that their child did in school with mathematics study. Move systematically through your class list so that you have regular contact with each family and let parents know that you are aware and care about their child. Notes to parents need not be any more complicated than this example.

Dear Morris Family,
Ray weighed and measured the hamster today and wrote it up in the Math Book. It was exciting to see Ray's enthusiasm.

Sincerely,
Lee Allen

COOPERATIVE MATHEMATICS

Kindergarten children learn mathematics best when they engage in concrete activities with other children. Working together, they use mathematics as a tool to solve the natural problems that arise in their encounters with the physical and social world. There are two important, interrelated assumptions for teaching contained in this approach that influence kindergarten mathematics activities.

The first assumption is that kindergarten children should have legitimate opportunities for social interaction in connection with their active learning of mathematics. They learn about quantity as they compare and contrast physical relationships and many of their activities with other children revolve around these experiences. As they encounter each other's varied viewpoints, they extend their own view and decenter from it.

The second assumption is that kindergarten children should have opportunities to participate in activities that create cognitive dissonance. Indeed, children's social interactions create more opportunities for cognitive dissonance as children predict, observe, and compare their views with those of others. Kindergarten teachers can provide conditions in which cooperative mathematics can flourish when they plan activities for children to pursue independently in dyads and when they work with children in small-group activities that use contrasting concrete materials.

Sex Differences in Mathematics Achievement

Inasmuch as boys and girls come to school with different patterns of socializing and game preferences, it is no surprise that researchers are finding that boys seem to achieve better than girls in mathematics after the elementary school years (Maccoby & Jacklin, 1974; Serbin, 1978). There is a general acceptance that boys' visual and spatial skills are largely responsible for this difference, whereas girls generally appear to perform better at verbal tasks. This appears consistent with the fact that as many as 90 percent of the children in school remedial reading programs are boys. While most schools offer such programs, in striking contrast, few schools offer remedial mathematics programs.

Contrary to popular belief, researchers also find that boys seem to be at least as social as girls, but in a somewhat different way (Maccoby & Jacklin, 1974). While boys will often congregate in larger peer groups, beginning as early as nursery school, girls tend to retain one or two social contacts at a time and are found in smaller social groups.

These are general research trends that summarize an immense number of studies and are subject to some exceptions. It is useful, however, to plan instruction that will counterbalance these factors and help prevent handicaps later in school. It makes sense to plan for all children to have visual-spatial experiences and for those who need it to have extra help. It makes sense also to plan for all children to have experiences in large-muscle group games that require collaborative planning and afford opportunities to practice alternative strategies.

Organization and Grouping for Instruction

If you want to create the best possible learning situation for all of your children, then you will offer mathematics instruction to small groups and individual children, based upon their needs, just as you do in reading or science instruction. The full-day schedule provides time to organize in this way while leaving time for other worthwhile experiences. Kindergarten teachers can offer children the varied physical experiences that they need as a foundation for more abstract learning in mathematics, science, or social science.

FOUNDATIONS IN MOTOR ACTIVITY

Mathematics concepts depend upon visual-spatial relationships that children experience in the physical world. Children develop visual-spatial skills when they have many and varied motor experiences, including music and movement, large-muscle games, and building activities in which they explore all three dimensions. The teacher's task is to try to provide these activities for all of the children in various ways and at different times, and to help those who may need extra encouragement.

When teachers notice some children who need more exposure to these kinds of activities, they can find ways to extend the time that children will spend in an area. They can encourage participation by (1) inviting the child or children to work with the teacher in a particular motor activity at a specific time and (2) physically moving near the child or children who are in an area that is helpful for improving visual-spatial skills.

The floor-block building area, part of the sociodramatic area, is one place where girls and other underrepresented children need teacher encouragement if they are to gain some of the large-muscle, three-dimensional skills usually associated with mathematics. It is also worthwhile to have large hollow wooden building blocks outdoors, either stored in a shed or rolled out each day. The playground and gymnasium are other places where more reticent children can be encouraged to participate.

Games can help children to build visual-spatial skills, including games with balls and hoops, climbing and jumping games, and collaborating with others in group games, free from the pressure of hard competition. Various group games, skills games with marbles, and tag games have been used successfully (Cratty, n.d.; Kamii & DeVries, 1980).

Particularly in a full-day kindergarten, it is important to schedule more than one opportunity for such large-muscle activity each day. In some settings, large climbing and balancing equipment, gymnastics mats, a parachute, tricycles, and hollow blocks have been collected in a large indoor playground-gymnasium in order to assure such activity, even in inclement weather.

Motor experiences take place as children use concrete materials for mathematics education. Five-year-olds readily play with place values and the concept of base when they have concrete referents. For example, the Dienes multibase arithmetic blocks (Educational Teaching Aids, 1985) and a homemade die or dice can easily become a place-value game using bases between two and ten. It is much easier for young children to work with base-two blocks than with base-ten blocks, simply because base two has fewer variables.

The original Dienes blocks are calibrated pieces of natural wood in which the cubic-centimeter unit block has the value of x^0; the long block, x^1; the flat block, x^2; and the "block" block, x^3. In base two, the wooden blocks have the relationship shown in Figure 7.1.

In base three, the long block is equal to three units, or three cubic centimeters, and the long block in base ten is equal to ten units. If a player collects ten units in throwing the dice, then she can trade them for a long block in base ten. However, if using base three, these ten units are worth one flat block and one unit block (see arrows in Figure 7.2).

It is a delight to see five-year-olds' enthusiastic absorption as they trade two units for a long when they play in base two, or three units for a long

Figure 7.1: Dienes Multibase Arithmetic Blocks: Base 2

Block	Flat	Long	Unit
2^3	2^2	2^1	2^0

when they play in base three, and four longs for a flat when they play in base four, and five flats for a block when they play in base five. In base ten, ten units (ones column) can be traded for a long, ten longs (tens column) can be traded for a flat, and ten flats (hundreds column) can be traded for a block (thousands column).

Initially, children (and many adults) need to physically remove from the storage box the exact units that they have drawn, match them with their existing collection, and then trade up to the next larger size of wood in the base. After a while, the children learn to anticipate a trade "in their heads" and trade up by exchanging part of their existing collection, eliminating the intermediary motion. When you see this anticipation taking place consistently for a few children, you can try providing centimeter graph paper on which they can record their final set of wood, marking the equivalent cubic-centimeter squares. Adults who despaired of ever comprehending bases, or who thought they understood but in fact had only relied on memorized formulas, have found authentic understanding of the concept after playing with Dienes blocks.

On another level, children understand multibases when you provide a model that they can complete:

> TEACHER: If this is a grain of sand (unit) and this is a pebble (long), then this is a rock (flat) and next would be a . . .
> CHILD: Mountain!

Figure 7.2: Dienes Multibase Arithmetic Blocks: Base 3

Block	Flat	Long	Unit
3^3	3^2	3^1	3^0

Beginning to use the blocks must come only after many prior activities with one-to-one correspondence and concrete experiences with concepts including larger than, smaller than, any, some, either-or, biggest-smallest, pairs, groups of two, sets of two, and simple seriations. After a few weeks, when many small groups have played in base two and some children seem ready to move ahead, it makes sense to bring out base three for them. Do be particularly sensitive to the more timid children who may not select this activity during the interdisciplinary activity periods. Invite them, set a time with them, and be with them when they need encouragement.

FOUNDATIONS IN RULES

Mathematician and philosopher Alfred North Whitehead (1960) contends that mathematics consists of establishing rules and understanding their relationships. The "gambling-counting-trading" game with Dienes multibase arithmetic blocks and simple ball games help children build toward a sense of codifying rules. Elementary Science Study's Attribute Blocks, Color Cubes, and colored loops are useful also as children build a notion of rules. Kindergarten children can establish their own rules and try to guess the rules that their friends create with the Color Cubes and the colored loops. Figure 7.3 describes a sequence of activities for building rules.

These activities involve classification in a cheerfully charged, suspenseful atmosphere of, "What's going to happen next?" The teacher models, the children predict, the children replicate, and then the children construct their own rules so that other children and the teacher can try to guess them. In this activity, children are dealing with class inclusion, intersection of sets, and class exclusion in very concrete ways. Each session involves five to ten minutes of direct instruction and some flexible follow-up time when children can play independently, on their own and with one another.

In setting rules for others, including the teacher as well as other children, the children experience a healthy sense of power. They are also on the way to dealing with placing the same number of cubes in each "playground," beginning with a one-to-one correspondence, then by counting, and then by adding and subtracting. Clearly, different children will demonstrate by their use of the materials when they are ready for next steps. The loops and cubes also lend themselves to "community planning" kinds of activities, as they represent zones and functions.

Holt and Dienes (1973) suggest a rule-building game called "Sand-Castles," a maze game that you can play in snow or sand. The object of the game is for children to take an efficient route, avoiding "tolls" at the vertices. This is similar to the African children's game of "networks," in which

Figure 7.3:   A Concrete Activity Sequence for Building
Rules

-Shake a covered box of Color Cubes and ask children what
 they think might be inside. Take out one cube and ask,
 What do you see?" "Guess what else might be inside."
 After a few extractions, children begin to build a
 cognitive map of the possibilities. At a separate time,
 it is useful to follow the same procedure with the
 Attribute Blocks themselves and the People Pieces, which
 also vary in size and shape as well as color.
-Lay out a red loop and a blue loop so that they do not
 touch. "Let's pretend that this is a red playground and
 that this is a blue playground. I have a rule that I
 can put red cubes in the red playground and blue cubes
 in the blue playground. Here is a green loop. What
 cubes can you put in the green loop? In the yellow loop?"
-Lay out the red loop and the blue loop so that they
 overlap each other in part. "I can put red cubes in
 the red part and blue cubes in the blue part. Now,
 there is this part (overlapping) which is both blue and
 red. Let's put cubes in it. Which ones can be there?"
 "Now use the green and yellow playground loops."
-Lay out the red loop and the blue loop. "Guess what
 rules I am using." (Place blue cubes in the red
 playground loop and red cubes in the blue playground
 loop.) "Here is a green playground loop and a yellow
 playground loop. Place the green and yellow cubes,
 using the same rule that I just used." Then, "Make up
 your own rule and let us try to guess what it is."
-After building these activities over several sessions,
 you might place cubes outside, but adjacent to,
 the same-color loops.
-A "People Sorting" game uses a similar procedure
 (Downie, Slesnick, & Stenmark, 1981, p. 28). Children
 themselves enter, or leave, a large loop of yarn laid
 out on the floor. They base their movement upon some
 attribute such as wearing something green or not
 wearing glasses. They guess each other's rules.

---

children attempt to duplicate a pattern in sand without lifting one's finger
or repeating a path (Zaslavsky, 1973). Here again, children create their own
rules and rules for each other, using a simple sequence. Any activities with
simple mazes help to develop these skills. The perceptual model of indirect
progress is represented in these activities, which sharpen children's visual-
spatial skills in challenging ways.

Playing with color matrices is a helpful parallel activity. Children might
begin by looking at a pattern of cubes, having someone remove a cube, and
then guessing which cube is missing. Reversing two cubes in a matrix,

children can attempt to locate the change for each other. In addition to playing with rules, children are also developing scanning skills.

Other patterning activities include pattern duplication with parquetry blocks. Children can use mirrors to vary and extend this activity for each other. In this way, they also build rotational and reversal skills. In this context, children can use decorative stencils, turning them in different directions; make their own potato prints, rotating them; and employ other created patterns. These activities contribute to the children's sense of space. They need plenty of time for exploration and self-directed repetition.

Since mathematics is a rule-bound occupation, as are group games, children need to have opportunities to explore and test rules in many games that they play. You will need to see that girls as well as boys participate in many rule-bound games in groups on a regular basis. A study by Piaget (1965) indicates that children develop an understanding of rules as they live through repeated social interaction and feedback from their peers. Often cognitive dissonance is involved when children experience such feedback.

Five-year-olds imitate rules in games, but they apply these rules incompletely, although with confidence. Therefore, children need repeated opportunities to test the rules, to see how they work, to make and play with rules, and to see how their actions affect other people.

The parallel between the rules of children's games and the rules of mathematics is too important to set aside. This is particularly true with respect to boys, who traditionally have greater involvement with group sports, building with large floor blocks, and woodworking, activities that tend to improve their visual-spatial development. Moreover, one researcher has hypothesized that "boys, more than girls, are encouraged to engage in problem-solving activities" (Fennema, 1981, p. 98). Kindergarten teachers need to be aware of these factors and plan for girls as well as boys to build with large blocks, engage in group sports, and continue their woodworking and other problem-solving activities. Teachers can use regular planning sessions and the times that they circulate around the classroom as opportunities to reinforce the participation of all the children in cooperative mathematics; block building; finding, setting, and solving problems; and other relevant activities.

FOUNDATIONS IN RELATIONSHIPS

One might infer that mathematics is to discursive, logical forms what music is to nondiscursive, imaginative forms. As an expressive form, each discipline uses unique abstract symbols and deals with relationships.

In mathematics, you are helping children to understand relationships in space, shape, and size and to develop the ability to represent these relationships through symbols. However, learning mathematics is more than acquiring a rapid command over "number facts" and basic arithmetic computation. Machines are able to do that better than people.

Children will need help in understanding how and when to use the tool that mathematics is, as well as to apply computation skills where they are relevant. It would be unfortunate to get bogged down in either-or controversies: Children need to learn meanings as well as skills, just as they need to learn content as well as process skills in science study. Skills function to serve meaning and not as ends in themselves.

First, kindergarten children need a variety of relevant experiences that they can explore in active ways (Hawkins, 1965; Nuffield, 1967). Second, they need adult help in order to

Clarify relationships
Find, set, and solve problems
Compare and contrast observations and findings
Learn specific skills
Record their findings
Interpret and use symbols

Concrete objects, task cards, and books, whether employed separately or in combination, do not insure that children will learn. You will need to juxtapose elements at the proper times, with adequate preparation and appropriate follow-up activities, in order to help children have an enriched sense of the world.

The Nuffield Mathematics Program, developed with children, offers a framework that is useful with young children and is integrated into the discussion that follows. Other approaches, in addition to the Dienes multibase arithmetic blocks and the Attribute Blocks, will include activities that use Cuisenaire rods, the VeriTech material, the ongoing Equals project, and Cruikshank, Fitzgerald and Jensen's (1980) analysis of an early childhood measurement sequence.

Children learn about relationships among space, shape, and size by active participation. Relationships are relative; therefore, children need contrasting experiences, some of which will be detailed in the following sections.

Space

Kindergarten children explore space in a variety of ways. Visual and plastic arts, block-building, and construction activities provide them with data. When they try to fit into boxes, tunnels, toys, last-year's coat, father's shoes, or an area near the teacher, they learn about space.

Topology is a good way to study spatial properties. For example, the sizes of markings made on a deflated balloon will change when the balloon is inflated, but the topological relations — the relative ordinal positions among any set of points on the markings — remain the same. Children learn this kind of spatial order through repeated transforming actions, just as they learn to recognize a particular person intuitively on the basis of a profile view (Copeland, 1984; Piaget & Inhelder, 1963; Sauvy & Sauvy, 1974). Both the social and the physical components of this development have their roots in the baby's development of object permanence.

Some of the activities that help children build this intuitive sense of spatial order include work with clay, yarn, rubber bands, and other malleable materials. The operations children perform with these materials — molding, tying, sewing, weaving, stretching, compressing, and so forth — foster the acquisition of early geometric concepts upon which projective and Euclidian geometry can develop.

The concepts of enclosure and boundary are also introduced through some of these activities, as well as through building with blocks, puzzling over mazes, and engaging in various mapping activities, such as those that involve Color Cubes and colored loops. Experiences that call upon the child to differentiate by categories like part of/not a part of, inside/outside/on, and before/after/in between provide excellent opportunities for inductive learning of these ideas.

Proximity and continuity concepts can develop through countless daily activities that involve tying knots, stringing beads, and various science activities with evaporation and condensation. Such learning grows whenever an experience calls for being close to or far away, in front of or behind, above or below, and to the left or right.

While children's sense of topology will develop intuitively, their sense of relative length and number of surfaces or angles will develop later. For example, the notion of continuity required to see a line in geometry as an infinite set of points is beyond the kindergarten child's sensorial or perceptual experience. You help children to extend and deepen their topological experiences when you provide concrete materials that children can transform and plan activities in which they can feel and see contrasts in texture and appearance. Children need a chance to talk about what they are seeing and feeling as they are using materials.

Examples of topological activities are given in Figure 7.4. These activities focus on contrasts and changes. For example, pouring is a most concrete example of change. It is especially important to provide children with containers of varied shapes and sizes as well as a series of containers of standard size gradations, which will help children learn about volume. Children acquire the concept of conservation of quantities only after many experiences in which they have observed and have themselves created transformations of shape, size, and space that are reversible.

Figure 7.4:   Topological Activities

-Tie, twist, or weave yarn or raffia that has two
  adjacent colors or two adjacent textures. These
  activities help to sharpen the sense of proximity.
-Build patterns cooperatively with a friend using beads,
  blocks, stickers, or geoboards, first back to back and
  then comparing patterns, a potential cognitive
  dissonance experience.
-Touch an unseen object and match it with corresponding
  pictures to sharpen images of boundaries.
-Use varied art media.
-Engage in large-muscle creative movement activities
  with props such as hoops, ropes, discs, and cloth, to
  help develop a feeling for boundaries, enclosures, and
  proximity.
-Rotate shapes and objects and play with symmetrical
  signs to stimulate relative thinking (Waters, 1973).
-Play "hide-and-seek" in relative-location games with
  dioramas. For example, Karplus and Thier (1967) use a
  toy figure, "Mr.O," who describes to anyone trying to
  find him whatever he sees from wherever he is located,
  whether or not he may be moving or seated on a moving
  vehicle. Kindergarten children and their teacher can
  play with the observer notion, placing objects in front
  of "Mr.O," and setting him on both stationary and moving
  vehicles. Young children can deal with an imaginary
  observer on much the same level as an imaginary friend
  who can be blamed for misdeeds. The outside observer
  points up for children that, depending upon your viewpoint, there may be more than one way to describe a
  situation. The cognitive dissonance in this tension
  between viewpoints is an important turning point in
  learning. Lavatelli (1970) also suggests activities that
  develop relative spatial concepts. She uses table
  settings and house, garage, and tree dioramas, often in
  connection with pictures.
-Pour water, sand, or beans through funnels, sieves, and
  tubes, into containers.

Shape

Children can explore shapes in a variety of ways. When children match
and compare similar and different shapes, and series of shapes whose sizes
vary, they build discrimination skills. When they fit shapes into corresponding openings, they have shown readiness to solve two-dimensional and, later,
three-dimensional puzzles. They move from elaborating pegboards with rubber bands to geoboard activities.

Geoboards that are circular or triangular as well as square can be used by kindergarten children. Wherever possible, it is useful for two or more children to work together when they are independent of the teacher. Sharing sequenced teacher-made picture task cards, they can work on parallel, equivalent geoboards and later on boards that have different proportions, an experience in concrete topology. Then the children can compare their parallel work, another occasion where they are likely to encounter cognitive dissonance.

Children can explore how many different three-, four-, five-, or six-sided figures they can create on the geoboard. They can replicate street signs, such as the octagonal stop sign. When used to compare shapes and sizes, geoboards lend themselves to the study of perimeter and area concepts, beginning with nonstandard measures.

Tangrams are puzzles composed of seven shapes that children can assemble in numerous ways. They require children to move outside of preconceived frames of reference and proceed through indirect progress, using trial-and-error manipulation. These puzzles are difficult to do when children begin with the seven pieces and try to replicate the preprinted patterns. The Elementary Science Study has developed a sequential approach to learning tangrams that begins with two shapes rather than seven. Using a series of cards, the puzzle proceeds with controlled variables until children reach seven shapes.

In addition to controlling variables, there are a number of steps that help children to develop the indirect-progress skills that make it possible to work with all seven shapes. The following steps, adapted from the Tangrams cards, can also be used with such materials as the Developmental Learning Materials' cubes and cards and parquetry blocks:

1. There is a one-to-one correspondence between the printed pattern outline, which has been demarcated, and the pieces. Pieces are placed *on* the outline.
2. There is a one-to-one correspondence between the printed pattern, which has not been demarcated, and the pieces. Pieces are placed *within* the outline.
3. There is a one-to-one correspondence between the outline and the pieces, and children assemble the pieces *next to* the outline.
4. Children replicate the pattern of shapes that are the same configuration but different in size.

When the variables have been controlled and increased gradually in these ways, most kindergarten children can move into the third step. Some children may be able and interested enough to pursue the less concrete fourth step.

Particularly for children with perceptual difficulties, it is very important to control variables and analyze tasks so that they have an abundance of experience similar to the first two steps. Kindergarten children enjoy the Tangram cards immensely and move through them with increasing enthusiasm and often with incredible speed.

You can increase children's sense of independence by providing self-checking devices and a buddy system of children who have different skills. For example, the Mini VeriTech (1977a, 1977b) booklets contain printed patterns that children compare and categorize. They are sequenced and self-checking when children place patterned block pieces in a boxed frame and compare them with an overall pattern. Children who use these materials enjoy recording their own progress by marking a card each time they complete a page. The catalogs of materials companies such as Developmental Learning Materials (1985) and Educational Teaching Aids (1985) include various self-checking devices that help children to "appreciate" themselves. Additional suggestions appear in chapter 9.

The VeriTech materials appeal to the perceptual skills of kindergarten children. As with Tangrams, many children become obsessed with these materials, perhaps because they share the common trait of being sequenced very gradually. Unlike the Tangrams, however, the VeriTech booklets begin at a visual rather than a physical stage; moreover, because they are self-correcting, they have a kind of problem-solving potential. Children can review their work if it is not matched, and try alternatives to create a match. The single-correct-answer quality of the materials, however, could be seen as a limitation when compared with a deeper view of problem solving, which classically involves the possibility of coming up with alternative solutions. Because these materials are visual, you will need to help kindergarten children "bridge" this imagery to ideas that grow out of their physical and social activities.

The Attribute Blocks have been mentioned in previous sections. They are blocks of different shapes that also vary in color and size. When you plan to have children study shape, it is useful to control other variables by using the same color and the same size in order to focus on shape as the only variable. This method is useful whenever you want children to perceive an individual variable, whether in the study of mathematics, reading, or science. When trying to teach a new shape, the Montessori technique of using an a:b:b:a pattern is helpful, for example: "This is a rectangle (a) and this is a parallelogram (b). This is a parallelogram (b) and this is a rectangle (a). Please, you take a rectangle . . . and then a parallelogram (handing each in turn to the child). And take a parallelogram and then a rectangle. Please give me a rectangle . . . and now a parallelogram. First, please give me a parallelogram . . . and now a rectangle."

However, even before children have labels for shapes, they can sort them into the same or different categories. As they do so, you can use the names. Children will probably learn most labels easily in this incidental way if you control the number of variables at any single time.

Size

Relative size and absolute size form still another relationship for study. Kindergarten children become involved with such phenomena as the size of a group of children or a portion of strawberries, the length of a truck, the height of a building, and how much is enough money for ice cream. They are concerned with being bigger than or smaller than; having more than and receiving less than or fewer than; and having the least or the most. These concerns reflect their daily activities in school and at home and pave the way toward understanding numbers and counting.

They can use nonstandard measures to find out more about themselves, their height and weight, the length of their feet, and the length of their strides. They can use strings, blocks, crayons, or a favorite doll as nonstandard measures. They also can compare size and density with balance scales, do float-or-sink activities, and use a meter stick to mark the arc of a pendulum.

Your role as teacher is to integrate each new variable gradually and to help children with the needed language as they engage in activities. Gross observations and approximations become refined through predictions, repeated observations, trying out new actions, and revising views. When children have opportunities to work in this way, their cognitive development progresses via the healthy tension of cognitive dissonance.

Using a balance scale is one such activity. A teacher and four- and five-year-old children can sort heavy and light objects by touch (Biggs, 1971), observing the balance scale's movements for feedback. The teacher can ask them to guess, for example, the difference between a small metal object and a large piece of styrofoam. When they look at the styrofoam, they may well predict that it will be heavier; but when they test it on the scale they will find that the smaller metal object is heavier. They can verify their observations by repeated testing. When contrasts take place between appearance and performance, children notice and are stimulated to raise questions. These same kinds of contrasts may be evident in their science study, for example, when they use magnets or compare flotation in fresh and salt water.

As children classify materials and have many experiences with one-to-one correspondence, their seriation skills can grow. Here are some useful activities for children to do:

> Match keys to padlocks. As the number of items increases, the teacher
> can encourage children to seriate, beginning at first with large and

small locks, then with three locks, and adding materials as children seem ready for more.

Decide how much water, sand, or grain to pour into transparent cups and then seriate each in turn. (This is different from asking a child to fill the next cup with a bit less or more. It is best to give a child the independence to decide how much to pour, in order to experience a degree of control. Seriation can be done by comparison.)

Further Development of Relationship Concepts

Understanding the concepts of space, shape, and size is an important foundation on which real comprehension of mathematics can be built, not an end in itself. The activities that follow will help children to progress along this path by giving them further experience with these concepts and encouraging them to represent and manipulate relationships through symbols.

SURVEYS

Surveys grow naturally from classifying and seriating activities and are good ways for investigating size, as well as other factors. The survey is a useful activity because children can be active, work cooperatively, set problems, suggest ways to represent findings, and use both nonstandard and standard measures, as they are able. Different children can learn similar concepts and receive practice through variant forms, whether the content is classified as science or social science. Surveys are an essential form in which mathematics is applied to the content areas. Various survey ideas that have been successfully used with kindergarten children appear in Figure 7.5.

While kindergarten children enjoy participating in and collecting data for surveys, not everybody will need to participate in every survey. Having the entire group sit while each child places a marker next to his or her birthday month or favorite snack can take a very long time, during which most of the children could be doing more productive things than watching the seemingly eternal repetition. Many teachers have found that working with a group of about eight children provides enough repetition to represent the communal process, while it avoids too much waiting, which creates demands on the teacher for managing children's inattentive or disruptive behaviors.

After your children have made a variety of surveys, pairs of children might be ready to cooperate in collecting data independently, after you plan together the purposes of the survey with the partners and discuss their suggestions. For example, if the survey involves asking individual classmates in which area of the classroom they prefer to work, the children would need some guidelines about when they should approach another child or when it would be intrusive. They will need to have agreed upon the answers for the following questions before they begin:

Figure 7.5: Survey Activities

-Birthdays each month among children in the group.
-Bedtimes.
-Family size. (This activity has been discussed in
  greater detail in an earlier section.)
-When I grow up I would like to be...(career choices).
-Favorite or preferred...
    Food in general, or cookie, or ice cream flavor, or
      snack in school
    Television program
    Storybook this week
    Writing implement (pencil, marker, pen, crayon, etc.)
    Vehicle to drive (truck, automobile, spaceship,
      motorcycle, etc.)
    Activity area in school
    Age (older, younger)
    Color (in general, or sneaker or shoe color, etc.).
-Number of pieces of mail received at home on Monday.
  (This is a useful homework activity.)
-How many cards can you hold in each hand?
-How high can you leap to place paint from your hand
  onto a chart?
-How many cars of each of several colors are in the
  parking lot? Which color is the least present?
  Which color is the most popular?
-How many cars, trucks, motorcycles, and so forth,
  pass the school during several five-minute time
  samplings? Use pegs or a tally to keep track. (This is
  ideal for a collaborative small-group independent
  activity.)
-Number of teeth lost by children this month, or to date.
-Number of children wearing long or short sleeves today.
-Ways that mother or father travels to work (automobile,
  train, bus, motorcycle, bicycle, walk, etc.).
-Ways that children in class travel to school (walk, bus,
  automobile, etc.).
-Parents who smoke or do not smoke; adults in the school
  who smoke or do not smoke.
-Changes over time, for example, pet length and girth,
  baby visitor, plant growth, container markings where
  water has evaporated each day, shadow lengths at
  different times during the day outdoors. (See chapter
  6 for additional ideas.)

- How will we keep a tally (marks, moving pegs)?
- Who will do what? In what order?
- Will the same person do each task throughout the activity? If we take
  turns, how do we switch roles?
- When will we have enough samples?
- When will we be finished?

When developing a survey with a group of children, it is useful to ask them to estimate what they are likely to find. Realistic estimations will be phrased in terms of more than, less than, the most, the fewest, and so forth, rather than actual numbers. After recording their predictions, the children enjoy the anticipation that builds until they can compare their original projections.

In addition to recording predictions, you will need to select an appropriate way to represent the findings in graphic form. There are several ways in which you might represent your activity. For example, you might use a horizontal or vertical bar graph format in which each segment represents one response. If you use this technique, be sure that each segment — whether it is a card, sticker, tooth outline, marking, or photograph of a child — is the same size for each datum. This is important so that anybody who looks at the graph or chart can make comparisons easily. Figure 7.6 is an example. (See also Figure 6.5.)

The next step is to develop a language experience chart of some sort that describes and analyzes the survey. For example, charts summarizing surveys on family size and eye color might look like this:

Ali has two people in her family.   (2)
Bob has five people in his family.   (5)
Cal has seven people in his family.   (7)
Di has the same number as Bob.   (5)
Ev has the same number as Ali.   (2)
Fran has four people in his family.   (4)
Cal has the most people in his family.   (7)

Three people have green eyes.   (3)
Six people have blue eyes.   (6)
Fifteen people have brown eyes.   (15)
Most people have brown eyes.   (15)
The fewest people have green eyes.   (3)
Many people have blue eyes.   (6)

Figure 7.6: Graph of a Survey of Lost Teeth

Before you know it, the children are using, writing, and comparing numerals. While surveys are one form of activity in which numbers burst into life, in addition to Dienes multibase arithmetic blocks and Attribute Blocks, there are a number of other approaches that nourish this development.

MEASUREMENT

Various measurement activities, by using nonstandard and then standard measures, can become parts of larger surveys. In themselves, measuring activities, because they employ some tool, prove to be active and involving for kindergarten children. These activities are powerful levers for children's building of quantitative relationships.

Cruikshank, Fitzgerald, and Jensen (1980) suggest measurement activities in various categories, along with a useful sequence of difficulty. Such sequencing begins with direct measures and continues with indirect measures, first using nonstandard measures and then standard ones. Another sequence begins with the measurement of length and continues with area, volume, weight, time, and temperature, in turn. Ideally, these activities are tied to the content areas, such as social studies and sciences, as well as the reading and writing programs.

Since measurement defines the relationship between a phenomenon and the measuring tool, a direct, nonstandard measure is the most fundamental form, that is, $a = b$. Many examples have been mentioned already, and some others would be, "What is the same length as this book? This Cuisenaire rod? This crayon?" "What is longer than this book? Shorter than this rod?"

You would need an indirect measure, however, to test the relationship between a bookcase and a closet, since it is unwieldy to move the bookcase each time you might want to establish the nature of the relationship. Will the bookcase fit into the closet? Rather than remove all of the books and move the case, the children might be able to come up with a suggestion for using an indirect continuous measure such as a length of string; thus, $a = b : b = c : a = c$. The area of a surface might be measured in a similar way by cutting a paper outline of an object and comparing the outline with a second object.

Three elegant activities in which children use direct measures and can experience cognitive dissonance about the conservation of quantity appear in Figures 7.7 through 7.9.

CUISENAIRE RODS

Cuisenaire rods use visual, spatial, and tactile senses. They help young children to move from the concrete manipulation of materials to dealing with quantitative relationships and actions with numbers. This process takes place only after they have experienced many of the active uses of relative quantity in their daily pastimes.

**Figure 7.7: Cognitive Dissonance in the Direct Measure of
                       Volume: I**

Purposes: Encourage children to predict, observe, and
  compare. Create possibility for cognitive dissonance.
Materials: Transparent jars of different sizes and
  shapes, measuring cup, paper strip taped along the
  length of each jar, rice, and marker
Organization: A small group or 8-12 children work with
  the teacher.
Procedures: Pour one measured cup of rice into a jar,
  shake it down, and mark the height on the paper strip.
  Repeat for each jar.
   Ask children what they see when they compare the
  lengths on the markers in different jars. Why are some
  the same and others different? Accept answers and
  consider them seriously.
   Repeat estimates and measures a few times. (This is
  important because some children may not be able yet to
  conserve a quantity when it changes in appearance.
  Repetition gives children the chance to discover that
  the discrepancy does not exist because of incorrect
  measurement.)
   Children can record their findings in their math
  notebooks as drawings and direct measures of tape
  length.

Adapted from M. Baratta-Lorton, Mathematics Their Way
Menlo Park, CA: Addison-Wesley, 1976), p. 136.

It is useful to nail an edge of quarter-round molding onto one table in
the mathematics area, so that the Cuisenaire rods will not slide off too easily. It makes sense to use this area for small-group instruction. After five or
ten minutes of instruction, you can leave children with ten to twenty minutes
of follow-up activities that are both independent and cooperative.

At the outset, children need plenty of time to freely explore and build
usual and unusual structures with the rods, which should be set out in the
mathematics area for several weeks or longer. During that time, some children may sort them by color intuitively, and some may notice that the same-
color rods are the same length. When you have observed any pattern building, you might begin with one group of those children to play a grab-bag
game in which each person has a brown paper sack, as follows:

"Pick up a white rod, feel it, and place it in your bag. Now, pick up
    an orange rod, feel it, and place it in your bag."
"Shake them up. Now you will be able to see with your fingertips. Pick
    out the white rod. Put it back. Now pull out the orange rod. Put
    it back. That was easy for you."

Figure 7.8: Cognitive Dissonance in the Direct Measure of Volume: II

Purposes: Encourage children to predict, observe, and
  compare. Create possibility for cognitive dissonance.
Materials: Two eight-ounce transparent containers, one
  low and broad, one tall and skinny; brown paper sacks;
  beads or marbles of the same size
Organization: A small group or 8-12 children work with
  the teacher.
Procedures: Place a brown paper sack with a hole in the
  top over each of the containers. Ask a child to drop
  a bead from each hand into each of the holes in the
  paper sacks, at the same time.
     Ask the child, "Are you putting the same number of
  beads into each sack, one each time?"
     As the child continues, ask, "Are there the same
  number of beads in each jar?" (Children may deny that
  both containers have the same amount of beads when
  they can see the beads, but invariably give
  conservation responses when they cannot perceive the
  inequality of the level of the beads in the
  containers.)
     Repeat a few times, occasionally alternating using the
  paper sacks and leaving the containers uncovered.
  Eventually the discrepancy between the responses they
  give in the two situations becomes apparent to them,
  and they say excitedly, "It's got to be the same; I
  put the same in each jar! It doesn't matter how it
  looks."

Adapted from C. S. Lavatelli, Piaget's Theory Applied to an
Early Childhood Curriculum (Cambridge, MA: American
Science and Engineering, 1970), p. 112.

"Next, pick up a red rod, feel it, and place it in your bag. Shake it well.
    Now, pull out a white rod. Put it back. Now, pull out a red rod.
    Look at that! You can see with your fingertips."

The orange rod is the longest, equal in length to ten white rods. The
white rods are the shortest. The red rods are equal in length to two white
rods. When you use this sequence, first the white and then the orange rod,
you provide the greatest possible contrast and children build a tactile and
visual image of quantitative relationships.

Fingertip retrieval with these three lengths of rods may be enough for
one direct instructional episode. Keeping it brief and seeing that children
feel successful means that children will look forward to the next session in
which you begin the same way and then gradually add the yellow rod (half

the length of the orange), the green rod (equal in length to three white rods or a red and a white), and finally the purple rod (equal in length to two red rods).

At a separate time, after reinforcing the tactile relationships with the grab-bag game, you might ask children how they could tell somebody who was not in the grab-bag group their methods for tactile retrieval. You also might notice that they are sorting often by color, on their own. As relevant, the following questions are helpful:

- What can you build with these rods?
- What can you build with the purple rods? (Ask about other colors.)
- Which rods are the same length as one another?
- Which rods are longer than the green? Shorter? (Ask about other colors.)
- If the green rod were a train and you used red rods and white rods as cars in the train, what different patterns of cars could you make?
- If the purple rod were the length of your train, what different combinations of cars could you use to equal the length, to be the same length, as your purple train?
- What if the yellow rod were the length of your train? (Ask about other colors.)

Figure 7.9: Cognitive Dissonance in the Direct Measure of Weight

---

Purposes: Encourage children to predict, observe, and compare. Create possibility for cognitive dissonance.
Materials: Balance scale, clay
Organization: A small group or 8-12 children work with the teacher.
Procedures: Weigh two clay samples of equal weight and same shape. Confirm equivalence with children: "Are you sure that they weigh the same amount?" "Check again to be sure."
Ask children to change the shape of one clay sample. "Are they the same weight?" "Let's weigh them to be positive."
Children who believe that the change in appearance is a change in quantity are puzzled when they weigh the samples and prove to themselves that they are equal. With repetition and other experiences, they will come to understand that the quantity remains constant.

Adapted from C. Seefeldt, _Teaching Young Children_ (Englewood Cliffs, NJ: Prentice-Hall, 1980), p. 253.

Five-year-olds have comfortably spent as much as half an hour substituting two rods for one. They are ready to hear you describe this process: "When we put these together, we call it adding their lengths." As children compare and contrast lengths, it is clear that there are differences between individuals. Some children may need more time than others to handle the rods at each phase. Some may need weeks, while others may take months of exploring and making patterns with the rods.

The concrete materials may help, but they do not substitute for the children's personal construction of the relationships. The ultimate recognition and readiness are in the child and not in the materials.

At the very least, it makes sense to offer varied materials and activities. When you and the children have explored many possibilities with trains, you might have some centimeter graph paper and colored markers or crayons handy so that each child who wants to do so can pick her or his favorite train to record in the mathematics notebook.

At this point, the children are on the threshold of manipulating numerals, if they have not already done so spontaneously. The use of graph paper as a discontinuous form provides children with a contrast to the continuous form of the rods. You will find many suggestions for using graph paper with the rods, for playing with "trains," and for engaging in cooperative games in Davidson's *Idea Book for Cuisenaire Rods at the Primary Level* (1977).*
Your children may experience a touch of cognitive dissonance in the game, "Filling Spaces with Rods." In this activity, two or more children can fill an area, transform the rods in that area so that they lie end to end, and then compare their patterns at various stages with those patterns that other children have made.

Whenever children can predict, transform materials, and compare and contrast their results, they have an opportunity to make new connections. Materials provide an additional benefit because children can arrive at their conclusions through contrasts and the basic problem-solving technique of trial and error, in this case with some inevitable inductive discoveries. You will notice that children who have more opportunity for inductive learning also acquire a stronger sense of power. Their findings are not based on an authority figure decreeing a "correct answer," but on their own constructed understanding, which they can verify by returning to the materials.

After manipulations, train constructions, and other active pursuits, some children may be ready to consider addition. While they add, they can use the Cuisenaire rods as a self-checking device that confirms whether or not the mental construction is true. You may find a few kindergarten chil-

---

*Pages that are most useful for the kindergarten level, arranged here in the sequence I recommend, are 55, 61, 63, 69, 75, 83, 91, 87, 95, 115, 121, 123, and 147.

dren able to engage in this concrete activity rather late in the school year.

Initially, children will spend plenty of time playing out the combinations of plus-one and doubles of numbers (Kamii & DeClark, 1984). At each new phase, it is useful to begin instruction with the rods and then to have them available for self-checking. You will find that it is easy to individualize instruction within your mathematics instructional groups because you can pose different problems to different children. This can be helpful for individuals who are returning to school after an illness or for those who need more time or special help with a procedure.

COMMERCIAL AND TEACHER-DESIGNED GAMES

Games also are useful in building toward numbers and the operations of addition and subtraction. There are several "syntaxes" or varieties of games that kindergarten teachers have used successfully. Among these are board games with cards, spinners, dice, or markers. The very simple "Candyland" (Milton Bradley Co.) involves a board, markers, and color-coded cards with one or two color moves. In "Chutes and Ladders" (Milton Bradley Co.), each child takes a turn spinning a card numbered from one to six, and moves a marker along a grid of one hundred spaces toward the last space. "Parcheesi" (Selchow & Righter) is another type of board game that uses a die and markers.

Whether you use these types of formats or design your own versions, do consider that it helps to reinforce children's reading readiness if you begin at the top of the game board and move from left to right. In addition, you may want to have fewer than one hundred items, and eliminate reverse movement penalties.

Card games are still another format. An immediate concern is that if children have to hold four or more cards in a fan shape, there may be some coordination problems. Consider creating a simple card stand by sawing a lengthwise groove in six-inch lengths of one-by-one wood stock. (Teacher-designed games are discussed at greater length in chapter 9.)

Ordinary adult playing cards can be used by kindergarten children and can be adapted for different levels of use. Teachers usually begin with part of the deck. When children can identify the numerals, two children at a time can independently play a more-than or less-than game variation of "War." In this game of chance they match pairs of numbered playing cards to see which is greater. Kamii and DeClark (1984) describe a game of "Double War" where each first-grade child plays with the sum of two cards, using a deck limited to values up to four. With either numerals or suits, children can play "pairs" games in which they seek pairs that are alike after the cards have been placed facing down. While both of these games are designed for the person who achieves the pair to keep the pair, you might consider a "Feed the Hungry Hippopotamus" box in which pairs can be placed communally. This cuts down on competition.

"Go Fish," where children ask each other for a particular card by number in order to collect and discard pairs of cards, is another simple card game which children can play cooperatively with discontinuous teacher supervision, once they have had instruction. "Dominoes" requires that children match equivalent sets of dots on wooden or plastic pieces, although you can sometimes find domino cards. Games of bowling pins also call upon counting.

An African game, commercially available as "Kalah," stimulates children to plan ahead. You can make this game board easily out of a regular twelve-hole egg carton, with an attached "bowl" or box at either end made from two halves of the upper part of an egg carton. To begin the game, a specific number of beans is placed in each of the twelve pots. Two children take turns. Following specific rules of movement, each player works toward moving as many beans as possible out of her pots and into her own "bowl," where the beans may remain. The person with the most beans in her bowl at the end of the game wins. African children play this game using pebbles and holes in the ground (Zaslavsky, 1973, 1979).

"Kalah" is included among the offerings of the Math/Science Network, "an association of 800 scientists, educators, engineers, community leaders, and parents who work cooperatively to increase the number of women interested in and qualified for scientific and technical careers" (Downie, Slesnick, & Stenmark, 1981). A project of theirs called Equals focuses on encouraging underrepresented groups to study mathematics by offering stimulating, gamelike cooperative activities that involve problem-solving strategies. A few of their activities that are particularly adaptable for kindergarten children include the following:

"Balloon Ride." Ten ropes (toothpicks) hold down the balloon (a teacher-made game board) and two people take turns cutting either one or two balloons on each turn; whoever cuts the last rope gets a free ride.

"Guess." The teacher thinks of a number between one and ten and asks children to guess it. As they guess, the teacher's feedback is "too big" or "too small." Guesses are recorded on a chart. After each guess, children are asked to note which numbers have been eliminated. After the teacher has taken a turn at being the giver of feedback, the children can take turns giving feedback and the teacher can be a guesser.

"Geoblock Activities." Working in pairs, one child builds a structure that the other child cannot see. The builder tells the other how to build the same structure at the same time. Then they compare structures and switch roles.

"Double Design." Using graph paper, one child creates a design unseen by his partner. He then gives his partner verbal directions to reproduce the design. The results are compared and the roles switched. How close are they? What additional information would have been helpful?

The latter two activities stimulate cognitive dissonance. They are similar to the bead-patterning and Cuisenaire rod comparisons mentioned earlier. The Equals project employs important problem-solving principles. Many of the activities extend beyond the kindergarten, and even the ones that have been mentioned here are modified somewhat for use in the kindergarten.

BLOCKS, COMPUTERS, AND OTHER CONSTRUCTIONS

Kindergarten children can construct many important quantitative concepts and put various relationships in fresh perspective as they play with commercial and teacher-designed games that stimulate them to focus on controlled variables. These experiences, many of which we have just discussed, help children to move into counting with numbers and toward performing operations with numbers. We will discuss several more in this section.

The one material that serves best as a multidisciplinary concrete tool for learning is undoubtedly floor building blocks, typically found in most kindergartens and only rarely in primary classrooms. Floor blocks help children to experience a range of mathematical relationships that include classification, seriation, spatial relationships, and number concepts.

Through collaborative use of blocks, children face the need to appreciate another person's viewpoint. These collaborative experiences contribute to their capacity for decentering themselves and building their capacity for relative thinking. This generic material leads to other constructions, such as woodworking, that reflect the development of relationships.

The computer is another type of generic equipment that serves science and mathematics education at the same time that it has uses in the arts and language. Computers are beginning to be present in kindergarten classrooms, and it is likely that their use will increase. It therefore makes sense to consider how they are being used and what relevant decisions you may need to make in kindergarten work as you approach the end of this century.

Blocks

Wooden blocks for young children have been used in schools since Froebel introduced them in the nineteenth century. The most frequently used wooden floor blocks today have a 1 : 2 : 4 relationship with each other, as opposed to the original Froebel blocks that could become a twelve-step staircase. The Montessori blocks and the comparatively small Cuisenaire rods could become a ten-step staircase.

These internal relationships are worth mentioning because they all reflect the concern of their inventors for children to be able to construct relationships. As a kindergarten teacher, it makes sense for you to be aware of relationships represented in available materials. While children will build most of these relationships inductively as they use the materials, it is worthwhile for you to be open to the fleeting moment when you can raise an appropriate question that can stimulate problem solving:

- Why do you suppose that is happening?
- What else have you tried?
- Which one is just the right length? The same length? Shorter? Longer?
- If you could invent a block that would be perfect for that part, what would it look like? Are there any objects in our room that you could substitute?

Children need to use problem-solving skills when they build with blocks. This activity is an opportunity for children to identify their own real problems and then to work out possible solutions. Since the materials allow the children to set the parameters themselves, they can feel successful and autonomous. The process of using blocks evolves through a number of activities (Provenzo & Brett, 1983):

Beginning explorations
Attempts to build up and out
Creation of patterns
Exploration of balance and symmetry
Attempts at bridging
Learning about enclosures
Decorating and designing
Dramatic play with structures

Some research on children's block building suggests that developmental stages in block building parallel Piagetian stages of cognitive development (Reifel, 1984b).

Children learn varied solutions such as that placing larger blocks under smaller blocks improves balance, and that bridging requires adding onto a structure after excluding smaller and equivalent pieces. Because this medium is so versatile, children can use their imaginations and build creative structures. Encourage this imaginative tendency with occasional suggestions: "Close your eyes. Imagine what your structure will look like. When you open your eyes, try and change it to fit your imagination." The floor blocks particularly stimulate dramatic play because children can create enclosures into which they might fit or in which they can use accessories (see chapter 5).

The Patty Smith Hill blocks stimulate dramatic play because they can be held together with metal rods and bolts, enabling children to build tall and large enclosures that are sturdy. Large hollow blocks, which are readily available, serve a similar purpose. In contrast are the smaller types of building materials such as Lincoln Logs, Tinker Toys, Bristle Blocks, Lego, and Construct-o-Straws. While the large floor blocks engage children's large muscles, both the floor blocks and the smaller construction materials stimulate problem solving and skills in managing three-dimensional space.

Balance the exposure of the children in your class to various construction experiences. If a child has not used floor blocks for a week or so, it is reasonable to share that observation: "You haven't used the floor blocks for a long time. When do you plan to work there?" Also consider inviting a particular mix of compatible children to work there at the same time. It is important to be conscious of which children have been underrepresented in the block activity and to encourage them with your presence and appreciative comments when they are using the materials.

Woodworking

Woodworking is another activity in which you may need to encourage underrepresented children to participate. Working with wood and real adult-sized tools serves to develop many skills. Adult-sized tools are easier to use because the weight and size of the tools helps children to have more balance and control as they work.

In addition to learning how to use the carpentry tools and apply measurement skills to real problems, children learn to plan a few steps ahead. Some of these steps reflect the perceptual model of indirect progress, which children can apprehend as they try out different approaches. The simple tools connected with woodworking also represent indirect activity—the way in which simple machines function. For example, consider the following:

Hammer. Children learn to apply leverage when they extract a nail with a hammer.

Brace-and-Bit. The brace-and-bit drills holes with an indirect motion.

Screwdriver. Some of your children can apply the leverage used in screwdrivers also.

Saw. Children learn that they need to draw the saw across the wood, held in a vise, toward themselves about three times in order to establish a groove. Then they can learn to apply a downward motion to saw into the wood, which should be carefully selected soft pine lumber.

When children use tools, they have direct experiences with the principles of physics. As with other acquired skills, some children will need more direct help than others.

In the beginning, children are quite content to hammer nails into a single block of wood. Later on, when they use more pieces and varying sizes, they face the problem of finding just the right size nail to hold the pieces together. If you have precut wooden wheels, you create another reason for children to measure carefully in order to attach the wheels so that they will turn together. They need to measure lengths of wood that can help them execute their plans, however simple they may be. While kindergarten children usually build up or out with woodworking, a few of them create enclosures.

Offer children dignity and respect for their work. For example, you can provide sandpaper so that they can have a smooth product. Sandpaper is easier to use when it is tacked to a hand-sized block of wood or attached to a commercial sandpaper holder. Another way to show valuing of their products is to have a nail-set available to sink nails below the surface of the wood and help give a finished look. Sometimes children like to paint their work. You also might consider displaying finished pieces on a colored-paper or cloth background.

Woodworking is an activity that needs continuous teacher supervision; therefore, it should be scheduled when you are not committed to direct, continuous instruction elsewhere but can be nearby, aware, and available. The workbench should be placed out of the way of traffic, so children can concentrate more safely. The use of adult tools is prestigious and certainly a privilege that can be available only to those children who prove that they can use them safely. As with block building or any other construction work, some basic behavioral expectations are reasonable. Materials should be handled carefully, not thrown, and children need to respect the work of other children and treat it carefully to avoid damage.

Computers

Kindergarten children can learn to become comfortable around computers. It is particularly important for girls and other groups underrepresented in the world of science and technology to develop a comfort level. Computer familiarity, rather than literacy, is a realistic goal for kindergarten children.

In some kindergartens, "Big Trak" (Milton Bradley Co.) is available (Swett, 1984). This is a vehicle with a number board on top that children can program in order to move the vehicle in different directions in multiples of its length. Teachers and children can measure the toy and place tape marks on the floor at intervals equal to the toy's length, creating a kind of nonstandard, numberless number line. This is an example of a direct, continuous measure. They also can engage in estimating and comparing where the computer will stop the vehicle. Playing with Big Trak can be an enjoyable and worthwhile activity, but some teachers are disturbed by the military-type insignia and have painted over them in order to deemphasize this aspect. "Turtle Tot" (Harvard Associates) is a more expensive form of equipment that children can program in a similar way.

Some kindergarten teachers are using commercial games that have been created for the computer. Some of these are really electronic workbooks. Once the novelty of the machine passes, children are left with the need for a single correct answer. When you review software, it is preferable to look for material with which children can "interact," independently and with each other, as well as material for which they can set rules. A good example is the LOGO graphics package that uses a hand-held programming device called a "mouse" and requires that children estimate, explore, and compare their representations.

Since some ability to identify numerals and to differentiate at least a few keys on a keyboard is necessary for these activities, it is a good idea to have the children work in pairs. Most schools also have an aide available. At the very least, you will need to provide some intermittent adult presence. Indeed, one way to gauge whether or not an activity is too difficult for your children is to observe the degree to which they can work with some independence and increasing autonomy. Some researchers have suggested that the precision required for using computers is more than many kindergarten children need or want (Barnes & Hill, 1983).

Whatever you plan in the way of computer experiences for children, monitoring their attentive or off-task behavior will help you know when the activity is relevant or appropriate. For example, when you find that children need repeated reminders to return to the task, you might suspect that the activity is beyond their comprehension or too restrictive. The computer can serve your human purposes in the kindergarten only if you are a critical user and apply your own humane values as a guide to practice.

Even in the longer kindergarten day, there is more to do than there is time for all of it. You will therefore need to make choices with children in your setting. The most worthwhile activities encourage kindergarten children to be active and autonomous and give them the chance to modify their environments. When you use mathematics as an applied tool, you can feel secure in the knowledge that children can be active in their own learning. When you offer opportunities for the powerful learning process of cognitive dissonance to occur, and provide contrasts through materials and games, children "break out" into numerical and other relationships with comfort and energy.

8

Aesthetics, the Arts, and Playfulness

AESTHETICS IN THE ARTS AND LIFE

The capacity to have aesthetic experiences and to appreciate and create art forms is part of what defines us as human beings. When we talk about, criticize, and trace the history of art forms, we engage in an indirect activity, which is different from the aesthetic experience of art. An aesthetic experience of, or creation of, something is a direct rather than an indirect way of knowing.

Aesthetic experience is available to all people as part of the broad range of ordinary human experience, as well as in exposures to art forms. For Dewey (1934, p. 11), "Even a crude experience, if authentically an experience, is more fit to give a clue to the intrinsic nature of esthetic experience than is an object already set apart from any other mode of experience." Aesthetic experience exists within, but also beyond, the "artistic" disciplines such as music, the visual arts, dance, and literature, including drama. These as well as all art forms have the potential for helping us to have an aesthetic experience and to see the "familiar" in "strange" ways (Dewey, 1934; Gordon, 1961). The experience is not guaranteed in the form itself but in the readiness of a consuming human being. Let us consider an example that may help to distinguish the art form itself from the aesthetic experience that comes out of ordinary life.

Driving past a six-story loft building in a city, you might see two workers using a roof-mounted pulley in a hoisting operation. The coordinated rhythm of their bodies rising and their muscles hardening to draw down the rope is poetry in motion. It is reminiscent of the scene in which the tent was raised in Walt Disney's film *Dumbo*; thus the film's expressive form can evoke in you an experience that closely imitates reality. Through skillful drawing and musical accompaniment, the film evokes the same sense of strength, rhythm, and synchronic harmony in the tension of the hoisting movement. In both cases — seeing the real workers as well as watching the animated, musically accompanied Disney workers — you may have an aesthetic experience. Clearly, however, the workers themselves were not an art form in the sense that the film was formed art.

While you might arrive at an insightful perception of the real-life workers, the filmmakers might communicate the same insight through their formed work. Your perception of both the real event and the artistic product is concrete, a direct experience. The art of Disney lay in an ability to perceive, to have insight into the aesthetic experience of the real perception, and then to capture his own insight by transforming it into the film's animated form. By integrating music with visual forms, he was able to help us see the familiar in a strange way. He was able to draw attention to certain elements of line, rhythm, and tempo. He was able to enrich our perceptions.

There are no guarantees, however, that we can have an aesthetic experience unless the artist has successfully created a form that can help us share some of the artist's experience. Philosopher Martin Buber (1958) proposes that there is an aesthetic experiencing for both the artist while creating and the connoisseur while appreciating, a direct relationship between the two human beings in a particular moment, which he terms an "I-Thou" relationship. Another philosopher, Suzanne Langer (1953, 1957), suggests that there is an opportunity for enrichment and fresh "insight" in a work of art.

In this context, aesthetic experience, including the "formed" arts as well as ordinary life, is available in some way to all people, regardless of age or intellectual capacity. Art is neither elitist nor a "frill," but an intrinsic perspective that is possible in all human activity.

AESTHETICS AND EDUCATION

Human insights can be communicated and perceived in varied forms. Even though a work may use several media, a "primary" realm (Langer, 1957) will stand out. When we look at "dance theatre" or multimedia "concept art," it is clear that one is basically kinetic, dealing with motion, and the other is basically visual.

Langer (1957, p. 78) proposes four major types of art products: plastic (visual), musical, balletic, and poetic. People perceive one or another type of form as it stands out as a figure against the background of a larger activity. In this way a primarily temporal or kinesic or auditory-poetic-linguistic or visual variant can affect people. These nondiscursive (sensory, emotional, surreal, imaginative) processes can reflect a rich range of perceptual models (underlying ways of connecting experiences) that would be less fully knowable if only discursive (logical, linear) tools were employed.

In order to be exposed to the full range of experiences in school, children need to have opportunities to use the artist's nondiscursive tools as well as the discursive tools of scientists, mathematicians, and others. Teachers should integrate these nondiscursive tools across the range of children's experiences, in order to stimulate flexible thinking and the creation of new connections.

Many of the children's aesthetic experiences will come through their play with materials and each other. Kindergarten children can create insightful forms, even if those forms are somewhat episodic rather than closed. Beginning with random approaches, they create forms with varying degrees of purposefulness. Their coordination and skills will grow. Part of the teacher's role will be to stimulate succeeding levels of challenge and communicate an appreciation of small benchmarks. Some suggested activities have been mentioned in chapter 5, in the section on sociodramatic play, as well as throughout the book. Others involve

Sensitizing. Provide a verbal description and appreciation of what you perceive is a child's intentional combination of materials.

Modeling Fluency. Elaborate on symmetrical or unusual structures, replicating what children have done.

Modeling Originality. Create original work of your own, such as bulletin boards, decorative programs, or haiku poetry, in the children's presence.

Flexibility. Create new forms or explore aloud alternative ways of solving problems.

The additional time of the full-day kindergarten permits teachers to work in greater depth within the arts and to broaden all program areas as children integrate them with artistic activity. Most kindergarten teachers take major responsibility for the arts within their own classrooms. Occasionally, a kindergarten teacher who is particularly skillful in music education will share these skills with another teacher, providing a special music time that can supplement, but should not replace, music as a regular part of classroom experience. It is unfortunate that music appears to be an area in which many teachers feel a lack of confidence; however, there are varied activities that teachers can do with children which do not require extraordinary skills.

In cases where a specialist teacher in the arts can be requested, teachers tend to prefer a music specialist. In one public-school early-childhood center, the staff gave priority to a specialist teacher who worked in creative rhythmic movement and music. In another full-day kindergarten center where many teachers played the guitar or piano, there was an instrumental music teacher who taught groups of children to play the violin by modeling and ear training, using an adaptation of the Suzuki method. Where separate special education classes are present at the kindergarten level, the specialist music, movement education, and physical education teacher programs have served to mainstream children with special learning needs.

It is rare to find an art specialist in full-day kindergartens. Most kindergarten teachers have included art activities as a major program component traditionally and feel comfortable using specialist resources in other areas. The visual arts in particular always have been the major form of symbolic representation in kindergartens. This chapter, therefore, highlights ways of working in the arts that supplement practices in the field that are strong. In kindergarten education the major role of the arts is to build on a strength which children bring to school — their capacity for successful aesthetic experience.

MUSIC

Music is a nondiscursive symbolic repository of perceptual models in its perceptual immediacy, direct involvement, and connectedness. One philosopher has seen "mathematics as conceptual music and music as sensuous mathematics" (Polanyi, 1963, p. 38). There is a sense in which "only music can achieve the total fusion of form and content, of means and meaning, which all art strives for" (Steiner, 1970, p. 29). Music can communicate basic human feelings to a baby before words are understood.

Music should be a part of life, not merely background. Music should be listened to purposefully. No matter how long or how well someone describes music, we will never really grasp it unless we play it and hear it directly.

Creating Music

Children can explore rhythm directly through body movement and percussion instruments in a rhythm "band" that includes such items as drums, triangles, Chinese gongs, shakers, sticks, tambourines, and everyday objects. Melodic and harmonic patterns are available through singing and playing other musical instruments. Children experience the dialectical perceptual model directly through musical counterpoint, part singing, and rhythm instrument orchestration.

It is important for you to intersperse plenty of free-form exploration with instruments, each time that children use them. It will be easier for you and the children to listen if you begin with a few instruments of fine tonal quality and gradually add to this stock. When a "stop-and-place-instruments-on-the-floor" signal is understood before the instruments are distributed, you create a chance to share ideas.

An experimental attitude on your part will encourage experimentation. You also can empower yourself and the children by communicating your acceptance of the notion that everyone can be expressive and creative with sound.

Children can classify and counterpose instruments of different pitches and music of varying rhythms and tempos. Since they frequently confuse volume, pitch, and tempo, children can profit from your help in providing direct contrasts of these different variables. After they have heard models, they can intuitively counterpose the musical concepts.

One of the most available and versatile of all music-making instruments is the human voice. Singing songs can turn an ordinary moment into something filled with expectation and camaraderie. The important element for children is their feeling of belonging and participation. Rather than trying to "teach" a song precisely, line by line, try to "infect" children with songs, by singing them on many spontaneous as well as planned occasions. Folk songs, with their natural repetition, are especially relevant for kindergarten use.

If you are among the many people who believe they cannot sing on pitch or carry a tune, perhaps you have noticed that young children are unaffected by this. Thus, you may feel comfortable accompanying activities with a song or chant, whether at the beginning of a whole-group meeting or during transition periods.

You also should remember that children's musical creations combine naturally with their sociodramatic play and creative dramatics, increasing their richness and expressiveness.

Appreciating Music

Children can appreciate as well as create music. In either case, music is a symbolic form and some elements require instruction so that they can become figures standing out against a background of sound.

Children learn to appreciate music when you systematically attempt to build their perceptions. You can set the tone through scheduling and creating a climate for listening. Sometimes controlling lighting or using a fragrance can set a tone conducive to listening. In one full-day kindergarten program, the twenty-minute rest period after lunch takes place in a dimmed room where classical music is played. Children keep rhythm as they use their individual mats and enjoy Mr. Mozart Week or Mr. Beethoven Week (Sheila Terens, personal communication, 1984).

You can control variables in other ways. You can play recordings or arrange for live performances in which children hear individual instruments and then the instruments in combination with others. Sometimes melody, rhythm, or mode can be highlighted in isolation.

Hearing brief samples of music from different cultures is another way you can highlight and contrast unique forms. Kindergarten children can distinguish between European and Eskimo music. If children have heard a story or seen a videotape about Eskimos, hearing their music can augment that activity.

We have been conditioned culturally to expect certain music to evoke certain kinds of images. Working with young children who are not as fixed in their connections, you may be able to keep open their appreciation by encouraging them to select relevant pictures from a large collection of varied pictures. When they see that you accept a variety of alternative associations, they build confidence in your support of diversity.

MOVEMENT EDUCATION

People have a veritable need to move, despite the fact that, as they grow older, they have movement socialized out of them. Moving through space and observing the movements of other people and objects are both direct aesthetic experiences. Incidentally, experiences with movement are the foundation for mathematics and the development of science concepts. Children may apprehend the perceptual model of dialectical activity as they have experiences related to these disciplines as well as in music, movement, and the visual arts. Creative rhythmic movement is also a starting point for dramatics, which is part of poetic language experience, as well as an outgrowth of sociodramatic play.

Children enjoy many activities with rhythm and rhythmic movement. Rhythms are varying interrelations of tempo and pulsations that we perceive as patterns. These rhythmic patterns are repetitious signals that we perceive as "wholes" that exceed their "parts." Much of musical experience reflects this quality of transposing "emotive" wholes, a direct experience with the perceptual model of synergy.

It is valuable to do movement activities and play with rhythm alone as well as with melody. In order to keep open their opportunities for new discoveries, teachers can use a drum to accompany the children rather than ask the children to keep in step with it. With more experience, children can try to adapt to teacher-initiated rhythms.

These practices extend and support children's imagery processes. Body movement is a medium that is a primary source for symbolic expression and can, when carefully developed, become an important additional way in which to legitimize and develop children's expressions. If possible, consider videotaping children's efforts as a way of providing them with both appreciation and feedback.

To begin, you can encourage children to

Come to me in any way you like.
Come in a new way. Come in a different way.
Come in a high way. Come in a low way.
Come as if the bottoms of your feet were covered with glue. As if you were wearing a heavy crown. As if you were carrying an injured bird. As if you were very angry. As if you were on the moon . . .

You can ask individual children to isolate and variably combine parts of their own bodies: "Move only your elbows. Your shoulders. Your head." They can isolate levels: "Move in as high a way as you can, in as low a way as you can." You can ask them to control their direction: "Move in the straightest way you can. The most curving way you can." "Move in the flat, as if there are transparent walls in front of and/or behind you." "Move in the deep as if there are transparent walls on either/or both sides of you." When teachers emphasize the validity of finding alternative ways to move, children can directly experience the perceptual model of indirect progress.

The possibilities for discussion and moving are vast. The children's use of space and rhythm are kaleidoscopic. They enjoy the challenge of "coming to you" in different and creative ways. They enjoy using such props as hoops, ropes, scarves, and costume parts. One group of kindergarten children explored the use of their bodies in space, both alone and with partners. The sampling of activities shown in Figure 8.1 took place over a period of many weeks.

When children have had many opportunities to explore moving through space and isolating body parts, directions, and levels, they begin to elaborate these activities. The teacher's role is to appreciate and encourage kindergarten children to explore new contrasts.

CREATIVE DRAMATICS: A POETIC ART

Creative dramatics grows out of children's rich experiences in music and movement activities, sociodramatic play, and children's literature. It is at once social, substantive, verbal, and aesthetic activity.

Figure 8.1: Movement Activities

Angles. When your feet stay in the same place without
moving, your body can lean. That's very special.
 Now try a different way to lean. Take a partner, and
try leaning with him or her.
Bubbles. Imagine that you are inside a bubble. Show how
you could move so that the bubble won't break, so that
you can stretch part of the bubble, ever so gently now.
 As you move inside your bubble, show how you can pass
other people in their bubbles without touching, then
with touching.
Moving. Move toward somebody.
Move away from that person in a new way.
Meet somebody else in a new way. (Repeated)
(Adapted from P. Press, personal communication, 1974.)
Directions. With a partner, try moving together toward
the labels on our wall, first toward the north, holding
hands.
 Hold your partner by the elbow and move in a very tall
way toward the west. Oh, Alan has found an interesting
way to hold Jan's elbow. Betty is making a new line
with her head. Jo is showing us the west side with her
ear also. It's beautiful to see so many different ways.
 Move toward the south with your partner in a very low
way, as if there is a low tunnel. Find a new way to
move together. You're leaving that tunnel in so many
different ways. Danny, that's a new way that you never
tried before--very clever idea. Evan, how original.
Gloria looks so relaxed and comfortable. Hal looks as
if he's done a great deal of hard work.
Mirrors. Next, let's be mirrors. Take partners and decide
which of you will begin. It could be whoever is nearest
the east side of the room. Now, one of you move very
slowly as you hear the drum begin. Partners, try to copy
that person. What nice new movements. Slowly, carefully
now. Ian and Lil, move there so you have more space.
 Now, the lead partner, change, and be the mirror to
your partner. (Repeat.)
Personal Analogy. Everybody go to the end of the room.
Now, come to me in a new way. That's fine, so many
different ways--some high, some low, somebody sideways.
Oh, it's good to see you.
 Try a new way now, and move backward to where you
started. Try a new way to come sideways. Find a new way
to return sideways. So many new ideas. Martin was
really following his neck. Nora, what an original way to
use your shoulder.
 Let's rest for a minute and talk. What were you
thinking of that can move sideways? What else can move
sideways? (Pointing to four children.) Try to be that
thing. (Repeat procedure.)
 Let's think together about some things that can move
backward. Yes. Uh-huh. Interesting. What a fine
idea. The objects can bend and stretch? Let's try
(Pointing to six children) to move backward as those
things do. Become those things.

In sociodramatic play, children's favored, repeated plays may become more formalized as creative dramatics. The drama can continue to retain an evolving, episodic format around this kernel of common experience and interaction. These plays express actions, feelings, and problem issues. It is a group authorship in flux, as it were. It may never be written down or, with help from older children or adults, it may evolve into written form.

The collaborative efforts of children as they explore space through rhythmic movement activities and experiment with the sounds and interplay of music can also enter into creative dramatics. In one kindergarten group, a teacher noticed that a few children's rhythmic movements complemented one another. While the remainder of the group observed with her, several children developed partner, trio, and quartet movements. As they enjoyed this cooperative effort of using space together, they began to develop pantomimes. They explored ways to add tempo and dynamics to their pantomime activities. They pantomimed and guessed parts of trips that they had taken to the zoo, bakery, and a bottling factory. They "became" parts of cooking processes, electrical experiments, and appliances and pantomimed volcanic eruptions. Some of the pantomime activity pressed itself into sounds and dialogue.

As the activity grew increasingly elaborate, the emergence of dialogue marked its transformation into creative dramatics. These explorations spanned a period of several months, during which three or four sessions lasting from ten to twenty-five minutes were held each week.

Kindergarten teachers can highlight elements, variable forms, original efforts, and growing sensitivities and skills. They can notice when children's actions become more spontaneous and authentic or when they are contrived and restrained. Letting children know that all sincere expressions are acceptable will help them become as spontaneous and authentic as possible, as will recognizing and appreciating each child in relation to his or her own progress.

A contrasting source for children's creative dramatics comes from the outside in, as compared with the more internal evolution just described. For example, the folk-song game "Up On the Mountain" involves partners first swinging each other and then becoming "frozen" into statues (Landeck, 1950, pp. 110–11). Teachers can emphasize the variety, originality, and specific elements of these "frozen" statues. (Incidentally, children may directly experience centrifugal force before they "freeze." A great deal of such tacit knowing takes place when they dance and use playground equipment such as swings, seesaws, and slides. Thus, their three-dimensional imagery builds in many ways.)

Some poems and cumulative folk tales lend themselves to dramatization. "The Three Billy Goats Gruff" is an all-time favorite. Children find high drama, suspense, and glee in stories with this sort of manageable threat.* Kindergarten children need practice in role playing. In order to stimulate their expressive language, teachers can begin by taking roles themselves. Shaftel and Shaftel (1967) also make many suggestions for role playing social values, which can be adapted for kindergarten use.

Increasingly, children elaborate their play, adding simple costumes and props. Cleary's *Ramona the Pest*, the story of a laughable mischief-maker with whom children identify, and *The Pied Piper* (Jacobs) are the sorts of stories that kindergarten children can dramatize. Everyone can have a role in *The Pied Piper*. Siks (1985), Ward (1960), and McCaslin (1980) are among the sources for specialized techniques and materials.

It is important to make space in which to move. If there is one area in the classroom where whole-group meetings can take place, it may be possible to enlarge this area for children's creative rhythmic movement and creative dramatics activities by simply moving furniture. Pairs of children can take turns moving the chairs and tables to the side, perhaps stacking them. It is helpful and safer when everybody knows which furniture needs to be moved, where it needs to go, and how it should be carried.

THE VISUAL AND PLASTIC ARTS

Space for the visual and plastic arts should be set aside near a water source, in order to cut down on traffic and mess, and should be labeled as an arts area. It should contain the following materials:

An easel and brushes of varying thickness so that children can choose their own style. Each child should have a fresh set of tempera colors, at least two or more of their own choice, in order to provide contrasts.

A pencil hung from the easel or the table painting area so that children can sign their own names.

A drying rack and plastic aprons.

A table and four to six chairs.

Storage shelves, including shoe boxes of uniform size, shirt boxes, huge ice cream cylinders, and/or packing crates.

Newspapers for covering table or floor surfaces, in order to cut down the washing up of markings, glue, clay residues, and cuttings.

---

*Some teachers have used role playing in this and similar folk tales as part of helping children to practice saying no, as a deterrent to child abuse. A recent piece, "Scared and Hurt" (Kuhmerker, 1984), briefly summarizes many of the issues in child abuse, which you might adapt to role playing.

Clay and varied accessories, including dowels of varying diameter for
rolling; jar covers, cookie cutters, sticks, and a stylus for marking;
and plastic knives and wires for cutting. Pine cones and other
large, textured seeds can be used for pattern making.

Collage materials including shop window dressings, discarded wallpaper books, closeout fabric sample booklets, merchants' discards,
wrapping paper, candy wrappers, packaging materials and containers, discarded buttons and trimmings, washers, screening,
mesh, wires, and wire ties.

There should be bulletin boards and displays, including framed openings to hold children's two-dimensional work and attractive arrangements
on which to display three-dimensional work. Hang hoops, wire, or twine
to accommodate mobiles and other hanging displays.

Teachers should keep a personal card file containing varied visual and
plastic arts projects. There also should be a camera on hand, for photographing children at work, as well as their projects. Share the slides and
snapshots with children, their parents, and others.

Three-Dimensional Arts

The three-dimensional arts deserve a closer look since they appear less
often than drawing or painting. The visual-spatial skills that children strength-
en through problem-solving in three-dimensional art work also affect their
mathematical skills. Many more kindergarten children need to have access
to molding materials such as clay, plaster of paris, papier-mâché, wire and
foil, and pipe cleaners. They also need to spend much more time using
construction materials such as floor blocks and carpentry materials.

WOODWORKING.   Woodworking can be used in kindergarten, often
by midyear. In the full-day kindergarten, there are more opportunities to
plan for this activity. There is more discussion of woodworking in chapter
7. For detailed ideas, also see Skeen, Garner, and Cartwright (1984).

CLAY.   Clay may be one of the most popular of the plastic arts. One
research study reports that five-year-olds spend more time with clay sculpture, an average of 19.7 minutes per session, than any other art medium
(Haskell, 1984, p. 183). Clay provides sensory comfort as well as a sense of
power. Where possible, children's finished work can be fired in a kiln. One
class received additional inspiration when a sculptor, the grandmother of
one of the children, worked in their room one day.

SEWING AND WEAVING.   Another category of three-dimensional art activities includes mesh weaving; sewing designs that children have drawn, first on cards and later on felt fabric; simple macramé; and cooperative rug murals. Paper clips and paper straws can be used for weaving, and jersey loops can be used to make potholders.

MOBILES AND BUILT-UP SCULPTURE.   Mobiles and built-up sculpture can be created in the kindergarten. Mobiles can be made from coat hangers, hoops, and other items. Constructions built from a clay or styrofoam base with interesting collections of junk are ways for children to experiment with various materials. They face challenging problems with balance as well as design and texture.

COLLAGES.   Collages have three-dimensional as well as two-dimensional aspects. For these as well as other activities, teachers would do well to become selective junk collectors. In addition to materials already mentioned, children can use onion skins, various dry beans, eggshells, and a variety of macaroni products.

Two-Dimensional Arts

Variety is important if you want to keep interest fresh and create new problems to solve in the arts area. For example, at different times during the school year, you might offer string or shadow drawing, printing with textured materials, or potato printing with children's original designs. When you provide repeated, well-spaced exposures, you will observe different outcomes, due to children's intervening experiences, their growing coordination, and their ability to plan.

If you run out of paper for painting, grocery bags and the classified columns of newspapers can serve as free substitutes. Freezer wrapping paper or barber-chair paper rolls are less expensive substitutes for fingerpaint paper.

Film techniques are part of some kindergarten programs. Children can use felt-tipped pens to draw directly on 8 mm film. They can take photographs with inexpensive cameras and display their pictures in books or on bulletin boards. The Aesthetic Education Project, administered by the CEMREL Corporation in St. Louis, developed some photography activities for children through a federally funded program. Children took photographs of parts of objects, such as an old automobile. Although the object was not identifiable in the photograph, the photograph was an interesting design in itself. Research findings showed that children were able to learn to accept more unusual photographs (Roger Edwards, personal communication,

1975). Children also seemed more accepting of diverse and unusual viewpoints.

There are unlimited possibilities for materials to be used artistically when you and the children learn to see the strange in familiar surroundings. When that happens, your major problem may be to find space to store everything. Materials should encourage diverse, personal use. This use is quite different from static pattern-making, picture-coloring, and copied cutting and pasting pastimes.

The Teacher's Job

Kindergarten children need a great deal of exploration with the materials of the visual and plastic arts. Different children need more or less practice in holding pencils, chalks, crayons, brushes, and scissors. Occasionally, a child, perhaps with special learning needs, will need help in applying glue. You may find it useful to hold a child's hand when he is using glue or scissors so that he can see how it feels. For children who are left-handed or have special needs, provide left-handed or four-fingered scissors. If a child is beginning to use the scissors with two hands, use masking tape to attach an end of the paper to the table, so that the child can do the cutting as independently as possible.

The purpose of instruction is to build independent skills as well as to avert frustration and defeatism. A five-year-old who has an ambitious scheme to transform a milk container into a truck may need a great deal of sensitive adult support for the execution of her project. If it appears that you may end up doing all the work, it may be best to help the child find an alternative.

Your major job is to encourage children to use materials in imaginative ways, including multimedia work. With careful questioning and the use of analogy, teachers can help children extend their ways of working in the arts. As you do so, it will be apparent when children need technical help and help with coordination. Any time you find yourself feeling that absolutely every child must use a particular material or create a particular product, you might suspect that a truly artistic experience is missing. Remember the teaching assumption that has been stated previously: Different children doing different things at different times can have equivalent experiences.

Finally, you can serve as a museum curator when you frame or mount children's art work and written work with dignity and display it on walls, the backs of room dividers, and the spaces between windows or doors. You can cover boxes with contact paper, wallpaper, or cloth, and stack them to provide a three-dimensional display area for children's constructions, clay work, artifacts, and collections. One educator suggests displaying children's unit-block work on a turntable that can be rotated, to add to spatial aware-ness (Haskell, 1984, p. 52). Another way of valuing children's work is to shine a lamp on such a turntable display or on some other three-dimensional arrangement so that you can create interesting shadows.

String wire or twine across a corner, or across a room from wall to wall or corner to corner, and hang up such things as hangers and hoops for mobiles, splatter paintings, puppets, weaving, straw sculpture, or children's own poetry, dictated or copied. Sometimes you can move a storage shelf or screen to set off a new area, so the contents of that area become a new focus for the children's attention.

Children themselves can help create such "museums," which become an integral part of their experience of success rather than an alien form. These personally involving experiences provide a readiness for trips to a school exhibition or art fair and to school or library-based "feely" museums. School librarians, collaborating with teachers, are working increasingly to develop these kinds of experiences. You are indeed fortunate if there are such collections of activities or hands-on museum opportunities nearby. Model sites such as the Please Touch Museum in Philadelphia or the Exploratorium in San Francisco are uniquely endowed extensions of more modest local efforts.

As you work in these varied ways, do keep in mind that aesthetic experience is part of daily life as well as a distinct experience with art media. Young children often begin to learn about new things through their artistic experiences. Much of their artistic imagery serves as a bridge to other subject areas through common perceptual models.

9

Language, Psycholinguistics, and Reading

Language teaching and learning are a natural part of most activities that are rich in content. Language is a tool skill that grows out of, and adds meaning to, content areas. Repetition and practice, necessary for acquiring skills and using a tool, occur naturally, in various forms, throughout the full-day kindergarten.

In this chapter we will consider what a language and reading program looks like in a full-day kindergarten. We will discuss the knowledge base of a language program, focus on ways in which children acquire language skills, and outline the four components of a reading program for kindergarten children.

INDUCTION AS A WAY OF KNOWING LANGUAGE

Any one of us can look around and see that normal children are learning the language that they hear around them, yet most adults do not remember learning to speak. It just happened comfortably for most of us, without self-awareness.

It is more important for young children to use language naturally than to focus merely on being aware of how they are using it. When teachers tap the satisfaction that new speakers experience and nurture this naturalness, children should be able to extend and expand their language skills with comfort and satisfaction.

Theoretically, it should feel no more difficult to learn to read than it was to learn to speak. After we look at some basic ways in which children learn to speak, we can consider how to apply these methods as children learn to use various language skills.

193

In a nutshell, children learn to speak through the process of *induction*. First, children perceive a model that is repeated. For example, every time Deb touched the button on her aunt's coat, her mother said, "Button. That's a button. See the button on the coat? Button." After lots of touching, seeing, and hearing the word and object together, in the second phase, Deb began to make the sound of "buh," to great acclaim and appreciation. She imitated the sound with adult feedback of "button" until she expanded her utterance to approximate the whole word.

A similar process takes place as children begin to use sentences and learn sentence structures (syntax). A kind of rubber-band stretching takes place. The "rubber-band" image fluctuates as the child reduces the adult's syntax. The adult in turn expands the child's statement. With continuing interaction, the child begins to expand her syntax, stretching toward the adult's fluent, more complex syntax.

Some researchers have identified a continuing process of adult-child "expansion/reduction/expansion/lesser-reduction" (Brown & Bellugi, 1964). The power of contrasts and analogies in the child's active construction of language has been underscored by Ervin (1964, p. 186) and Wittgenstein (1958, p. 35). As children perceive contrasts, their ability to use language becomes more flexible. The significance of such contrasting syntactic patterns in language learning is noted also in work as varied as that of Bruner (1966), Cazden (1972, 1981), Chomsky (1965), Fries (1963), Gleason (1965), Miller (1969), and Montessori (1965).

At the same time, expansion is not guaranteed in and of itself but depends upon the social interaction between the adult modeler and the child that is stimulated by the activity. The stimulation of the content — the meaning shared — provides a deeper structure than the mere order of words in an utterance (N. Chomsky, 1972).

Now, it follows that the process of natural, inductive, early language development could be used to help children develop their continuing linguistic skills. When modeling of the "rubber-band" variety has been used, by informal repetition of sentences that are syntactically equivalent but with varied content, children have been able to induce a more efficient or expanded use of spoken language (Fromberg, 1976; Gleason, 1981; Yonemura, 1969). That is, when teachers have used concrete, materials-based, playful game situations that are tied to certain contrasting pairs or trios of sentences, children have been exposed to a planned — rather than the usual random — modeling of contrasting sentences. Examples of such "syntax model games" can be found among the works just cited.

In summary, induction in learning syntax (or reading words) includes the following processes:

Repeated models of contrasting patterns of words in sentence pairs. (Ideally, this occurs in gamelike situations.)

Imitation by the children as they play the game, followed by expansion (without expressed evaluation) by the adult.

Induction of the syntax by the child, evidenced by use in game playing.

TRANSFORMATIONAL-GENERATIVE GRAMMAR AND LANGUAGE EDUCATION

The significance of syntax — the structural relations of patterns of words in sentences — bears some attention in the longer kindergarten day. With more time, teachers have more opportunities to engage in longer, more involved conversations with children and thus to model more complex language.

It is instructive to notice that the playfulness of young children is an important factor contributing to the development of creative linguistic possibilities. Babies learn the rules that hold language together. They frequently overregularize these rules logically and creatively, even when they are unconventional. For example, a toddler might say, "I runned home."

These contentions are consistent with a Piagetian view of young children as active participants in the acquisition of knowledge. In the child's personal construction of his world, innate human possibilities interact with environmental experiences. The inductive process in this interaction extends knowledge beyond experience.

As adults and children interact, working and talking together about activities, children acquire and strengthen their use of the conventions of forming sentences. Teachers can consciously use the expansion, coordination, subordination, or other alterations of sentence pairs in the context of activities. As children have more exposure to language and find reasons to use varied sentence forms, their language becomes more efficient. Individual speaking and writing styles are the result of such experiences.

Notice that if we expect children to understand words like *but, because, which, that, if-then, or, and, of, all, some,* and *any,* denoting relation and subordination, they will need to hear them contrasted with other words in sentences. Many of these concepts are essential to an understanding of mathematics and other content areas and deserve our systematic inclusion in concrete situations that make sense to children.

C. Chomsky (1972), in a study of young children's acquisition of language, used pictures with contrasting pairs of sentences, rather than bare word testing, as a way of diagnosing children's comprehension of these variations. It is helpful to harness the power of contrasts as you use inductive strategies, trusting children's receptivity.

COMPONENTS OF A READING PROGRAM

There are entire volumes and courses of study devoted to the abundant variety of reading programs. Rather than a review of the field, this section presents one point of view about reading instruction in a full-day kindergarten. This point of view proposes that there are four essential components in a systematic instructional program — (1) language experience, (2) writing into reading, (3) children's literature, and (4) phonemic instruction — and that these components should be applied flexibly for different children. Keep in mind that you can help children develop their language skills while they engage in meaningful activities.

Component 1: Language Experience

The language-experience approach to writing and reading has been around for many years. In it, kindergarten teachers write down, in the children's presence, what children dictate to them. They may write on paintings that children have created, on chart paper following a shared experience, and on labels for the physical environment of the classroom. After such experiences, children and their teachers may save their written observations and findings.

In preceding chapters, there are examples of such writing in the content areas. Almost any everyday experience can become an "experience chart." This practice saturates the kindergarten children visually with the medium of writing, in much the same way that they have been saturated aurally with their native spoken language.

On these occasions, teachers find that it is important to record precisely what children say, so that the written form captures the children's spoken language, even if it is not standard English. In this way, bilingual children or children with dialectal differences have a chance to feel that their spoken language is acceptable. They also have the repeated experience of seeing their ideas recorded and their experiences saved and retrieved. In the pursuit of literacy, children "need their own writing to be done for them just as they need other people's writing to be read to them" (Smith, 1983, p. 84).

Large sheets of paper, with or without accompanying pictures, can be used to record procedures that a group follows, say, in a science activity or in cooking. Furniture in the classroom can be labeled, as can doors, windows, and the directions of east, west, north, and south. Children can wear labels on their clothing that explain their roles in sociodramatic play, such as "doctor," "baby," and "mother" (Mackay et al., 1978, p. 7). In addition, children can play with letters or words on flannel boards and magnet boards.

With enough modeled repetition, many children begin to sort out the concept of spaces as the delimiters of words. They need repeated, focused exposure to the left-to-right orientation of the English language. They will observe, however casually, that the teacher always forms each letter from the top to the bottom and from left to right. When key words that have unusual configurations appear often, some children sort them out. With many such experiences, some children begin to induce the sound structure of words, while others build a sight vocabulary.

When you feel that a child might like to discuss a drawing or painting, you might ask, "Would you like me to write what you were thinking while you were drawing?" or "Do you want to tell me about your picture so I can write down what you say?" Be aware that the youngster might not have planned or produced a representational drawing; therefore, it would be inappropriate to ask, "What did you draw?" since that could suggest that representation or a particular standard was required as the only acceptable form.

A group of pictures with brief dictated narratives can be bound into a class book. It can be on a particular topic, such as "Looking Out the Window," "Wheels," "Dinosaurs," or "Motors." Such a book might circulate at the reading area or even overnight at home. Other activities can include shopping lists, plans for parties, notices of special events, schedules of daily activities, special instructions, letters to a sick child, a thank you note to a toy donor or a visiting senior citizen, and invitations for parents to assist on a class trip. Anderson (1968, p. 150) recommends a "News-Item Chart," a sort of newspaper broadside that could contain such information as, "Sue has a baby brother," "Ellen has a birthday today," and "Mary's grandmother came to visit last night."

A class message center or working post office, in which each child has a box, can be a place for children to receive mail, such as notices to take home, messages from each other, appointments with the regular teacher or special teachers, or greeting cards.

These are among the many things that children can write or dictate: picture captions, cartoon strips, songs, poems, stories, journal entries, jokes, riddles, telegrams, directions to follow, eyewitness accounts, personal recollections, personal essays, fables, editorials, and original nature booklets (Moffett, 1968, p. 116).

Occasionally, individual kindergarten children have made "talking compositions" on audiotapes. Some of these have become experience charts, recorded by an older child or an adult. Sometimes individual children will go back and retell their stories on the tape, embellishing or varying their material, as close as kindergarten children come to the act of revising or editing. For them the process itself and the satisfaction of the experiences, even though they may be episodic, incomplete, or rambling by adult standards, are more important than the final product.

Most kindergarten children are able to write their own names and recognize the names of other children, if they have had repeated opportunities to see them. Motivation to write their own names is high and is a welcome first writing activity. The book, *Rosa-too-Little*, by Felt, can only serve to add inspiration. In this book, a preschool city child secretly practices writing her own name in order to obtain a library card. After children can write their own names, teachers can arrange a trip to the local library, where children can receive library cards.

Children have strong personal motivation for improving their dictation and their own writing. Research shows that children enter school already knowing quite a bit about writing (Clay, 1982; Ferreiro & Teberosky, 1982; Graves & Stuart, 1985). The vagaries of the English language, however, dictate that about 15 percent of the words we frequently use simply do not fit regular patterns (Mazurkiewicz, 1964, p. 135). Children are more likely to recognize those words if they have seen them written and if they have some background in phonemic associations to guide them. Children who use invented spellings show significant progress in acquiring phonemic associations. Using invented spellings, kindergarten children have been able to keep interactive journals with their teacher.

The whole point of language-experience activities is to help children learn to use those tools that communicate meaning. Clearly, children who have good opportunities to react, feel trust, and experience delight in school activities have more about which to talk and write, and they also have more background to bring to reading the printed page. They enjoy using these tool skills to express their views of the world, their place in it, and their relations with other people.

Component 2: Writing into Reading

Carol Chomsky contends that, for the young child, "the natural order is writing first, then reading what you have written" (1971, p. 292). She points out that the child who selects a plastic letter *r* to represent *w* in the word *wet* is reminding adults that this is the way he pronounces his *r*'s. The developmental value of invented spellings has met with increasing acceptance by people who are concerned with early writing curriculum (Calkins, 1986; Clay, 1982; Smith, 1983; Temple, Nathan, & Burris, 1982).

You may be wondering how kindergarten children might be expected to write, even with invented spellings, before they can coordinate the task of handwriting to keep pace with their need to be expressive. The dilemma of bypassing the technical coordination of handwriting or the recall of word parts has been handled in several ways. For example, Montessori (1965) advocates writing words that have been read. Others, working with children who have special learning needs, report that hand holding while writing has served as additional sensorial reinforcement for reading (Fernald, in Smith & Dechant, 1961; Spalding, 1969).

The "talking typewriter" (Moore & Anderson, 1968) has been updated with the IBM computer materials prepared by Martin (Brandt, 1981). The original talking typewriter overcomes the need for handwriting, as very young children gradually construct the words at the same time that they learn to read them. As the typewriter keys are locked and unlocked, through trial and error, the keys are named and words are constructed; in short, the children begin to read and write. The "environment" in this setting is "responsive." In the updated computer version, prepared for use with kindergarten children, pairs of children work together at each computer. The computer work is supplemented with workbook exercises and writing with close adult supervision. The number of adults needed, computer costs, and the use of workbooks are limitations in this approach.

THE BREAKTHROUGH TO LITERACY PROGRAM

Mackay, Thompson, and Schaub (1978) attempt to bypass the need to coordinate handwriting and the recall of word parts in an intriguing way. Their *Breakthrough to Literacy* program of "sentence makers" has been used with thousands of children.

The kindergarten year, or whenever children are emerging as readers, is the ideal time to introduce the "sentence maker." This consists of a three-part oaktag folder, each part nine by eleven inches. The folder stands up to form a kind of private study carrel and folds flat for easy storage. The interior consists of nine rows of pocket slots into which children can match word cards that correspond to the words that are printed on part of the folder. A section of the folder is blank so that children can add "personal" word cards to these slots. Personal words are written by the teacher on an oaktag strip.

The teacher keeps scissors and an oaktag strip at hand, writes a word when a child asks for it, and cuts it off the strip. The child then places the word card in a plastic stand similar to those used in "Scrabble." The child may add other preprinted word cards and a question-mark or period card to the stand. The child may be able to recognize some of these words or may ask another child or the teacher to help find the needed card from a word card file or a pouch pocket storage device that hangs on the wall. The files duplicate the folder's word sequence. A labeled carpenter's drawer cabinet might serve equally well.

One child may read her statement to another child or the teacher and then write it in a notebook or on a drawing. In this way, the ideas will not be lost during the slow development of the coordination required for hand-writing. Moreover, even if a child is not yet able to write, she can still com-pose ideas on the stand.

One exciting aspect of this material is that a child can express ideas that have personal meaning, expressed as she would speak, using her own natural syntax. Inasmuch as the child's own expressions form the material for read-ing, the *Breakthrough to Literacy* method is part of the language-experi-ence tradition.

The teacher can integrate handwriting instruction with sentence mak-ing by simply stating what he is doing, while doing it, for example, "To write this 'o,' I start at the top, move counterclockwise, and close the circle." As the teacher repeats the directions and speaks in terms of curves and lines, most handwriting needs are satisfied. Occasionally a child will need the kinesthetic support of the teacher helping to move the child's hand while stating the directions. The letter *s* is one that children find particularly difficult.

In addition, the sentence maker contributes to the children's concrete understanding of syntax as they physically set words in the stand. The left-to-right sequence is reinforced by a mark at the left side of the stand. When they read back what they have selected, they frequently fill in "grammatical" words and their usual spoken syntax, even though the stand may contain only a few "lexical" words that have "high information content" in random order (Mackay et al., 1978, p. 96).

When the teacher asks the child to read each word card separately in the order set on the stand, the child gains an appreciation of the contrasting patterns of words in sentences. At times, a child may rearrange or insert new word cards as he sees the need for meaning in their order. This learning comes more directly in this way than from copying dictated script.

The teacher should understand that the child's written statements may reflect a much more profound level of interest than their face value. One child composed the sentence, "My dad said to me you go upstairs," reflect-ing his rejection of her presence and the denial of television privileges, quite a bit of drama for so simple-looking a statement (Mackay et al., 1978, pp. 109–10).

Researchers who have studied the beginnings of writing also have noticed that young children tend to produce simple inventories of words that interest them but do not necessarily mean anything together. Children also often express themselves with little concern for a possible audience (Temple et al., 1982).

The teacher also needs to understand, from a developmental standpoint, the child's abbreviated or "telegraphic" utterances with written words. For example, McNeill (1970) observes that the new speech of very young children has a unique syntax, and Chomsky (1971) notes "telegraphic" kinds of spelling patterns. Mackay et al. (1978) observe that, when children begin to write, their written syntax is a reduced version of their spoken syntax, but that it expands with experience. This is like the aforementioned "rubberband" process that occurs when children learn to speak.

Indeed, children learn to write much as they learn to talk: by observing repeated models. They learn the conventions of written language by hearing the writings of other people read to them. Author Eudora Welty (1984), speaking of her beginnings as a writer, discusses her mother's reading to her repeatedly at many times and places. Her understanding that books were products rather than "natural wonders" developed gradually, from simpler, magical, holistic views to more refined inductions.

Realistically, the experienced teacher accepts that children naturally shrink the symbolic "rubber band" in the form of "telegraphic" written utterances. The sentence maker materials serve to situate the activity of writing at the more concrete level of recognition, as opposed to recall. Even after a child has "graduated" from use of the stand after kindergarten and is writing at the recall level without the stand, teachers will notice that a child may "revert to simple sentence making for a time" (Mackay et al., 1978, p. 156). Later in the year, a few children may begin to play with transforming one word into another, an indication that they are at a "recall" level. Capital letters, other than in their names, are variables that are added after they have achieved proficiency with the sentence makers. These developmental phases are part of the child's natural rhythm of language development.

The many hundreds of kindergarten children whom I have observed using these materials viewed them as satisfying privileges that they had achieved. They composed their sentences, recorded them in notebooks, and illustrated their statements, creating their own illustrated narrative books. Within these same settings, they also played with blocks, dramatic materials, water, clay, crafts, and a full range of other concrete materials.

Breakthrough to Literacy is a personalized, creative, participatory alternative to workbooks and look-say types of basal readers that depend on rote learning and memory alone. In the context of the four components for a reading program that are presented in this chapter, as well as a rich language arts environment, the *Breakthrough* materials have served to satisfy the need that community and administrators may have to identify concrete reading materials for emergent readers.

COMPOSING

While writing develops in ways that parallel speaking and is stimulated by hearing written material read, the written work of beginning writers does have some unique characteristics. For one thing, even with the *Breakthrough to Literacy* materials, teachers should expect and value many examples of invented spellings. Since the act of composing, used in the sense of freedom to organize feelings and ideas in a personal way, is the single most important writing task to nurture, effective kindergarten teachers must be great appreciators of the trust with which young children present their work. Quite simply, teachers appreciate the flow, the enthusiasm, and the sense of accomplishment that young children bring to their work.

Necessarily brief statements are not returned with requests for expansion. They are appreciated. Inventories are not returned with requests for closure. They are appreciated. Creative spelling, handwriting, and punctuation are not turned into on-the-spot lessons. They are accepted. Technical instruction takes place at times separate from when young children feel the flush of accomplishment. Teachers will find that it is helpful to think of composing activities as being a set of interwoven phases: prewriting, writing, revising, and creating a final product.

The *prewriting* phase is a critical time for all teachers to work with children in harnessing and building enthusiasm and motives for writing. Children have plenty of motivation to express their experiences in symbolic forms, whether written, artistic, or dramatic. Philosopher Suzanne Langer (1948) has hypothesized that human beings actually have a need to symbolize. Through symbols, children can express the various ways in which they connect and organize their experiences. Kindergarten teachers generally focus on simply stimulating the flow of composing. At most, they might network related ideas or prepare a "project folder," a sentence maker of words related to a specific topic that individuals might choose to use.

You will find additional stimuli for prewriting activities among the discussions of questioning techniques and the uses of analogy in chapter 2, and the activities connected with the content areas of chapters 5, 6, 7, and 8. It is natural that writing and other symbol-making activities are entwined with the range of subject matter areas. Young children naturally integrate these activities. Effective kindergarten teachers are particularly sensitive to the integration and application of skills in content areas.

The *writing phase*, like its prewriting counterpart, can take place in many areas of the classroom, but an ongoing commitment to writing as composing can be underscored by creating a kindergarten writing area. The space should be set up away from traffic and should be labeled as a writing area. It should contain the following resources:

Tables, with six to eight chairs facing a wall, room divider, or carrel
A storage space for journals, writing folders, and *Breakthrough to Literacy* sentence makers for those who use them
A space and procedure for storing work in progress, e.g., clipboards or clothespins on a line of string from which to hang papers
A place to leave "finished" work for you to see
Writing implements, reserved exclusively for the writing area (These may change from time to time in order to highlight the area, e.g., when a special magic marker or stunning pencil is provided, one for each seating space.)
Paper supplies and teacher-made pad books (four to six sheets of paper stapled together) of varied sizes
A stapler

Teachers keep records that might include the following items: (a) A dated file of samples of children's completed writing in the form of single sheets or short pad books — some teachers have found it useful to save finished work in a large red manila pocket folder, one for each child, and place the collection of folders in a phonograph record stand or milk crate. (b) A dated schedule of reserved space in the writing center, allowing each child to work consecutively for at least three days at the start of each moderately (as opposed to fully) active work period; as each reserved space is vacated, another child may choose to use the space. (c) A personal task card file of their ideas for stimulating writing content and for energizing the writing center.

There should be bulletin board and hallway displays labeled "Kindergarten Writing — (month)" that might include broadsides, an occasional pad book, or labeled drawings arranged in an aesthetically appealing format. There might be photographs of kindergarten children engaged in writing or sharing their writing with others. It is useful to bring to the parents' attention the contents of items listed above.

The bulk of kindergarten children's writing products appear and increase after several months of the school year have passed. Sometimes the children's writing involves playing with words and sounds just as they have done in the course of oral language development. When teachers stimulate and appreciate children's written efforts, children feel comfortable enough to write about their personal experiences. Other products include labels for pictures that they have drawn in the arts area, one-page stories or pad book stories of several pages, or journal entries in the writing area.

The journal is an ongoing personal statement in which children write each day after the teacher has provided them with a bound notebook at about the same time that they would be ready for a "sentence maker"; that is, different children will be ready at different times. The most effective kindergarten teachers correspond nearly every day with children through the journal.

Before the kindergarten children arrive, Ursula Davis, a New York City public school kindergarten teacher, writes a daily one- or two-sentence letter to each child who has a journal. She might ask about how they like something, or about siblings or other everyday experiences, and the children write their answers in the journal. Often, they will ask a question in return, such as "Dear Ms. Davis, I have 1 sister. She is a baby. How many brothers and sisters do you have? Love, Alex." Sometimes children write in the journal and fold over a page to denote that it is private.

As teachers appreciate the process of children's writing efforts, they can highlight various aspects of the writing. For example, teachers reflect back what a child has written and ask the child for confirmation. They might ask what the child perceived to be the most important part of the story or why the child decided to write about this topic. They also might ask if the child plans to write about a similar or different topic next time. They might raise some of the questions that were discussed in chapter 2, using only those questions for which they really need an answer. Their best questions may be answered differently by different children. These strategies encourage children to trust the teacher enough to risk sharing honestly, and to develop their own critical thinking skills.

Occasionally, kindergarten teachers ask children to select their favorite piece of work so that it can be displayed in or circulated from the classroom reading area. Imagine the excitement of authorship and publication as a child glues a library card holder onto the cover of his own book!

Children can help each other with their writing as they share their work at peer conferences or in a larger group sharing time. Sharing ideas and written work with others helps children build a sense of audience. Some teachers have taped a mark on the floor to designate an area for peer sharing. By sitting there, any child is inviting others to share written work. At first, children may read simultaneously to one another. After the teacher has consistently modeled appreciation, the retelling of stories, and clarification questions, children learn to do this for one another; for example, a child who finishes reading to the class may fold her arms and ask, "What did I just say?" and then, "What questions do you have to ask about my story?" Lucy Calkins (1986) provides detailed ideas for teacher or peer writing conferences.

Beyond adding to their work, a *revising* or *editing phase* is usually not relevant for young children. Occasionally a child may see something months after he originally wrote it and marvel at how much more proficient his later work seems. To expect much more than this is to expect more self-awareness than young chidren are developmentally able to experience. An opportunity for self-directed revision might occur, long after a first flush of creative achievement, if a youngster were preparing some favorite writing on "special" paper for a display or sharing.

A final product for young children might involve collecting illustrated stories or an exchange of messages into a personal or class notebook. If children collaborate in creating a book of illustrated stories around a single topic, teachers can provide a special quality or size of paper on which children can copy a favorite piece of writing. These can be framed in oaktag or colored paper and hung on the school walls. More often, kindergarten children and their teachers are likely to be quite satisfied with episodic writing, simple phrases or sentences, and labels.

Component 3: Children's Literature

While *Breakthrough to Literacy* can serve as one material alternative to a basal reader series, it serves only part of the needs involved in a comprehensive reading program for the kindergarten. Children need to have multitudes of exposure to fine-quality literature throughout their lives, beginning as early as infancy. Therefore, before and in conjunction with their earliest writing experiences, children need to be acquainted with books and other forms of print through comfortable, stimulating, and exciting activities.

Difficult as it may be to imagine, there are children who enter kindergarten without such positive encounters with books. For these children, for others who may have become television addicts by the time they enter kindergarten, as well as for those who have had many positive associations with books or are already reading, it is essential that you as teachers provide a meaningful atmosphere and exposure to fine literature.

The reading area, described briefly in chapter 1, is a locale in which you can create a comfortable atmosphere where individuals can concentrate. It is a setting that you can embellish with "invitations" to expectancy and delight.

As you read aloud to the entire group at least once each day, you can extend this atmosphere. Kindergarten children are still young enough to appreciate sitting on your lap or close to you in a small group. At these times, it is natural to point to the words as you read.

In your role as questioner, you can use puppets, dramatization, and open-ended and imaginative discussions before and after the story time as ways in which to deepen meaning and positive associations for children. It helps comprehension when children can have some expectations about what you will be reading, so that they can have the pleasure of imagining what is to come and to predict playfully what may be ahead. You might ask them what questions they have about the book before reading.

When children hear poems and stories, the experience itself can be sufficient. The "turned on," totally absorbed atmosphere and the children's very posture tell you when they are aesthetically captivated. It is redundant to ask, "Did you like it?" when their behavior holds the answer. Certainly, if they are fidgeting, looking around, or trying to find stimulation in each other, you have clues that the story or timing is not relevant.

Hearing fine literature is a far cry from the farina-like basal series, which simply lack excitement, meaningful content, and, often, multicultural values. When you ask most children before they begin school what they think school is all about, they are likely to answer that they will learn to read and have homework. Therefore, the excitement of the child who is reading, "Oh! Oh! See! See! Look, Daddy, look!" is most likely due to an identification with the task of schooling and a sense of accomplishment, rather than an inherent joy in the content itself.

Beyond hearing fine literature read to them, children need to have fine literature to read themselves, as their skills develop. In the following pages we will discuss some examples of both types of literature for children. An asterisk (*) will identify sample books that kindergarten children can read by themselves. Figure 9.1 outlines criteria with which to select literature for those kindergarten children who are beginning to read. (Following the main bibliography at the end of this book are two sections on children's literature. The first is a listing of all titles that have been referred to in the text; most of these will need to be read to kindergarten children. The second section is a list of "great books" that beginning readers in kindergarten may be able to read on their own.)

When we look at books written for children that they find appealing, several forms stand out as distinctly attractive to children. Teachers have the important job of differentiating those that have integrity from those that are gimmicky or "supercute."

PERSONS IN FEATHERS OR FUR.   There are many stories about human problems and feelings that are masked by animal forms. The kindergarten child can identify with the characters and share the author's experience. *The Noisy Book** (Brown), *The Way Mothers Are* (Schlein), and *Charlotte's Web* (White) represent this genre.

These animals serve quite a different purpose than do the violence-prone and violence-immune characters that appear in some other books directed to children. While *Charlotte's Web*, laced with life-and-death

Figure 9.1:   "Great Books": Criteria for Beginning Readers

CRITERIA FOR SELECTION	CRITERIA FOR REJECTION
–Characters have integrity, are believable, and can be identified with.	–Characters are supercute, mawkish, of contrived.
–Characters represent wholesome human relationships.	–Characters promote prurience or violence.
–Values are integral to the material.	–Values are presented as moralizing.
–Egalitarian values are present, e.g., multiculturalism, sexual equality, etc.	–Values include stereotypes or lack of pluralism.
–There is a satisfying ending.	–There is an anxiety-provoking ending.
–There is significant and/or playful content.	–Content is trivial, mindless or exploitative.
–Language is used beautifully.	–Language is stilted or contrived.
–There is just one story in each book.	–The book is a series of stories or textbook materials conforming to a pre-established reading list.
–Illustrations are integrated with text.	
–Illustrations are aesthetically appealing.	

issues, involves the listener in an intimate friendship experience with a spider and farm animals, *The Way Mothers Are* underscores the intimacy of a warm family relationship through animals. *The Noisy Book*,* filled with repetition that children enjoy participating in, leaves the reader/listener with a sense of empathy for a convalescing dog and provides a satisfying ending.

At their best, these persons in feathers or fur, no less than human story characters that succeed as good literature, frequently involve the reader/ listener in significant human problems. Issues of growth and achievement; security and dependency; fear, assertion, and power; and life and death are universal themes that can engross a reader. The finest children's stories handle these issues with care for children, providing satisfying if not always happy resolutions. They do not titillate children and purvey suspense and violence as ends in themselves.

REALISTIC FICTION.   Anything that really could happen in a child's experience can be the subject of realistic fiction. Children have opportunities to see how other people, or animals who retain animal characteristics,

behave and feel in situations with which the young listener/reader can identify. Sometimes these situations occur at other times and places than the ones
in which your children live. These stories can help children to see familiar
events in new ways. *Benjie on His Own* (Lexau), about the securities and
insecurities of an urban black child being raised by his grandmother, and
Flack's *Angus Lost*, about curiosity, adventure, and security in familiar
things, present believable characters with whom children can identify. Both
authors stimulate readers beyond the surface action, touching significant personal realities.

The best authors use mostly direct conversation that focuses the reader
on the present time of the story. Often one main idea and character are the
focus of these stories. Children are able to validate the possibility of these
events and characters. Kindergarten children are satisfied with simple endings. Even if an ending comes as a surprise, it should be within the possibility
of a child to imagine it.

A book like Tresselt's *I Saw the Sea Come In* stands in contrast to the
stories in which character identification seems prominent. Tresselt presents
a realistic situation but creates an aesthetically powerful mood by the beautiful use of language. Indeed, spoken language is rarely as poetic as this example. Children need to have exposure to a variety of expressive forms, and
this variety is most likely to be found in the books that you will read to them.

FOLK TALES.   The cumulative form of the folk tale, in which each
successive event is added to the next and repeated, is frequently found in
literature for young children. This form is consistent with kindergarten
children's developmental needs. When the substance is appealing, the cumulative stories are most popular and are easily retold. The repetition helps
to make these tales readable. Children also enjoy the repetition since it offers them a sense of mastery due to their being able to predict what is coming. Examples of such stories are Flack's *Ask Mr Bear*,* Gag's *Millions of
Cats*, Tworkov's *The Camel Who Took a Walk*,* and the folk tales *Caps
for Sale** (Slobodkina) and *The Enormous Turnip** (Southgate). They all
have satisfying endings.

A repetitive form that has symmetry exists in McCloskey's *Blueberries
for Sal*, in which a human child and a bear cub inadvertently switch places.
A less plausible realistic fantasy is de Regniers' *The Giant Story*,* in which
a boy repeatedly tries out his imaginary power, to the satisfaction of numerous children. Children feel delighted to be able to identify with the main
character.

POETRY.   Successful authors appeal to children by communicating
appreciation for their characters and respect for their audience. There is a

kind of sincere "eye contact" made with children's very marrow. A. A. Milne is a master of this craft, as evidenced by his *Winnie-the-Pooh* books and his poetry classics, *Now We Are Six* and *When We Were Very Young*. He manages to touch most concerns and problems of childhood, except for the pain of major deprivation. When adults read "Sand Between the Toes," with coordinated tickles beginning with "sand in the hair," both reader and listener share a rare joy.

It is worthwhile for children to hear a variety of styles and forms of poetry. Adoff's poetry anthologies, including the works of Langston Hughes and Nikki Giovanni, provide a variety of settings and fine craft. Both children and adults appreciate Giovanni's metaphors in "Winter Poem."

Children certainly appreciate poetry that they hear. Narrative poems can serve as a basis for their creative dramatics, right alongside prose stories. Poetry is particularly adaptable to choral speaking, with subgroups taking turns, which helps reticent children to participate. In addition, when you group together poems that have a common theme or metaphor, children can experience similar themes from different perspectives, a powerful way to learn about different ways of knowing the world. Such groupings contribute to the development of critical education. Jacobs (1965) suggests using "poem cycles" along similar lines.

Your own enjoyment of a poem can be contagious. It is worthwhile to build a stock of familiar, favorite poems that you can integrate incidentally at the "right" moment, even if it is not storytime. Milne's "Happiness," Stevenson's "My Shadow," and Segal's "Be My Friend" are just right at certain moments. The daily storytime could include one or two or an entire session of poems for children to hear. Children have favorite poems and ask for repetition, just as they do with stories.

NONFICTION TRADE BOOKS.   Many nonfiction trade books are written imaginatively and entertainingly for young children. Illustrations in both fictional and nonfictional works are frequently well integrated with the text and add to the experience of the book for children. However, as much as these features serve to capture a child's interest, the primary purpose of nonfiction is informational. In addition to information about the world in general, puzzles, riddles, jokes, magic, recipes, and games are found among nonfiction trade books for kindergarten children.

PERIODICALS.   Periodicals for kindergarten children have been published that consist largely of illustrations with just a few labels and captions. Rather than use these as a whole-group, didactic reading activity, provide several copies of newspapers or other appropriate periodicals that children can choose to read in the reading area.

Component 4: Phonemic Instruction Through Games

When you provide literature for children to listen to, look through, and read in the kindergarten, the main purpose is to stimulate their enjoyment and appreciation of varied literature. Such positive experiences help children to build reasons to want to read. Although these kinds of exposures to literature, the saturation of their school environment with language-experience materials, and a sense of accomplishment in the use of the "sentence maker" stimulate many children to induce for themselves the process of reading, some children need a different kind of stimulation. They may need specific, focused technical help in decoding skills and using the sound structure of the English language. Phonemic instruction, which deals with the sound structure in an inductive way, is the fourth component in a comprehensive reading program.

Reading is useful and pleasurable. It is an essential economic and cultural tool. When children acquire this tool at an early age, independent, vicarious, and extended experience opens up sooner. However, rote decoding without understanding is meaningless exercise. How many times have you decoded a page of print without grasping the author's meaning? Even in the face of technological changes that may replace the constant need to read, it is inconceivable to imagine a postliterate world. While this is not the forum for arguing whether or not children should learn to read, it is the place to talk about when it should be taught and how.

PUTTING READING IN ITS PLACE

Through the years, early childhood educators have argued over whether to begin teaching reading in the kindergarten, first, or second grade. The "talking typewriter" was one attempt, among others, to teach nursery-age children to read. Children in Montessori classrooms receive reading instruction in the nursery years if their teacher judges that they are ready for it. There have been "progressivists" who have recommended that children wait until they are seven years of age, when their eyes mature. The most common practice is to begin with six-year-olds, based upon the Morphett and Washburne study (1931), which recommended reading begin at the mental age of six years, six months.

Prevailing practices merit review at this time. First, nursery-age children have been able to learn to read. For example, Durkin (1966) reports that many children have entered kindergarten with independent reading skills already established. Also, most children learn to read in our society before they are seven years of age, apparently without an increase in ocular problems. As a matter of fact, with recent advances in the diagnosis of perceptual learning disabilities, teachers are finding that about 15 percent of children in the school population have such impairments even before they have been expected to read. Therefore, causes of reading problems also exist elsewhere than in the act of recognizing printed symbols.

It is a constant wonder, in the light of research findings into the great range of capacity within a chronological age group, that adults continue to be concerned with the starting *age* for reading instruction. It would be better to regard "readiness" to read as a lifelong state. When this view is taken, your job as teacher boils down to diagnosing a child's skill at a given time and providing instruction at the next level of complexity.

Educators such as Hunt (1961) and Montessori (1965) speak of "teachable moments" and "sensitive periods" when the time is ripest for learning particular skills. Vygotsky (1962) contends that "instruction usually precedes development. The child acquires certain habits and skills in a given area before he learns to apply them consciously and deliberatively. . . . Therefore the only good kind of instruction is that which marches ahead of development and leads it; it must be aimed not so much at the ripe as at the ripening function" (pp. 101, 104). Adults are likely to be more aware of sensitive periods when they have been missed and children subsequently develop remediation needs. In a review of reading readiness, researchers suggest that readiness is a "dynamic" condition, reflected in the "flexible" interaction between teacher and child, rather than a rigid date (Downing & Thackray, 1971).

A part of the timing problem in teaching reading during kindergarten is that educators have frequently asked, "What might children better be doing with their time besides reading?" I am not sure that children could be doing anything more important with their time than to learn as much as they can in ways that make them feel human and competent. At the same time, I feel strongly that a program that focuses on the three R's, to the exclusion of rich experiences and meaningful content, is a program that tries to place disembodied tools into a child's hands. Attempting to develop skills in such a sterile atmosphere is like dosing babies with medication that kills the necessary bacteria along with the unwanted ones. While the babies' resulting digestive upsets may be reversed, we cannot be so certain of reversing as readily the "school game" of feigned attention as a façade for boredom that children learn as a by-product of content-poor early schooling.

The fact remains that learning to read is not an end in itself but a tool skill that can help to capture, support, and extend the range of possible meaning for children. It is particularly unfortunate that the pressure on minority-group children to learn to read has taken a linear direction, largely excluding inductive methods and meaning that the children can value.

It is worth looking at the most efficient ways of helping children to acquire reading skills, while retaining a medium in which content-rich activity continues to take place. The sooner children reach a level of comprehension in their reading that approaches their level of interest, the sooner reading can function as a tool. Early success breeds a feeling of competence and purposeful, natural use of this tool. As with any skill, coordination and comfort in its use accrue with practice. Strong motives to read grow out of a sense of competence, solid activities, and stimulating dialogue.

For these reasons, when children need help in recognizing the sound structure of printed symbols, many teachers offer systematic instruction in decoding skills, using the same processes that took place in the early development of spoken syntax. This instruction, however, is a small part of children's exposure to language enrichment activities.

READING PHASES

Reading specialists generally identify three main phases: recognizing printed symbols, comprehending the author's meaning, and utilizing this understanding.

Very briefly, recognizing the printed symbol requires sensory and perceptual faculties. Various conventions are understood, such as the notions that

> A word that is heard can be designated by spaces between groupings of letters.
> Symbols represent words.
> The same symbols often have the same sounds.
> Symbols are presented in a left-to-right sequence in English.

Fries (1963) suggests that the reader develops a range of habitual responses to a specific set of contrasting patterns of graphic shapes. Practice strengthens habits. Smith (1978) sees reading as learning to exclude those graphic elements that are immaterial to meaning by acquiring a habit of expectancy in relation to symbols.

Comprehending the author's meaning requires memory, association, anticipation, and generalization skills. Inasmuch as the reader brings connotative meanings to the material (Freud, 1965), it has been said that the reader who brings more to the material will get more out of it (Chall, 1967; Smith, 1978).

Just as decoding skills precede and grow parallel with comprehension skills, comprehension precedes and grows alongside readers' utilization of what they have read or heard. Beyond comprehension, reading can add to experience as readers use the understanding they already have gained to act, think about, or simply enjoy this new material. For example, reading that makes people laugh draws upon their past experience.

PRACTICE

Since practice strengthens habits, and real habits are self-motivated, your role as integrator and appreciator is to help children look forward to reading. Practice, in and of itself, does not make learning to read take place, but it does provide the time for the inductive processes that do.

At this time we should note that children who are able to learn faster require less practice. However, the more opportunities children of the same general age have to develop skills, the wider the range of abilities among them will grow. Therefore, any grouping that exists should be for a specific short-range purpose, such as a particular phonemic skill of contrasting cat and can, or the particular interest in discussing sports books of varied complexity.

When laypeople and many teachers talk about learning to read, they most often refer to practice in the decoding phase. The many methods of teaching decoding that have been used by teachers fall into two major types: the "whole" or analytic method and the "part" or synthetic method.

The "developmental basal series" marketed by many publishers are built on the method variously referred to as the "whole-word," "look-say," and "sight-word" approach. Children begin to read with whole words that may or may not be *regularly* spelled (i.e., words that have a one-to-one correspondence between each letter and a single sound, such as *fat* or *sun*, are spelled *regularly*; those that do not fit this description, such as *look, come, said*, and *house*, are *irregularly* spelled).

When children begin with irregularly spelled whole words that they are expected to memorize, they usually notice reduced cues such as the initial letter of the word, the outline of the word's letters that ascend above or descend below the line, the length of the word, or a nearby picture. One educator suggests that "sight memorizing" whole words in this way is like teaching a language that has no alphabet, where each word is a separate symbol (Tudor-Hart, 1966, pp. 28–29). In light of this observation, it is worthwhile to remember that language is first an auditory, sound-based skill, and only later becomes a visual, print-based skill.

Although some children will easily infer the regularities in the relationships between sound and print, others will need varying degrees of carefully planned instruction. When teachers begin with the whole-word method, they usually introduce "sounding out" toward the end of the first year, or after children have achieved a body of "recognition" words.

"Phonics" is the school-based instructional program for sounding out words. In phonics instruction, children are taught isolated sounds, such as "b-uh" as the sound you make when you see the letter "bee." Vowels are marked phonetically so that children can differentiate *a* as in *fat* from *a* as in *fate*. The children are told the generalizations and are expected to apply them deductively. However, I have contended throughout this book, and explicitly in chapter 3, that kindergarten children learn more readily when inductive approaches are utilized.

When we look at phonics instruction, we can see an example of how "readiness" is not related simply to maturation. Readiness to learn to read by using the deductive means of "phonics" is quite different from readiness to learn to read by using the inductive means of "phonemics." Particularly with young children, readiness needs to be directed toward, and defined by, a particular method of instruction.

The "part" or synthetic methods vary along a continuum from the traditional "phonics" instruction, with an initial introduction of isolated sounds, to "phonemic" instruction, in which contrasting patterns of sounds are bound within words. Variations in programs relate to such issues as

- Do children need to learn letter names before sound values?
- Should capital letters be used in initial teaching?
- Should nonsense syllables be employed for instructional purposes?
- Should words be built from left to right, as in Stern and Gould's (1965) use of *ma/n*, or right to left, as in Gattegno's (1968) or Fries's (1963) or Bloomfield & Barnhart's (1961) *an* to *man*?

My own viewpoint is that children can learn to read without calling letter names first. A great deal of time that involves rote learning has been devoted to calling out alphabet letter names. It does not hurt to know the letter names, but it is simply not worth belaboring. Functioning rather than labeling is primary. Of course, knowing the alphabet will help children with dictionary skills, and most of them learn the alphabet easily if they have not picked it up before reading.

Using lower-case letters in beginning reading helps children to perceive more differentiations than with capital letters alone. To start out using both capital and lower-case letters is to expect an act of conservation of sound for young children, an added burden. It is an act of faith as well as conservation to imagine that *G* and *g* have the same sound value.

I would recommend the use of whole words alone at the earliest moment in systematic phonemic instruction; therefore, building from *an* to *man* or *at* to *mat* keeps us a bit more consistently honest than the "ma/n" approach.

Since children learn to use both whole and part methods in reading, there are many connecting paths that join these two camps, if you consider the psychology of reading as a combined act of sensation, perception, and comprehension. For example, when very young children look at television, road signs, and labels on boxes, they are responding on the basis of whole-word recognitions with particular context clues. When children copy words and sentences from printed material in which they are interested, they are combining both approaches. The "language-experience" and writing approaches to reading instruction support both whole and part methods of teaching reading. In addition, after children have developed independent word attack skills, they become able to read more rapidly as they use reduced configurational clues.

SKILL LEVELS

Before looking at inductive decoding games and some principles underlying them, it will help to define a few levels of skill that teachers consider as they select specific games. *Independent reading* will refer to the ability of a child to decipher new words with a significant range of sound-symbol relations at hand. *Beginning reading* will refer to the process of "breaking the code" and acquiring these relations. *Prereading skills* will refer to the multisensory and cognitive support systems that contribute to beginning reading. The inaccurate assumption that reading readiness begins and ends in a workbook or any other preset program should be dispelled by an activity-based program.

THE ROLE OF THE TEACHER IN DECODING GAMES

Decoding games have been played as a vehicle for systematically presenting phonemic contrasts so that children can induce the patterns. These games use concrete materials with controlled variables. They are part of a larger experiential setting where children can become saturated with written as well as spoken language. Using a game format helps children to share responsibility (Hyman, 1978, p. 161) for their learning. There are five principles involved, as follows.

PRINCIPLE 1: CONTRASTING PATTERNS.   When teachers use inductive decoding games, a primary principle is to provide contrasting patterns of phonemes in whole words. The phoneme is the smallest range of sound that can change the meaning of a word. For example, the transformation of the word *mat* to *that* represents a single phonemic substitution. While *th* is written with two graphemes, it is a single sound, or phoneme.

A new phonemic variable needs to be contrasted against a background of known elements if it is to stand out and create a contrasting pattern. When there are too many variables, it is more difficult for children to induce the new phoneme.

Wherever possible, include self-checking devices in order to help children be more autonomous. Self-checking devices include puzzle pieces that fit; a picture on the opposite side of a card so that a child can check accuracy;

and opportunities to match responses against other possible responses, such as a visible chart.

PRINCIPLE 2: WHOLE WORDS. A second principle is that you need to model the new phoneme several times in the functional context of a word. When you avoid "naked consonants" by verbalizing phonemes in a functional context, subsequent blending problems can be avoided. For example, it is practically impossible to state a consonant sound alone. It comes out as a "buh" or "kuh" or "suh." When children who are taught to read by using phonics or sounding-out methods meet a new word, the "naked consonants" slow them down so that "suh-tuh-o-puh" for some children becomes distorted as *supper* rather than *stop*.

PRINCIPLE 3: CONTROLLED VARIABLES IN SEQUENCE. The third principle is that the simpler and more commonly used phonemes should be taught before the more variable and less commonly used phonemes. For example, the common sounds of the vowels such as in *bat, bet, bit, but*, and *lot* are simpler to learn than the name sounds of the vowels such as in *bake, beat, be, boat*, or *rule*, which require accompanying patterns. Similarly, consonants such as the *c* in *cat* and *face* or the *g* in *gas* and *gem* are more complex than *m* or *b*, which do not require conservation ability.

You might consider a "vicariousness index" as a corollary to the simple-to-complex sequence of sounds. Concrete materials would be used before pictures at the prereading level, and pictures would be used in the transition to written symbols. When children have trouble, simply go back toward the more concrete level.

PRINCIPLE 4: PLANNED FLEXIBILITY. The fourth principle is derived from the third. For example, in case you have planned an activity that is too difficult or too simple for your children, you should be prepared ahead of time to adapt in either direction, with either a simpler or a more complex alternative. To adapt during an ongoing activity, consider the sequence of phonemic complexity. At the beginning reading level, it is useful for you to keep writing materials handy so that you can provide a simpler alternative or add new words as you see a need arise.

You will need to be flexible about the range of abilities in your classroom, too. Many children learn to read without apparent effort, under widely different conditions. They induce the contrasting patterns of phonemes and are able to become independent readers rather smoothly. However, many others require varying amounts of systematic help in acquiring this skill. The professional teacher's greatest contribution is systematic help only when it is needed. If a child can already decode, then that child should be encouraged to select reading materials from among the fine literature that you have been able to collect.

PRINCIPLE 5: BUILD COOPERATION.   Whenever possible, it is useful to avoid, play down, or minimize competition in these games. It is more helpful to the children when you appreciate their growing skills and focused efforts. If children in kindergarten can perceive their own learning to read in a neutral, straightforward manner, perhaps fewer learning blocks will occur.

You can avoid or reduce competition by creating cards beforehand so that, for example, all the "Bingo" cards finish together. With board games, instead of each child moving a marker toward a goal, the entire group might move a single marker toward the goal, for example, "E.T. Goes Home." A competitive atmosphere may be a signal to you that children's self-confidence has been shaken.

DECODING ACTIVITIES

It is easiest for children to play decoding games when you model the games by simply doing them. Open each session by reading the new words alone first, thereby showing the children a new phonemic variable contrasted several times against known phonemes. Then model the game by taking a sample first turn.

Let's say the game involves contrasting patterns of words. The original concept is preprinted on oaktag, which remains visible to the players throughout the game, for example:

> bat : ban
> mat : man
> fat : fan
> pat : pan

A look at specific games will clarify this procedure.

PAIRS.   The game of "Pairs" or "Concentration" is particularly adaptable to any skill level. It could almost be an entire sequence in and of itself. In addition, children are highly motivated to focus on the cards that are turned face down, as they try to pick a pair. For this game, it is also possible to set different tasks for children who are playing together.

At the prereading level, a set of cards could match pairs of pictures that begin with the same sound as boy, box, or ball, or milk, man, or mouse. The model chart would consist, not of words, but of rows of other pictures that begin with one or the other sound. Still another game could be pairs of pictures that end with the same sound as hammer, fur, and car, or pairs of pictures of words that rhyme. Thus, children will be using pictures to discriminate sounds.

First, however, children need to learn to play the "Pairs" game itself. Use the following procedures:

> Model the action yourself.
>
> The first child takes a turn and turns over two cards, then replaces them if they do not make a pair.
>
> Be sure that other players see the cards that the player has turned over, before they are replaced.
>
> As the others take turns, each player tells what he or she turns up.
>
> Each player replaces the cards in the same locations if they do not match.

It is an exciting moment when the cards do match, and you can add, "You really are concentrating." The child can then place the matched pair in the group's cooperative storage container, which could be called, for example, "The Pairs Bank."

You can increase the chances for your children to be successful by constructing two identical pairs for each of three contrasts. The game can build gradually toward ten pairs. The earliest cards may be simply those pictures, shapes, or colors that are the same; or pairs of animals or flowers; or outdoor-indoor picture pairs. "Number Pairs," in which children match cards with the same number of objects on them, has been used successfully with young children (Joyce McGinn & Fredda Lynn, personal communication, 1973). Since children should not have to wait a long time for their turn, from two to four players is a sufficient number. When playing with children who have played at matching pairs and are at the beginning reading level, you might add, to an ongoing set of pictures or shapes, a pair of cards with the common sound of "a" pronounced on it, with the total number of cards newly reduced for this occasion. This procedure makes for a smooth transition. When *at* is added, then *mat*, with one set of four cards in each new game, the *a* cards can be retired. Figure 9.2 presents one possible way of sequencing words in phonemic games.

Most kindergarten children are able to handle and enjoy this activity by mid-year. By the time that *at* has retired and four or five different initial consonants with four cards each have been added, the children are ready for a reduced number of variables, the return of *at*, and the addition of *an*. The *an* family, for example, can build words with many of the same initial consonants. In this manner, the game of pairs continues to expand through the other simple consonant-vowel-consonant (cvc) word patterns such as *tan*,

Figure 9.2 A Possible Sequence of Words in Phonemic Games (Beginning Reading Level)

```
                    a:at
              at:mat:sat:pat:fat (etc.)
              pat:pan,fan (etc.) or pin,fin (etc.)
              pat:pit,sit (etc.) or pit,pin (etc.)

Adding one new variable in each game:

(First Game)     2 X 4 = a    a    a    a
                         at   at   at   at

(Second Game)    2 X 4 = at   at   at   at
                         mat  mat  mat  mat

(Third Game)     2 x 4 = mat  mat  mat  mat
                         pat  pat  pat  pat

(Fourth Game)    3 x 4 = mat  mat  mat  mat
                         pat  pat  pat  pat
                         rat  rat  rat  rat

(Sixth Game)     2 X 4 = pat:pan
                         rat:ran
                         fat:fan
                         mat:man
```

tap, *tag*, and so forth, one at a time, over a period of weeks. It is worth noting that younger children find it easier to transform *mat* to *man* than *mat* to *met*. The medial vowel seems to be sequentially more advanced.

The cvcc (consonant-consonant-vowel-consonant) patterns, such as the words *flat*, *slit*, *stop*, and *plum*, build in a similar way, as well as the cvcc patterns such as *felt*, *soft*, and *bend*. Words such as *plums* and *sends* are natural extensions of these sound patterns. Here we see a progression of common phonemic patterns in which there is a one-to-one correspondence between sound and symbol. This sequence has been loosely adapted with reference to a variety of linguistically based reading works (Bloomfield & Barnhart, 1961; Fries, 1963; Gattegno, 1968; Stern & Gould, 1965).

As children become more proficient, word families can be added gradually and in turn:

Words that end in *ill*, *ick*, and *ack*
Patterns such as *hat:hate*
Patterns in a separate activity, such as *bit:bite*
Commonly used digraphs, such as *shut*, *chip*, *this*, and *think*
Vowel digraphs represented in patterns such as *set:seat* or *got:goat*

For example, well beyond the cvc stage, the following model may comprise one game of "Pairs":

$$
\begin{array}{rcl}
\text{bet} & : & \text{beat} \\
\text{met} & : & \text{meat} \\
\text{net} & : & \text{neat} \\
\text{pet} & : & \text{peat} \\
\text{set} & : & \text{seat}
\end{array}
$$

If you try to teach several vowel digraphs together at one time, you defeat the natural induction process. Presenting more than one new variable usually depends upon deductive applications of general principles; therefore, it is inappropriate for kindergarten children. It is more natural for children to acquire their decoding skills inductively in the functional setting of a game, with one new variable added at a time.

There are "Pairs" games that can be played with children who are at the independent reading level. Few kindergarten children achieve this level, however, except the early readers who have arrived already reading.

In the course of becoming an independent reader, a child may acquire the ability to recognize some words as whole entities without really having grasped the underlying phonemic properties. There may be no comprehension problem; however, because a child has acquired the sight word does not necessarily mean that he can apply the component patterns in other words. This is one of the diagnostic problems that teachers face in later remediation situations.

At the independent reading stage, some children may need to practice with *er*, *ir*, and *ur*, or *scr* and *thr* combinations, within the context of whole words. You can contrast these various phonemic patterns by using the game of "Pairs" as well as other games described in the next section.

OTHER CARD GAMES.   Several card games such as "Slapjack" and "Go Fish" can be similarly adapted to developing sequential skills. At the prereading level, pictures can be used to acquaint children with the game format and to help them focus on similarities and differences in the sounds.

For example, in a "Slapjack" game with three children, you can ask one child to focus on pictures that begin with the same sound and another to focus on word endings. Some children show a sense of cooperation in this setting and help each other when a picture opportunity is about to be missed. This is a difficult game for most children at the prereading level, designed only for those children who manifest readiness for finer sound discriminations.

In the "Go Fish" game, each player receives four cards from the deck.

Then they ask each other for a card that goes with one of the pictures that they are holding. Before the game begins, you should share common labels for the group to use so that the picture of the mouse is not taken to be a rat, or the dish to be a plate. As each child receives a pair of pictures whose labels rhyme, that pair is set aside. Otherwise, the child "fishes" for an additional card.

Card games serve as an opportunity for you to provide initial instruction through a brief modeling of the game, taking only a minute or two. They give you great flexibility because you can add or remove cards to make the game simpler or more complex. They also provide an opportunity for the children to play later with each other independently, usually for ten to fifteen minutes or so. In this way, the children are practicing a particular skill in a playful way. A detail to keep in mind is that young children have difficulty holding a "fan" of cards. You can saw a lengthwise groove in a short piece of wood in order to provide a convenient stand for the cards, similar to a "Scrabble" stand.

Lotto board games are a good transition to beginning reading because the cards are open for all participants to see. These games capitalize on the fact that children can match word forms before they can read them. A useful lotto sequence includes (1) picture-and-word:picture-and-word; (2) picture-and-word:word; and (3) word:word.

You will need to control the gradual addition of phonemic variables carefully if these card games are to be instructional rather than mere review or testing. This should not be a major problem for you or the children, as long as you keep a flexible perspective. You can provide a model for the contrasting phonemes in these games, much as you did for the "Pairs" game, using a preprinted model chart. You will not be alone in this, because children will occasionally model for other children and show them how to play a particular game.

BOARD GAMES.   Board games represent still another form in which decoding instruction can take place. You can adapt games that use:

> Dice or a die made of a wooden cube
> A set of cards
> A spinner card
> A set of tokens

These games can be adjusted to the various reading levels that have been mentioned previously. Dice or spinners direct players to move a token along a path that is marked on the board. When the commercial "Twister" game is adapted, for example, the markings on the spinner card and the playing "board" represent phonemic patterns that the children are ready to use. You can construct your own "Twister" boards by attaching together four large paper bags from the food market with masking tape.

In other games, one-inch wooden cubes can serve as substitute dice, with words taped onto the cubes. You can prepare a set of cards that direct the movement of pieces to sections of the board marked for particular words. When cards or cubes are marked for directions, you can change the game more easily by changing the cards or cubes rather than an entire board.

There is also a flexible aspect to using cards with a spinner device that points to where a player will go. Each of several concentric circles can be designated for each of the players. In this way, you can individualize the game.

There are many imaginative, colorful themes and arrangements that you can use when you custom design board games for the children with whom you work. "Snoopy Goes Home," "Rainbow with a Pot of Gold," "Baseball," "Haunted House," "Care Bears," and popular television character themes can be developed. Since it is time consuming to develop these games, it is worthwhile to use sturdy materials, to cover them with clear plastic, and to create "universal" boards on which you can change cards, spinners, and dice. These materials become part of your collected stock of other direct activities that children can find so stimulating.

GAMES WITH OBJECTS.   You will need games with objects, particularly for those children who need help with visual and auditory discrimination in their daily activities. Children can sort objects that begin with the same sound as *house* and *hat* into the brightly colored "horse" box while they place objects that begin with the same sound as *feather* and *fig* into the "fruit" box. Also, they can sort objects that rhyme. Notice how the use of models that contrast, rather than the isolated sound or letter name, are sufficient for you to grasp how the sorting works.

Another sorting device that has prestige appeal in the child's culture is a cabinet of small transparent plastic drawers usually found in carpentry shops. You can tape a word beginning with a different sound on each drawer. Inside the drawer are miniature objects that begin with the same sound. Children can empty a few drawers onto a cloth and sort the objects into the drawers, or remove objects from a drawstring bag and sort them into the drawers.

SOUND AND WORD READINESS
For a few children who enter kindergarten, sound itself needs to be reinforced as a conscious "figure" in their background experiences. In recent years, teachers have become concerned that some children are coming to

school needing such experiences. For these children, instruction may re-create the earliest kinds of interactions between parent and child, when the parent mentions body parts, labels objects, and sings Mother Goose rhymes.

Just as the new parents' language and music help to bring the baby into the world of sounds, you can help children to differentiate sounds through speaking and singing with them. Just as the teacher of very young children bathes them in *verbal* labels and descriptions, kindergarten teachers need to soak them with *visual* labels and descriptions in functional ways. You can extend children's awareness of language as an auditory stimulant by the general sound awareness of their environment. Children can simply close their eyes, focus on sounds, and then share their imagery.

When children compare and seriate sounds and then translate these comparisons into creative movements through space, they are building their imagery system and their ability to transpose experiences from one sensory source into another. In a parallel way, written symbols involve the translation of meaningful auditory experiences into visual symbols.

When children can interchange words more freely, there is much greater flexibility and scope to their speech. Similarly, when children have the sense that they can interchange phonemes more freely, their reading skill gains more flexibility and scope. The teacher who helps a child to use contrasting patterns as a basis for self-correction through comparison does much to help that child toward becoming an independent reader.

In activities that focus on contrasting sound patterns, children are using *recognition* skills. Recognition skills are easier to apply than *recall* skills. After children have played at recognizing and classifying objects by sound, there-fore, ask them to find other objects in the room, or in a box, that rhyme with *hair* and *bear*, or begin with the same sound as *wolf* and *wish*. Teachers frequently use the playful, "I Spy" game, with a challenge to find "something that begins with the same sound as *Deborah*," or "someone whose name ends the same as the name *Eden*."

In still another step, children can recall objects that are not visible. For example, riddles with rhymes require skills in recall: "I love the beach but I cannot eat it. I can eat a (peach)," or, "This begins with the same sound as *Daddy*, and I can play with it. It is a (doll or dog)." Riddles delight youngsters, particularly those that they create beyond the range of adult sophistication. Kindergarten children are active participants in these kinds of activities.

After children have dealt with objects and pictures and learned through repetition that the teacher uses the terms *word* and *object* to mean the same thing, most will gain a consciousness of *word*. Young children and dis-advantaged children, however, may perceive phrases or sentences as welded rather than as words that function as interchangeable parts.

The sense of "wordness" begins at the auditory level, when you label and discuss objects. The idea of a word takes on added meaning when the children see you write words. It helps children to understand when you talk about what you are doing as you are doing it.

You can point along a line of print as you read a story. "Big Books" (Hunter-Grundin & Grundin, 1983) are a help. It is an interesting variation to read stories or poems using an overhead projector, pointing to the words as you read (Anderson, 1968; Moffett, 1968). This medium helps to focus attention. To further support this idea of a word, you can ask the children beforehand to guess how many words they will hear and then to share their findings (Mackay, Thompson, & Schaub, 1978).

On a visual level, you cannot take it for granted that all children understand that a space signifies the separation between words. Children have to be exposed to this notion. Nor can you expect them to orient their reading and writing in left-to-right, top-to-bottom directions unless they have learned it functionally.

From the earliest times, teachers of young children have written a child's name on his drawing and talked about it. Whenever writing is under way, note aloud that it begins at the left. When you create board games, make the tokens move from the left to the right and from the top of the board downward. Notice that many commercial board games start at the bottom of the board and so are less suited for reinforcing the left-to-right, top-to-bottom orientation that young children need to acquire.

With all this repetition, it is still natural for kindergarten children to make written or visual reversals occasionally. Most of this passes by the time a child reaches the age of seven years.

ORGANIZATION OF THE FOUR COMPONENTS

You can see children make significant progress in the four components of a kindergarten reading and language program when you have a longer day. Ideally, the language arts and reading can be pursued throughout the school day. While you have provided a reading area, a writing area, and a teacher's instructional area, reading and language activities go on in many other areas of the classroom as well.

Steps in Integrating Sentence Makers

Children can choose to use the *Breakthrough to Literacy* sentence makers throughout the activity times once they have received their own personal sentence maker. The following are the steps that teachers have found helpful:

IDENTIFY CHILDREN.   After the first six or ten weeks of the school year, when children have learned the classroom traffic patterns and procedures, identify a small group of two to five youngsters who have shown during language experience activities that they have a recognition vocabulary of twelve to twenty words.

DICTATE AND COPY.   Ask each child to dictate a statement that you can write on an illustration he or she has made. Draw the child's attention to how you are writing, commenting on the top-to-bottom, left-to-right movements and the lines and curves. Write one line at a time and ask the child to copy it directly below your writing. Notice which children write with ease and interest and where you may need to provide handwriting help.

INTRODUCE THE SENTENCE MAKER.   Bring together a small group and show them a sentence maker. Talk about a sentence that they would want to set on the stand. Demonstrate setting a sentence on the stand, then read it. Demonstrate how to replace the words in the folder. Then encourage children to compose a few sentences together, taking turns setting out the words and reading them. Each time they finish a sentence they can take turns slipping the word cards back into the folder.

PERSONAL SENTENCE MAKER.   After several sessions in the small group, distribute personal sentence makers to the group members and review procedures for use and storage.

CIRCULATE.   As you circulate during activity periods, review procedures as needed and provide help with personal words. Appreciate thinking and perseverance.

REVIEW WORD CARDS.   Every week or two, review the word cards in each child's sentence maker and remove those that he or she cannot read without the sentence context. This should take place with a relaxed attitude. Appreciate what the child can read.

IDENTIFY CHILDREN.   Using these procedures, introduce other small groups or individuals to the sentence makers.

Small-Group and Individual Instruction

Language arts and reading instruction in the full-day kindergarten is largely auditory and social. Many legitimate opportunities exist for children to talk to each other and to the teacher in small groups and one to one. In fact, most instruction takes place in small groups and with individuals rather than with the entire class. If some children come to you already reading independently, it is a waste of their time to sit with other children who are engaged in sorting sounds or matching words. At other times, however, they might be in a discussion group with the other children because they share a common interest in animals or motors.

In order for the writing activities to remain relevant and inviting, children and teachers need to pace themselves in flexible ways. Therefore, small-group and individual work make sense. During these contacts, teachers accept children's work as they write about their own experiences in divergent ways. Whether a teacher has the sentence makers available or uses a writing process without them, the important purpose in either case is to help children ease the flow of their own ideas and feelings into written forms. Lessons in decoding or other technical skills should take place at separate times.

Integrating Literature

The kindergarten child's language can grow in a context of rich opportunities to make new connections in active ways. A most important part of this context is exposure to a fine quality of children's literature, thoughtfully displayed and dramatically presented by the teacher. Reading material should be available for children to select and look at independently as well as at daily whole-group storytelling times. Among its many values, literature serves children as a model and an inspiration for writing.

Children develop personal motives for reading when they have the time and opportunity to choose from stimulating materials. In the longer school day, kindergarten teachers simply have more time and opportunity to share their joy in reading and love of beautiful language. Kindergarten children can participate in "book clubs" in which small groups of children share their pleasure in reading about similar topics of interest. These activities advertise the pleasure of particular books. After all, the major point of language instruction is to create comfortable self-directed readers and writers.

As you work with kindergarten children in language instruction, it is important to remember not to expect instant results. The impact of whatever you have done to expose children to activities for which they appear receptive may become apparent to you days or weeks later. Since they develop so quickly, your wait is limited. You can feel successful when you have helped children to feel successful and competent by appreciating what they have tried to do as well as what they have accomplished.

PART III

Conclusion

10

Establishing a Full–Day Kindergarten

ONGOING ARGUMENTS ABOUT FULL–DAY KINDERGARTEN

Impact on First Grade

If you could be a fly on the wall of the teacher's room and hear the first-grade teachers talking about the new graduates of the full-day kindergarten program, you might hear the following interchange:

MS. A: Something must be going on in that longer kindergarten day! I'm not so sure it wasn't easier before this all started. Most of the children come in reading or readier to read, but there are still some children who need lots of work, so I end up right back where we used to be before the full-day kindergarten. I want to be sure that everybody gets my approach to phonics in a systematic way. But these children seem so much more restless and less willing to pay attention. I'm not sure that there is any advantage to the longer day. It just ends up being a babysitting service for parents, and more trouble for us.

MS. B: I couldn't agree more. You know, I have been having a rough time, too. I'll ask the kids to do something and, more often than not, they seem to get busy but I get the feeling that they're doing something else. We've really been locking horns quite a bit. Finally, I realized that they were ending up where I wanted them to be, but they got there in different ways. Since I realized that they were just doing it differently from the way children did it in the past, I have been more comfortable with them. But I still feel as if I'm pushing uphill about a lot of things that used to go so smoothly.

These teachers were revealing more than they might have intended. Ms. A implicitly admitted that most children who had attended the full-day kindergarten were advanced in their reading. She also showed that she was focused on the few who were least accomplished. She appeared able to use only a single approach to teaching reading and was not prepared to individualize instruction or to plan for small-group instruction. Ms. B admitted an early resistance to working in diverse ways, feeling more comfortable when everybody did things in the same way. However, she was able to appreciate that the children who came from the full-day program seemed to be more independent than children had been in the past, even if that meant a somewhat grudging adjustment on her part.

If only kindergarten teachers and informed principals could communicate better with first-grade teachers, it might just be possible to help them to focus on the children's accomplishments: accrued skill development and independent, diverse ways of working. Perhaps better continuity between the full-day kindergarten and first grade could take place if there were an adjustment period and staff development for first-grade teachers, such as

> Visits to the kindergarten by first-grade teachers
> Videotapes that emphasize how successful kindergarten teachers manage varied teaching with small groups
> Sharing of techniques and activities that kindergarten teachers use to stimulate children's independence and responsibility, with collaborative efforts made to adapt these for first-grade use

Other arguments for and against the full-day kindergarten surface in community attitudes toward the education of young children. Kindergarten teachers must deal with the inevitable disparagement of their function as "babysitting" or "only playing," countering it with explanations of what children are doing that is meaningful and valuable to their learning and overall development, including their transition to first grade.

Affluence and Achievement

A significant issue has been the impact of the longer day on children from different socioeconomic backgrounds. There is a growing body of evidence, based on standardized testing, suggesting that the greatest comparative benefit of the longer day seems to take place for children who are less affluent (Lawrence Public Schools, 1983, 1984). This does not negate the benefit, albeit comparatively smaller, that children from more affluent homes might experience.

The impact on all children should not be measured and compared only by test scores. There needs to be a reasoned consideration of how children, even affluent children, would be spending their time otherwise. There would likely be more time for television and less time for social interaction and collaborative work with other children. The myth of a doting parent or other adult playing games and having significant in-depth conversations with children at home needs to be exposed. That's usually not what happens. When both parents are wage earners; when families move often; when we live in a society that includes single-parent households, few siblings, increased isolation in expanded suburbia, and less contact with grandparents and other extended family, we need to rethink the myth of what children find when they come home. At the same time, we need to assure that children's time in school is used in worthwhile ways, to help them become increasingly human, civilized, and successful.

ADMINISTRATIVE CONDITIONS

With all of these considerations, it is reasonable to suggest that a full-day kindergarten can be a positive force for development. While it will not hurt children to continue in a half-day program that is appropriate to their development, it is my contention that children can benefit by participating in an appropriate full-day kindergarten. Having said this, there are some qualifying administrative conditions that characterize successful full-day programs.

ADJUSTMENT TO SCHOOL.   The first month of the school year should begin with a gradual introduction to kindergarten, starting with part of a morning and then half a day for a few weeks, before adding the full-day schedule. In some districts, teachers make home visits, meeting parents and children.

PARENT OPTIONS.   Parents can choose a half day. Since states do not mandate compulsory full-day kindergarten, this is not a legal issue. In practice, a handful of parents have taken this option initially. In the Hewlett and Lawrence, New York, school districts it was found that 3 percent of eligible families chose the half-day program in the first year that the full day was offered (Joyce McGinn, personal communication, 1984; Sheila Terens, personal communication, 1984). One or two parents declined the full day in subsequent years.

SCHOOL DISTRICT OPTIONS.   The school district professionals should reserve the right to decide if an individual child may need a different schedule. For example, when most kindergarten children in the full-day program have made an initial adjustment, a staff team may decide on a modified individual schedule for some. Individual children may be invited to attend the full day after a few months of half-day and extended-day participation. Sometimes an individual child will attend half a day on Mondays only and then full days during the rest of the week. In other cases, a family crisis may suggest to adults that an individual child needs to spend a few weeks mid-year on a shorter schedule.

PARENT SERVICES.   Teachers should confer with parents often. The principal and teachers can use parents as resources. They should plan with them for cultural activities at the school and keep them informed about, and involved with, curriculum activities. The school district can offer parent-education activities and parent/toddler programs, when there is an early childhood center.

STAFF DEVELOPMENT AND PLANNING.   Returning kindergarten teachers and newly hired ones should be involved together in planning the opening of school and the kindergarten program. There also should be a provision for ongoing dialogue concerning the program, particularly during the first two years. This requires additional "preparation" time for teachers, in order to stimulate this dialogue and to make individual preparations. After the program has been installed, there should be dialogue with the first-grade teachers who will be inheriting the kindergarten classes.

CLASS SIZE AND BUDGET.   Class size in the full-day kindergarten should not represent an increase from the half-day.
    The budget should be adequate to meet some of the following start-up considerations:

Additional classroom space. Furnishing a new kindergarten classroom may cost between $3,000 and $8,000.
Additional salaries. Allocations must be made to cover kindergarten teacher and lunchroom aide salaries and fringe benefits.
Additional expendable materials. The arts and writing consumables double in cost for each classroom.
Other facilities. Lunchroom services may need to be increased.
Transportation. The midday bus service budget will be smaller for a full-day program. Additional bus service will be needed at the start and end of the kindergarten day.
State aid. It may be possible to gain an increase in state aid.

HIGHLIGHTS OF THE FULL-DAY
KINDERGARTEN CURRICULUM

Once all of the emotional and political dust has settled, an ongoing argument regarding the longer day is that there is a need to outline how the additional time should be used and what the curriculum for the full kindergarten day should be. How much content and skill work should full-day kindergarten children do? This book has been an attempt to respond to this question, so in this section I will review the main components of the experiential, humane, full-day kindergarten curriculum that has been presented.

The full-day kindergarten curriculum design in this book focuses on four interconnected features: (1) skills and attitudes, (2) child development, (3) content in disciplines, and (4) interdisciplinary activity.

SKILLS AND ATTITUDES.   The additional time in the full-day kindergarten is an opportunity for children to have more extended instruction and develop a broad range of skills. Children learn these skills in playful ways as they use concrete materials and have content-rich activities.

Through the use of concrete materials, kindergarten children acquire mathematics concepts as they solve problems and learn about mathematical relationships that develop out of their active experiences. Cruikshank et al. (1980), Kamii (1984), and the Nuffield Mathematics Project (1970) are meaningful sources of mathematical ideas.

Language and reading development take place inductively as children develop self-directed motives for learning and using these skills. The four components of a full-day kindergarten reading and language program include (1) the environmental language-experience approach; (2) writing into reading, including the use of *Breakthrough to Literacy* materials; (3) a plentiful, exciting exposure to fine-quality literature; and (4) an inductive, playful approach to decoding games.

Problem solving and connection-making take place as children encounter cognitive dissonance and their teacher uses analogies systematically in teaching. Children become increasingly comfortable with ambiguity and differences of viewpoint, since they are setting problems as well as seeking solutions to questions that have more than only one possible answer. In turn, they become more able to question, transform their ways of thinking, and engage in critical thinking.

Social learning, skills, and attitudes develop through legitimate social activity; therefore, exemplary teachers plan cooperative learning activities, among children in the kindergarten as well as with children of different ages.

CHILD DEVELOPMENT.   Children learn best when certain conditions are present: inductive experiences, cognitive dissonance, social interaction, physical experiences, play, and a feeling of competence. Teachers who create such conditions are not "metacognitive nudgers." Rather, they respect children as human beings who learn by actively constructing their own thinking. Teachers create an environment where such learning can take place.

CONTENT IN DISCIPLINES.   Content matter for kindergarten activities is planned with consideration of the ways of knowing in disciplines and the generation of related interdisciplinary activities across time. These activities provide the content upon which children can apply and practice skills. Effective teachers plan such worthwhile activities at a pace that keeps content fresh and helps children to improve and expand their skills in ways that feel successful.

INTERDISCIPLINARY ACTIVITY.   There is an opportunity to reflect on the natural ways in which kindergarten children connect their experiences and to respect the interdisciplinary routes that they follow. Kindergarten teachers and children can use the tools of many disciplines in their activity-based program. Exemplary teachers engage in the reform of kindergarten education so that it takes on its own unique form, rich in content and in concrete activities in which skills and tools are applied.

PROPOSED WAYS TO PLAN: DAILY, WEEKLY, AND BEYOND

Effective planning requires knowing how often activities should occur. In Figure 10.1, activities are categorized by frequency, based on what teachers have generally found to be reasonable for each curriculum area. You may prefer more emphasis in some areas, and you may want to adjust the time spans. The timing of activities is based on an average expectancy because holidays and other events may take place at irregular intervals.

DAILY ACTIVITIES.   These include a whole-group story, gym and outdoor exercise, and music or movement education. Individual options at different developmental levels should be available in art, sociodrama, science, mathematics, and reading/language arts. There should be small-group instruction in reading/language arts, mathematics, science, social science, and in the arts.

WEEKLY ACTIVITIES.   A mathematics homework sheet should go home with each child. The class should take a brief trip near or in school,

Figure 10.1: Planning System for Frequency of Activities

ACTIVITY	FREQUENCY				
	Every Day	Every Week	Every 2 Weeks	Every Month	Once in a While
Story	W*				
Physical education	W				
Music & movement	W				
Reading	S,I				
Mathematics	S,I				
-Homework		W			
Writing	S,I				
-Experience Chart		3/wk.			
Arts	S,I				
Sociodrama	S				
-Role Playing		W			
Science	S,I				
Cooking			S	W	
Celebrations			W		
Fairs, performances					W
Trips					
-Short, 10-30 min.		W			
-Several hours				W	
Resource visitor			W		
Note to each parent				W	
New activity or material in each area		S			
New teacher-made game			S		
New display		W			
New snack food		W			

*W=whole-group activity; S=small-group activity; I=individual activity.

of 10 to 30 minutes. A new science activity, social science activity, and art material should be provided. Set up a fresh bulletin board or library display, or give a mysterious clue to a new topic or book. Create a new snack food preparation.

BIWEEKLY ACTIVITIES. Meet a resource person and develop interview questions on an experience chart together with the children. A new, teacher-made, customized game in reading or mathematics should be provided. Create an interdisciplinary cooking project, including multicultural, language arts, science, and mathematics involvement. This could be incorporated into a celebration.

MONTHLY ACTIVITIES. Take a class trip of a few hours or more. Plan a special event or celebrate birthdays, with summer birthdays conducted during June and September parties. Each parent should receive a personal one-line note from you regarding her or his child's school progress.

OCCASIONAL ACTIVITIES.   These include whole-class fairs, assembly program presentations, a class museum, or a parent breakfast.

PURPOSEFUL TEACHING

Effective full-day kindergarten teachers integrate their plans by purposefully applying their teaching values. Four major purposes of teaching, which have been discussed at length in this book, are

To encourage a sense of competence and successful achievement
To accommodate different learning strengths
To strengthen cognitive, physical, social, and emotional development
To encourage imagination

In order to encourage a sense of competence and successful achievement, teachers will spend most of their time during the longer day in instruction with small groups of children. There are some whole-group activities and individual teacher-child work.

In order to accommodate different learning strengths, similar content and skills should be taught in different ways. Kindergarten teachers need to recognize that kindergarten is often the first school experience for children; therefore, the kindergarten becomes the original model of mainstreaming. Children come to school with varied and special developmental learning needs. These needs are more readily met in a decentralized system of classroom management.

In order to strengthen cognitive, physical, social, and emotional development, teachers can build into activities the need for collaboration among children. There will be plenty of learning taking place in the full-day kindergarten, more than was possible in the half day, as children work cooperatively on projects with each other. Their collaboration can add strength and variety to their learning experiences.

In order to encourage imagination, there should be provision made for children to spend some time each day during which they can schedule and pace themselves, and during which they can choose to be alone or find privacy in the classroom environment.

REFLECTIONS

The full-day kindergarten is not a stepping-stone to first grade. It is not a traditional first grade begun one year earlier, nor is it an extended nursery school. Ideally, it is a unique time with its own distinct knowledge base and practices that reflect a continuum of child development.

If you begin to plan for a full-day kindergarten and you already have an integrated half-day kindergarten, you are likely to extend this integrated outlook to the full day. If, on the other hand, you have already been using largely whole-group instruction and lots of workbooks, worksheets, and teacher-directed activities, you are likely to extend this segmented outlook to the full day.

The time is ripe for reexamining such basic attitudes. You have an opportunity in either a full- or half-day kindergarten to reform kindergarten education so that it takes on its own unique form. This book has looked at the full-day kindergarten in terms of the quality of time and the real instructional time that children and teachers experience.

There are so many activities to choose from that your only problem will be an economic one — limited time and seemingly unlimited choices. Your responsibility remains one of trying to make the kindergarten year the best you can for your group. Since young children naturally construct meanings in their own ways, it bears reiterating one more time that different children doing different things at different times can have equivalent experiences. Therefore, the activities in which you engage together follow the methods of inquiry and ways of working across varied content fields. The form that experiences take is relative to the capacity of the learners. You remain with the task of choosing the most relevant activities from among those that are most reasonable.

You can take this opportunity to create a place and time in which young children can feel successful, can take responsibility for many activities, and can legitimately learn collaboratively with other children and with you, their teacher. If you take this option, then your children may well have an opportunity to look forward to great expectations in their lives.

References

References to Children's Literature

"Great Books" for Beginning Readers

Index

References

Abraham, K. G., & Lieberman, E. "Should Barbie go to preschool?" *Young Children*, January 1985, *10*, 12 14.

Adcock, E. P., et al. *A comparison of half-day and full-day kindergarten classes on academic achievement.* Baltimore: Maryland State Department of Education, 1980.

Anderson, V. D. *Reading and young children.* New York: Macmillan, 1968.

Aschner, M. J. "The analysis of verbal interaction in the classroom." In A. Bellack (Ed.), *Theory and research in teaching.* New York: Bureau of Publications, Teachers College, Columbia University, 1963.

Baratta-Lorton, M. *Mathematics their way.* Menlo Park, CA: Addison-Wesley, 1976.

Barnes, B. J., & Hill, S. "Should young children work with microcomputers — LOGO before Lego?" *The Computing Teacher*, May 1983, 11–14.

Barnes, S., & Edwards, S. *More effective and less effective student teaching experiences: Qualitative comparison of extreme groups.* Paper presented at the annual meeting of the American Educational Research Association, New Orleans, LA, April 1984.

Bertalanffy, L. von. *Problems of life.* New York: Harper Torchbooks, 1960.

Biggs, E. *Mathematics for younger children.* New York: Citation, 1971.

Bird, J. *Science from water play.* Milwaukee: Macdonald-Raintree, 1978.

Bloomfield, L., & Barnhart, C. L. *Let's read.* Detroit: Wayne State University Press, 1961.

Brandt, R. "On reading, writing, and computers: A conversation with John Henry Martin." *Educational Leadership*, October 1981, 60–64.

Briscoe, M. G. "Tides, solutions and nutrients." *Nature*, November 1, 1984, p. 15.

Brown, R., & Bellugi, U. "Three processes in the child's acquisition of syntax." In E. H. Lenneberg (Ed.), *New directions in the study of language* (pp. 131–61). Cambridge, MA: M.I.T. Press, 1964.

Bruner, J. S. *The process of education.* Cambridge, MA: Harvard University Press, 1961.

Bruner, J. S. *Toward a theory of instruction.* Cambridge, MA: Harvard University Press, 1966.

Buber, M. *I and thou* (2nd ed.). (T. G. Smith, Trans.) New York: Charles Scribner's Sons, 1958 (1923).

Burg, K. "The microcomputer in the kindergarten." *Young Children*, March 1984, 28–33.

Calkins, L. M. *The art of teaching writing*. Portsmouth, NH: Heinemann, 1986.

Cazden, C. "Language programs for young children: Notes from England and Wales." In C. S. Lavatelli (Ed.), *Language training in early childhood education* (pp. 119–53). Urbana, IL: ERIC, 1971.

Cazden, C. *Child language and education*. New York: Holt, Rinehart & Winston, 1972.

Cazden, C. (Ed.). *Language in early childhood education* (rev. ed.). Washington, DC: National Association for the Education of Young Children, 1981.

Chall, J. *Learning to read: The great debate*. New York: McGraw-Hill, 1967.

Chomsky, C. "Write now, read later." *Childhood Education*, 1971, *47*, 296–99.

Chomsky, C. "Stages in language development and reading exposure." *Harvard Educational Review*, February 1972, *42*, 1–33.

Chomsky, N. *Aspects of a theory of syntax*. Cambridge, MA: M.I.T. Press, 1965.

Chomsky, N. *Language and mind* (enlarged ed.). New York: Harcourt Brace Jovanovich, 1972.

Chukovsky, K. *From two to five*. (M. Morton, Trans. & Ed.) Berkeley: University of California Press, 1963.

Clark, K., & Clark, M. "The development of consciousness of self and the emergence of racial identity in Negro preschool children." *Journal of Social Psychology*, 1939, *10*, 591–99.

Clay, M. M. *Observing young readers*. Exeter, NH: Heinemann, 1982.

Copeland, R. W. *How children learn mathematics* (4th ed.). New York: Macmillan, 1984.

Craig, G. S. *Science for the elementary school teacher*. New York: Ginn, 1958.

Cratty, B. J. *Learning and playing*. Freeport, NY: Educational Activities, n.d. (post-1968).

Cruikshank, D. E., Fitzgerald, D. L., & Jensen, L. R. *Young children learning mathematics*. Boston: Allyn & Bacon, 1980.

Cuffaro, H. "Microcomputers in education: Why is earlier better?" In D. Sloan (Ed.), *The computer in education: A critical perspective* (pp. 21–30). New York: Teachers College Press, 1985.

Cullinan, B., Karrer, M. K., & Pillar, A. M. *Literature and the child*. New York: Harcourt Brace Jovanovich, 1981.

Davidson, P. S. *Idea book for Cuisenaire rods at the primary level*. New Rochelle, NY: Cuisenaire Co. of America, 1977.

Davis, A., & Dollard, J. *Children of bondage*. Washington, DC: American Council on Education, 1940.

Developmental Learning Materials Teaching Resources. *Instructional Materials Catalog*. Allen, TX: DLM, 1985.

Dewey, J. *How we think*. Boston: D. C. Heath, 1933.

Dewey, J. *Art as experience*. New York: Capricorn, 1958 (1934).

Dienes, Z. *Building up mathematics*. London, England: Hutchinson Educational, 1960.

Dienes, Z. *Mathematics through the senses*. Boston: Fernhill, 1973.

Dinkmeyer, D., & Dinkmeyer, D., Jr. *Developing understanding of self and others* (rev. ed.). Circle Pines, MN: American Guidance Service, 1982.

Disney, Walter (Producer). *Dumbo* [Film]. (J. Grant & D. Huemer, Adapters.) 1941.

Downie, D., Slesnick, T., & Stenmark, J. K. *Math for girls and other problem solvers*. Berkeley, CA: Lawrence Hall of Science, University of California, 1981.

Downing, J., & Thackray, D. V. *Reading readiness*. London, England: University of London Press, 1971.

Durkin, D. *Children who read early*. New York: Teachers College Press, 1966.

Educational Teaching Aids. *Mathematics catalog*. Chicago: Educational Teaching Aids, 1985.

Eisner, E. (Ed.). *Learning and teaching the ways of knowing: Part II*. Eighty-fourth yearbook of the National Society for the Study of Education. Chicago: Chicago University Press, 1985.

Elementary Science Study Teachers' Guides. *Animals in the classroom*. New York. McGraw-Hill, 1970. (a)

_____. *Pattern blocks*. New York: McGraw-Hill, 1970. (b)

_____. *Drops, streams, and containers*. New York: McGraw-Hill, 1971. (a)

_____. *Match and measure*. New York: McGraw-Hill, 1971. (b)

_____. *Attribute games and problems*. New York: McGraw-Hill, 1974. (a)

_____. *Eggs and tadpoles*. New York: McGraw-Hill, 1974. (b)

_____. *Growing seeds*. New York: McGraw-Hill, 1974. (c)

_____. *Primary balancing*. New York: McGraw-Hill, 1976. (a)

_____. *Tangrams*. New York: McGraw-Hill, 1976. (b)

_____. *Changes*. New York: McGraw-Hill, 1976. (c)

Elliott, J. *The implications of classroom research for the professional development of teachers*. Unpublished manuscript. Cambridge, England: Cambridge Institute of Education, 1979.

Engel, B. S. "Between feeling and fact: Listening to children." *Harvard Educational Review*, August 1984, *54*, 304–14.

Ervin, S. M. "Imitation and structural change in children's language." In E. H. Lenneberg (Ed.), *New directions in the study of language* (pp. 163–89). Cambridge, MA: M.I.T. Press, 1964.

Fagot, B. I. *Teacher reinforcement of feminine-preferred behavior revisited*. Paper presented at the biennial meeting of the Society for Research in Child Development, Denver, CO, April 1975.

Fennema, E. (Ed.). *Mathematics education research*. Washington, DC: Association for Supervision and Curriculum Development, 1981.

Ferreiro, E., & Teberosky, A. *Literacy before schooling*. (K. G. Castro, Trans.) Exeter, NH: Heinemann, 1982.

Festinger, L. *A theory of cognitive dissonance*. New York: Harper & Row, 1957.

Feuerstein, R. *Instrumental enrichment*. Baltimore: University Park Press, 1980.

Fleuegelman, A. *The new games book*. Garden City, NY: Doubleday, 1976.

Fox, G. T., Jr. *Why educational policies must redistribute the work of teaching, teacher education and educational research*. Unpublished manuscript, 1984.

Fox, G. T., Jr., Anglin, L., Fromberg, D., & Grady, M. *Collaboration: Lessons learned from experience.* Washington, DC: American Association of Colleges for Teacher Education, 1986.

Frederiksen, N. "Implications of cognitive theory for instruction in problem solving." *Review of Educational Research,* Fall 1984, *54,* 363–407.

Freud, S. *The interpretation of dreams.* (J. Strachey, Trans. & Ed.) New York: Basic Books, 1965 (1932).

Fries, C. C. *The structure of English.* New York: Harcourt Brace & World, 1952.

Fries, C. C. *Linguistics and reading.* New York: Holt, Rinehart & Winston, 1963.

Fromberg, D. P. *The reactions of kindergarten children to intellectual challenges.* Unpublished doctoral dissertation. New York: Teachers College, Columbia University, 1965.

Fromberg, D. P. "Syntax model games and language in early education." *Journal of Psycholinguistics Research,* July 1976, *5,* 245–60.

Fromberg, D. P. *Early childhood education: A perceptual models curriculum.* New York: John Wiley, 1977.

Frost, J. L. "Children in a changing society." *Childhood Education,* March/April 1986, *4,* 242–49.

Frye, N. *The stubborn structure.* Ithaca, NY: Cornell University Press, 1970.

Gattegno, C. *Teaching reading with words in color.* New York: Educational Solutions, 1968.

Genovese, E. P. *Roll, Jordan, roll: The world the slaves made.* New York: Pantheon, 1974.

Gilliland, K. "EQUALS in computer technology." *The Computing Teacher,* 1984, pp. 42–44.

Gleason, H. A., Jr. *Linguistics and English grammar.* New York: Holt, Rinehart & Winston, 1965.

Gleason, J. B. "An experimental approach to improving children's communicative ability." In C. Cazden (Ed.), *Language in early childhood education* (rev. ed.) (pp. 77–82). Washington, DC: National Association for the Education of Young Children, 1981.

Gleick, J. "The man who reshaped geometry." *The New York Times Magazine,* December 8, 1985, pp. 64ff.

Goodlad, J. I. *A place called school.* New York: McGraw-Hill, 1984.

Goodman, M. E. *Race awareness in young children.* New York: Collier, 1964.

Gordon, W. J. J. *Synectics: The development of creative capacity.* New York: Collier, 1961.

Gordon, W. J. J., & Poze, T. *Making it strange.* New York: Harper & Row, 1968.

Gordon, W. J. J., & Poze, T. *Strange and familiar.* Cambridge, MA: Porpoise Books, 1972.

Gordon, W. J. J., & Poze, T. *The metaphorical way of learning and knowing.* Cambridge, MA: Porpoise Books, 1973.

Gordon, W. J. J., & Poze, T. *The art of the possible.* Cambridge, MA: Porpoise Books, 1980.

Grant, G. S. (Ed.). *In praise of diversity: Multicultural classroom applications.*

Omaha, NE: Teachers Corps, Center for Urban Education, The University of Nebraska, 1977.

Graves, D., & Stuart, V. *Write from the start*. New York: E. P. Dutton, 1985.

Guilford, J. P. "Three faces of intellect." *American Psychologist*, 1959, *14*, 469–79.

Guttentag, M. "The social psychology of sex-role intervention." In B. Sprung (Ed.), *Perspectives on nonsexist early childhood education*. New York: Teachers College Press, 1978.

Harrison, B. G. *Unlearning the lie: Sexism in school*. New York: William Morrow, 1974.

Haskell, L. L. *Art in the early childhood years*. Columbus, OH: Charles E. Merrill, 1984.

Hawkins, D. "Messing about in science." *Science and Children*, February 1965, *2*, 5–9.

Hess, R. D. "Political socialization in the schools." *Harvard Educational Review*, Summer 1968, *38*, 528–36.

Hess, R. D., & Torney, J. V. *The development of political attitudes in children*. Chicago: Aldine, 1967.

Hill, S. "Beware of commercials: Young children may not need microcomputers." *Australian Journal of Early Childhood*, September 1985, *10*(3), 16–21.

Hofstadter, D. R. *Gödel, Escher, Bach: An eternal golden braid*. New York: Viking, 1980.

Holt, M., & Dienes, Z. *Let's play math*. New York: Walker, 1973.

Honig, A. S. "Television and kindergarten children." *Young Children*, May 1983, *38*, 63–76.

Horney, K. *New ways in psychoanalysis*. New York: W. W. Norton, 1939.

Humphreys, J. W. *A longitudinal study of the effectiveness of full day kindergarten*. Evansville, IN: Evansville-Vanderburgh School Corp., 1983.

Hunt, J. McV. *Intelligence and experience*. New York: Ronald Press, 1961.

Hunter-Grundin, E., & Grundin, H. S. *3L: Language, literature, and literacy*. Louisville, KY: Reading Development Resources, 1983.

Hyman, R. T. *Simulation gaming for values education: The prisoner's dilemma*. New Brunswick, NJ: University Press of America, 1978.

Hyman, R. T. *Strategic questioning*. Englewood Cliffs, NJ: Prentice-Hall, 1979.

Imhoff, M. M. *Early elementary education*. New York: Appleton-Century-Crofts, 1959.

Jacobs, L. (Ed.). *Using literature with young children*. New York: Teachers College Press, 1965.

Jennings, M. K., & Niemi, R. G. "Patterns of political learning." *Harvard Educational Review*, Summer 1968, *38*, 443–67.

Johnson, D. W., Johnson, R. T., Holubec, E. J., & Roy, P. *Circles of learning*. Washington, DC: Association for Supervision and Curriculum Development, 1984.

Johnson, J. E. *Characteristics of preschoolers interested in microcomputers*. Unpublished manuscript, Pennsylvania State University, Division of Curriculum and Instruction, University Park, PA, 1984.

Jung, C. G. *Analytical psychology.* New York: Vintage, 1970 (1968).

Kamii, C. K. "Obedience is not enough." *Young Children,* May 1984, *39,* 11–14.

Kamii, C. K., & DeClark, G. *Young children reinvent arithmetic.* New York: Teachers College Press, 1984.

Kamii, C., & DeVries, R. *Physical knowledge in the preschool.* Englewood Cliffs, NJ: Prentice-Hall, 1978.

Kamii, C., & DeVries, R. *Group games in early education.* Washington, DC: National Association for the Education of Young Children, 1980.

Karplus, R., & Thier, H. D. *A new look at elementary school science: Science curriculum improvement study.* Chicago: Rand McNally, 1967.

Koblinsky, S., & Behana, N. "Child sexual abuse: The educator's role in prevention, detection, and intervention." *Young Children,* September 1984, *39,* 3–15.

Kreinberg, N., Alper, L., & Joseph, H. "Computers and children: Where are the girls?" *PTA Today,* March 1985, pp. 13–15.

Kuhmerker, L. "Scared and hurt." *Ms. Magazine,* April 1984, *12,* 69.

Landeck, B. *Songs to grow on.* New York: William Sloane Associates, 1950.

Langer, S. *Philosophy in a new key.* New York: Mentor, 1948 (1942).

Langer, S. *Feeling and form.* New York: Charles Scribner's Sons, 1953.

Langer, S. *Problems of art.* New York: Charles Scribner's Sons, 1957.

Lasswell, H. D. *Politics: Who gets what, when, how.* New York: Meridian, 1958.

Lavatelli, C. S. *Piaget's theory applied to an early childhood curriculum.* Cambridge, MA: American Science and Engineering, 1970.

Lawrence Public Schools (Number Four School). *Full day kindergarten program evaluation.* Lawrence, NY: 1983.

Lawrence Public Schools (Number Four School). *Full day kindergarten program evaluation.* Lawrence, NY: 1984.

Levi-Strauss, C. *The elementary structures of kinship.* (J. H. Bell & J. R. von Sturmer, Trans.; R. Needham, Ed.) Boston: Beacon Press, 1969 (1949). (a)

Levi-Strauss, C. *The raw and the cooked.* (J. & D. Weightman, Trans.) New York: Harper Torchbooks, 1969 (1964). (b)

Lieberman, J. N. *Playfulness.* New York: Academic Press, 1977.

Luria, A. R. *The mind of a mnemonist.* (L. Solotaroff, Trans.) New York: Basic Books, 1968.

McCaslin, Nellie. *Creative drama in the classroom* (3d ed.). New York: Longman, 1980.

Maccoby, E. E., & Jacklin, C. N. *The psychology of sex differences.* Stanford, CA: Stanford University Press, 1974.

McDermott, J. "Geometrical forms known as fractals find sense in chaos." *Smithsonian,* December 1983, *14* (9), 110–17.

Mackay, D., Thompson, B., & Schaub, P. *Breakthrough to literacy.* New York: Longman, 1978.

McLuhan, M. "We need a new picture of knowledge." In A. Frazier (Ed.), *New insights and the curriculum* (pp. 57–70). Washington, DC: Association for Supervision and Curriculum Development, 1963.

McNeil, J. D. *Reading comprehension.* Glenview, IL: Scott, Foresman, 1984.

McNeill, D. *The acquisition of language.* New York: Harper & Row, 1970.

May, R. *Power and innocence.* New York: W. W. Norton, 1972.

Mazurkiewicz, A. J. *New perspectives in reading instruction.* New York: Pitman, 1964.

Merleau-Ponty, M. *The primacy of perception.* (J. M. Edie, Ed.) Evanston, IL: Northwestern University Press, 1964.

Meyerhoff, H. (Ed.). *The philosophy of history in our time.* Garden City, NY: Doubleday Anchor, 1959.

Miller, W. R. "Language acquisition and reading." In J. Walden (Ed.), *Oral language and reading.* Champaign, IL: National Council of Teachers of English, 1969, 31–47.

Mini VeriTech. *Early childhood series for: Perception, visual discrimination, concept formation.* Montreal, Canada: Brault & Bouthillier, 1977. (a)

———. *Figures and forms.* Montreal, Canada: Brault & Bouthillier, 1977. (b)

Minsky, M. *Computation: Finite and infinite machines.* Englewood Cliffs, NJ: Prentice-Hall, 1967.

Mitchell, L. S. *Here and now story books.* New York: E. P. Dutton, 1921.

Mitchell, L. S. *Young geographers.* New York: John Day, 1934.

Moffett, J. *A student-centered language arts curriculum, grades K–6: A handbook for teachers.* Boston: Houghton Mifflin, 1968.

Montessori, M. *The Montessori method.* (A. E. George, Trans.) New York: Schocken, 1965 (1912).

Moore, O. K., & Anderson, A. R. "The responsive environments project." In R. D. Hess & R. M. Bear (Eds.), *Early education* (pp. 171–89). Chicago: Aldine, 1968.

Morgan, R. *The anatomy of freedom: Feminism, physics, and global politics.* New York: Anchor Press, 1982.

Morphett, M. V., & Washburne, C. "When should children begin to read?" *Elementary School Journal,* March 1931, *31,* 496–503.

Morris, J. B. "Classroom methods and materials." In O. N. Saracho & B. Spodek (Eds.), *Understanding the multicultural experience in early childhood education* (pp. 77–90). Washington, DC: National Association for the Education of Young Children, 1983.

Muessig, R. H., & Rogers, V. R. "Suggested methods for teachers." In P. J. Pelto, *The study of anthropology* (pp. 81–116). Columbus, OH: Charles E. Merrill, 1965.

Myers-Walls, J. A., & Fry-Miller, K. M. "Nuclear war: Helping children overcome fears." *Young Children,* May 1984, *39,* 27–32.

Naisbitt, J. *Megatrends: Ten new directions transforming our lives.* New York: Warner, 1982.

Nieman, R. H., & Gastright, J. F. *Preschool plus all-day kindergarten: The cumulative effects of early childhood programs on the cognitive growth of four and five year old children.* Paper presented at the annual meeting of the American Educational Research Association, Washington, DC, April 1975.

Northrop, F. S. C. *The meeting of east and west.* New York: Macmillan, 1946.

Nuffield Mathematics Project. *Beginnings.* New York: John Wiley, 1967.

———. *Mathematics — The first three years.* New York: John Wiley, 1970.

Paley, V. G. *Boys and girls: Superheroes in the doll corner.* Chicago: University of Chicago Press, 1984.

Pehrsson, R. S., & Robinson, H. A. *The semantic organizer approach to reading and writing.* Rockville, MD: Aspen, 1985.

Peters, R. S. *Ethics and education.* Glenview, IL: Scott, Foresman, 1967.

Pfeiffer, J. *The thinking machine.* Philadelphia: J. B. Lippincott, 1962.

Phenix, P. *Realms of meaning.* New York: McGraw-Hill, 1964.

Piaget, J. *The psychology of intelligence.* (M. Piercy & D. E. Berlyne, Trans.) London: Routledge & Kegan Paul, 1950 (1947).

Piaget, J. *Play, dreams and imitation in childhood.* (C. Gattegno & F. M. Hodgson, Trans.) New York: W. W. Norton, 1962 (1951).

Piaget, J. *The moral judgment of the child.* (M. Gabain, Trans.) New York: The Free Press, 1965.

Piaget, J. *The grasp of consciousness.* Cambridge, MA: Harvard University Press, 1976.

Piaget, J., & Inhelder, B. *The child's conception of space.* (F. J. Langdon & J. L. Lunzer, Trans.) London: Routledge & Kegan Paul, 1963 (1956).

Piaget, J., & Inhelder, B. *The early growth of logic in the child.* (E. A. Lunzer & D. Papert, Trans.) New York: Harper & Row, 1964.

Piaget, J., & Inhelder, B. *Memory and intelligence.* New York: Basic Books, 1973.

Polanyi, M. *The study of man.* Chicago: The University of Chicago Press, 1963.

Porter, J. D. R. *Black child, white child.* Cambridge, MA: Harvard University Press, 1971.

Provenzo, E. F., Jr., & Brett, Arlene. (M. Carlebach, Photos.) *The complete block book.* Syracuse, NY: Syracuse University Press, 1983.

Raywid, M. A., & Shaheen, J. A. "Diversity: Surviving and thriving." *Early Years,* October 1983, pp. 28–31.

Reifel, S. "Children living with the nuclear threat." *Young Children,* July 1984, *39,* 74–80. (a)

Reifel, S. "Block construction." *Young Children,* November 1984, *40,* 61–67. (b)

Rensberger, B. "What made humans human?" *The New York Times Magazine,* April 8, 1984, pp. 80ff.

Richards, R., et al. *Early experiences.* Milwaukee, WI: Raintree-Macdonald Educational, 1976. (a)

Richards, R., et al. *Ourselves.* Milwaukee, WI: Raintree-Macdonald Educational, 1976. (b)

Robison, H. F., & Spodek, B. *New directions in the kindergarten.* New York: Teachers College Press, 1965.

Russell, H. R. *Ten-minute field trips: Using the school grounds for environmental studies.* (K. Winckelmann, Illus.) Chicago: J. G. Ferguson, 1973.

Sadker, D., & Sadker, M. "Is the O.K. classroom O.K.?" *Phi Delta Kappan,* January 1985, *66,* 358–61.

Sauvy, J., & Sauvy, S. *The child's discovery of space.* (P. Wells, Trans.) Baltimore: Penguin, 1974.

Seefeldt, C. *Teaching young children.* Englewood Cliffs, NJ: Prentice-Hall, 1980.

Serbin, L. A. "Teachers, peers, and play preferences: An environmental approach to sex typing in the preschool." In B. Sprung (Ed.), *Perspectives on non-sexist early childhood education*. New York: Teachers College Press, 1978.

Shaftel, F. R., & Shaftel, G. *Role-playing for social values*. Englewood Cliffs, NJ: Prentice-Hall, 1967.

Sheehy, E. D. *The fives and sixes go to school*. New York: Holt, 1954.

Shigaki, I. "Child care practices in Japan and the United States: How do they reflect cultural values in young children?" *Young Children*, May 1983, *38*, 13–24.

Siks, G. B. *Creative dramatics*. New York: Harper & Row, 1958.

Skeen, P., Garner, A. P., & Cartwright, S. *Woodworking for young children*. Washington, DC: National Association for the Education of Young Children, 1984.

Slavin, R. E., Madden, N., & Leavey, M. *Combining student teams and individualized instruction in mathematics: An extended evaluation*. Paper presented at the annual meeting of the American Educational Research Association, Montreal, Canada, April 1983.

Smilansky, S. *The effects of sociodramatic play on disadvantaged preschool children*. New York: John Wiley, 1968.

Smith, F. *Understanding reading* (2nd ed.). New York: Holt, Rinehart & Winston, 1978.

Smith, F. *Essays in literacy*. Exeter, NH: Heinemann, 1983.

Smith, H., & Dechant, E. *Psychology in teaching reading*. Englewood Cliffs, NJ: Prentice-Hall, 1961.

Sorauf, F. J. *Political science*. Columbus, OH: Charles E. Merrill, 1965.

Spalding, R. B., with Spalding, W. T. *The writing road to reading* (2nd rev. ed.). New York: William Morrow, 1969.

Spodek, B. *Developing social studies concepts in the kindergarten*. Unpublished doctoral dissertation, Teachers College, Columbia University, 1962.

Sprung, B., Froschl, M., & Campbell, P. B. *What will happen if . . . : Young children and the scientific method*. New York: Educational Equity Concepts, 1985.

Steiner, G. *Language and silence*. New York: Atheneum, 1970.

Stenhouse, L. (Ed.). *Curriculum research and development*. London, England: Heinemann, 1980.

Stern, C., & Gould, T. *Children discover reading*. New York: Random House, 1965.

Sullivan, W. "The Einstein papers: A flash of insight came after long reflection on relativity." *The New York Times*, March 28, 1972, pp. C1 ff.

Sullivan, W. "A hole in the sky." *The New York Times*, July 14, 1974, pp. 11ff.

Sullivan, W. "Strange, scroll-like wave is linked to biological processes." *The New York Times*, January 8, 1985, p. C3.

Swett, S. "Get good mileage out of Big Trak." *Teaching and Computers*, April 1984, pp. 26–28.

Synectics Education Systems. *Juggler flowsheet*. (Available from Synectics Education Systems, Cambridge, MA; n.d.)

Taba, H., Durkin, M. C., Fraenkel, J. R., & McNaughton, A. H. *A teacher's handbook to elementary social studies: An inductive approach* (2nd. ed.). Reading, MA: Addison-Wesley, 1971.

Temple, C. A., Nathan, R. G., & Burris, N. A. *The beginnings of writing.* Boston: Allyn & Bacon, 1982.

Tizard, B. "Problematic aspects of nuclear war." *Harvard Educational Review*, August 1984, *54*, 271–81.

Tobias, S. *Overcoming math anxiety.* New York: W. W. Norton, 1978.

Torrance, E. P. *Guiding creative talent.* Englewood Cliffs, NJ: Prentice-Hall, 1962.

Toulmin, S. *The philosophy of science.* New York: Harper & Row, 1960 (1953).

Tudor-Hart, B. "Reading and the acquisition of speech." In *The first international reading symposium* (pp. 24–33). New York: John Day, 1966.

Vygotsky, L. S. *Thought and language.* (E. Hanfmann & G. Vakar, Trans.) New York: John Wiley, 1962.

Vygotsky, L. S. *Mind in society.* (M. Cole, V. John-Steiner, S. Scribner, & E. Souberman, Eds.) Cambridge, MA: Harvard University Press, 1978.

Ward, W. *Drama with and for children.* Washington, DC: U.S. Government Printing Office, 1960.

Waters, B. *Science can be elementary.* New York: Citation Press, 1973.

Welty, E. *One writer's beginnings.* Cambridge, MA: Harvard University Press, 1984.

White, R. W. "Motivation reconsidered: The concept of competence." *Psychological Review*, September 1959, *65*, 297–333.

Whitehead, A. N. *The aims of education.* New York: Mentor, 1929.

Whitehead, A. N. *An introduction to mathematics.* New York: Oxford University Press, 1960.

Williams, L., & De Gaetano, Y. *ALERTA: A multicultural bilingual approach to teaching young children.* Menlo Park, CA: Addison-Wesley, 1985.

Wilson, E. O. *On human nature.* Cambridge, MA: Harvard University Press, 1978.

Winn, M. *The plug-in drug.* New York: Viking, 1977.

Winter, M., & Klein, A. E. *Extending the kindergarten day: Does it make a difference in the achievement of educationally advantaged and disadvantaged pupils?* Washington, DC: Bureau of Elementary & Secondary Education, 1970.

Wittgenstein, L. von. *Philosophical investigations.* (G. E. M. Anscombe, Trans.) New York: Macmillan, 1958.

Women's Action Alliance. *The impact of inclusionary materials in early childhood classrooms: A summary of preliminary findings from field testing the project R.E.E.D. materials.* Paper presented at Access to Equity: The First National Conference on Educational Equity for Disabled Women and Girls, Baltimore, MD, June 1982.

Yonemura, M. *Developing language programs for young disadvantaged children.* New York: Teachers College Press, 1969.

Zaslavsky, C. *Africa counts.* Boston: Prindle, Weber & Schmidt, 1973.

Zaslavsky, C. *Preparing young children for math: A book of games.* New York: Schocken, 1979.

Zukav, G. *The dancing wu li masters: An overview of the new physics.* New York: Bantam, 1980.

References to Children's Literature

All of the books in this section have been referred to in the text. Most of them need to be read to kindergarten children. Those books that kindergarten children might be able to read themselves are listed also in the "Great Books" for Beginning Readers section.

Adoff, A. (Ed.). *My black me.* New York: E. P. Dutton, 1974.

Anderson, L. *Mary McLeod Bethune.* (W. Hutchinson, Illus.) Champaign, IL: Garrard, 1976.

Beim, J. *Eric on the desert.* New York: Morrow, 1953.

Beim, J., & Beim, L. *Two is a team.* (E. Crichlow, Illus.) New York: Harcourt Brace & World, 1945.

Brown, M. W. *The noisy book.* (R. Thomson, Illus.) New York: Scroll Press, 1973.

Cleary, B. *Ramona the pest.* (L. Darling, Illus.) New York: Morrow, 1968.

Credle, E. *Down down the mountain.* (E. Credle, Illus.) Nashville, TN: Thomas Nelson, 1934.

de Paola, T. *Strega nona.* Englewood Cliffs, NJ: Prentice-Hall, 1975.

de Regniers, B. S. *The giant story.* (M. Sendak, Illus.) New York: Harper & Row, 1953.

Felt, S. *Rosa-too-little.* Garden City, NY: Doubleday, 1950.

Flack, M. *Angus lost.* Garden City, NY: Doubleday, 1932.

Flack, M. *Ask Mr. Bear.* New York: Macmillan, 1958.

Gag, W. *Millions of cats.* New York: Coward, McCann, & Geoghegan, 1938.

Greenfield, E. *Mary McLeod Bethune.* (J. Pinkner, Illus.) New York: Thomas Y. Crowell, 1977.

Jacobs, J. (Ed.). *Pied Piper and other fairy tales.* (J. Hill, Illus.) New York: Macmillan, 1968.

Krauss, R. *The growing story.* (P. Rowand, Illus.) New York: Harper & Row, 1947.

Lamorisse, A. *The red balloon.* Garden City, NY: Doubleday, 1956.

Lexau, J. M. *Benjie on his own.* (D. Bolognese, Illus.) New York: Dial, 1970.

Lipkind, W., & Mordvinoff, N. *Russet and the two reds.* New York: Harcourt Brace & World, 1962.

MacDonald, G. [pseud.]. *The little island* by M. W. Brown. (L. Weisgard, Illus.) Garden City, NY: Doubleday, 1971.

McCloskey, R. *Blueberries for Sal.* New York: Viking, 1968 (1948).

McCloskey, R. *One morning in Maine.* New York: Viking, 1952.

Miles, M. *Annie and the old one.* (P. Parnall, Illus.). Boston: Little, Brown, 1971.

Milne, A. A. *Winnie-the-Pooh.* (E. H. Shepard, Illus.) New York: E. P. Dutton, 1957.

Milne, A. A. *Now we are six.* (E. H. Shepard, Illus.) New York: E. P. Dutton, 1958.

Milne, A. A. *When we were very young.* (E. H. Shepard, Illus.) New York: E. P. Dutton, 1958.

Rey, H. A. *Curious George.* New York: Houghton Mifflin, 1973.

Rockwell, A. *Cars.* New York: E. P. Dutton, 1984.

Schlein, M. *The way mothers are.* (J. Lasker, Illus.) Chicago: Albert Whitman, 1963.

Schneider, H., & Schneider, N. *Follow the sunset.* (L. Corcos, Illus.) New York: Doubleday, 1952.

Segal, E. "Be my friend." In E. Segal, *Be my friend* [Poetry]. New York: The Citadel Press, 1952.

Sendak, M. *Where the wild things are.* New York: Harper & Row, 1963.

Slobodkina, E. *Caps for sale.* Reading, MA: Addison-Wesley, 1947.

Southgate, V. (Retold). *The enormous turnip.* (R. Lumley, Illus.) Loughborough, England: Wills & Hepworth, 1970.

Stevenson, R. L. "My shadow." In R. L. Stevenson, *The child's garden of verses* [Poetry]. New York: Platt & Munk, 1961.

Tresselt, A. *I saw the sea come in.* (R. Duvoisin, Illus.) New York: Lothrop, Lee & Shepard, 1968.

Tworkov, J. *The camel who took a walk.* (R. Duvoisin, Illus.) New York: E. P. Dutton, 1974.

White, E. B. *Charlotte's web.* (G. Williams, Illus.) New York: Dell, 1968.

Yashima, T. *The umbrella.* New York: Viking, 1970.

"Great Books" for Beginning Readers

Kindergarten children might be able to read the books in this section independently some time during the school year. Two asterisks (**) next to a book in this section indicate that some kindergarten children are likely to be able to read it after they have heard it read.

REALISTIC FICTION

Alexander, M. *Nobody asked me if I wanted a baby sister*. New York: Dial, 1971.

Alexander, M. *When the baby comes, I'm moving out*. New York: Dial, 1979.

Allen, P. *Who sank the boat?* New York: Coward-McCann, 1982.

Ayer, J. *A wish for little sister*. New York: Harcourt Brace & World, 1960.

Beim, J., & Beim, L. *Two is a team*. (E. Crichlow, Illus.) New York: Harcourt, Brace & World, 1945.

Borack, B. *Grandpa*. (B. Sheeter, Illus.) New York: Harper & Row, 1967.

Breinburg, P. *Shawn's red bike*. (E. Lloyd, Illus.) New York: Thomas Y. Crowell, 1975.

Edwards, Dorothy. *A wet Monday*. New York: William Morrow, 1976.

Keats, E. J. *The snowy day*. New York: Viking, 1962.

Keller, H. *Geraldine's blanket*. New York: Greenwillow, 1984.

Krauss, R. *The carrot seed*. New York: Harper & Row, 1945.

FOLKTALES

Emberley, B. (Adaptation). *Drummer Hoff*. (E. Emberley, Illus.) Englewood Cliffs, NJ: Prentice-Hall, 1967.

Flack, M. *Ask Mr. Bear*. New York: Macmillan, 1958.

Kahn, R. *Jump, frog, jump!* (B. Barton, Illus.) New York: Greenwillow, 1981.

McDermott, G. *Anansi the spider*. New York: Holt, Rinehart & Winston, 1972.
Sharmat, M. W. *I don't care*. (L. Hoban, Illus.) New York: Macmillan, 1977.
Slobodkina, E. *Caps for sale*. Reading, MA: Addison-Wesley, 1968 (1947).
Southgate, V. (Retold). *The enormous turnip*. (R. Lumley, Illus.) Loughborough, England: Wills & Hepworth, Ltd., 1970.**
Tworkov, J. *The camel who took a walk*. (R. Duvoisin, Illus.) New York: E. P. Dutton, 1974.**
Zemach, M. *The little red hen*. New York: Farrar, Straus & Giroux, 1983.

FANTASY

Blake, Q. *Mister magnolia*. London, England: Jonathan Cape, 1981.
Brown, R. *A dark dark tale*. New York: Dial, 1981.
de Regniers, B. S. *The giant story*. (M. Sendak, Illus.) New York: Harper & Row, 1953.**
Lionni, Leo. *Little blue and little yellow*. New York: Astor, 1959.
Most, B. *If the dinosaurs came back*. New York: Harcourt Brace Jovanovich, 1978.
Most, B. *Whatever happened to the dinosaurs?* New York: Harcourt Brace Jovanovich, 1984.
Raskin, E. *Nothing ever happens on my block*. New York: Atheneum, 1966.
Sharmat, M. W. *A big fat enormous lie*. (D. McPhail, Illus.) New York: E. P. Dutton, 1978.**

PEOPLE IN FUR AND FEATHERS

Brown, M. W. *The noisy book*. (L. Weisgard, Illus.) New York: Harper & Row, 1939.**
Brown, M. W. *Quiet noisy book*. (L. Weisgard, Illus.) New York: Harper & Row, 1950.**
Burningham, J. *Mr. Grumpy's motor car*. New York: Thomas Y. Crowell, 1973.
Eastman, P. D. *Are you my mother?* New York: Random House, 1960.
Eastman, P. D. *The best nest*. New York: Random House, 1968.
Gackenbush, D. *Claude and pepper*. New York: Seabury, 1976.
Hayes, G. *Bear by himself*. New York: Harper & Row, 1976.

NONFICTION

Aruego, J., & Dewey, A. *We hide, you seek*. New York: Greenwillow, 1979.
Azarian, M. *A farmer's alphabet*. Boston: David R. Godine, 1981.
Bang, M. *Ten, nine, eight*. New York: Greenwillow, 1983.**
Barton, B. *Building a house*. New York: Greenwillow, 1981.
Bauer, C. F. *My mom travels a lot*. (N. W. Parker, Illus.) New York: Frederick Warner, 1981.

Budney, B. *A kiss is round*. (V. Bobri, Illus.) New York: Lothrop, Lee & Shepard, 1958.

Crews, D. *Truck*. New York: Greenwillow, 1980.

Crews, D. *Parade*. New York: Greenwillow, 1983.

Gibbons, G. *Trucks*. New York: Thomas Y. Crowell, 1981.

Green, M. McB. *Is it hard? Is it easy?* Reading, MA: Young Scott Books, 1960.

Hoban, T. *Push pull empty full: A book of opposites*. New York: Macmillan, 1972.

Hoban, T. *I walk and read*. New York: Greenwillow, 1984.

Kalen, R. *Rain*. (D. Crews, Illus.) New York: Greenwillow, 1978.

Kalen, R. *Blue sea*. (D. Crews, Illus.) New York: Greenwillow, 1979.

Keller, C. (Ed.). *Pet jokes for kids*. (P. Coker, Jr., Illus.) Englewood Cliffs, NJ: Prentice-Hall, 1977.**

Lasker, J. *He's my brother*. Chicago: Albert Whitman, 1974.

Maestro, B. *Traffic: a book of opposites*. New York: Crown, 1981.

Mayer, M., & Mayer, M. *Mine!* New York: Simon & Schuster, 1970.

Rockwell, A. *Cars*. New York: E. P. Dutton, 1984.

Skaar, G. *Nothing but cats and all about dogs*. New York: Young Scott, 1947.

Welch, M. McK. *Will that wake mother?* New York: Dodd, Mead, 1982.

Wildsmith, B. *ABC*. New York: Franklin Watts, 1962.

Wildsmith, B. *1, 2, 3's*. New York: Franklin Watts, 1965.

Wildsmith, B. *Puzzles*. New York: Franklin Watts, 1970.

Wiseman, A. S. *Finger paint and pudding prints*. Reading, MA: Addison-Wesley, 1980.

About the Author

Doris Fromberg is Professor of education and Director of Early Childhood Teacher Education at Hofstra University in Hempstead, New York. After having been a teacher and administrator in public and private schools, she received an Ed.D. from Teachers College, Columbia University. She is also a field-based curriculum and administration consultant to school districts and has served as a Teacher Corps director. Her special interests are early childhood curriculum, teacher education, school climate, and classroom organization. She has published books, monographs, and articles. Among her recent publications are *The Successful Classroom: Management Strategies for Regular Elementary and Special Education Teachers* (New York: Teachers College Press, 1985), with Maryann Driscoll, and *Collaborating: Lessons Learned from Experience* (Washington, D.C.: American Association of Colleges for Teacher Education, 1986), with G. Thomas Fox, Jr., Leo Anglin, and Michael Grady.

Index